D1708374

The Growth of Responsible Government

THE GROWTH OF
RESPONSIBLE
GOVERNMENT

from James the First

to Victoria

by

A. H. DODD

*Professor of History, University College
of North Wales, Bangor*

Routledge & Kegan Paul
LONDON

First published 1956
by Routledge & Kegan Paul Ltd.
Broadway House, Carter Lane, E.C.4
Printed in Great Britain
by W. & J. Mackay & Co. Ltd., Chatham

Contents

Prefatory Note

This book has grown out of lectures given for the last dozen years or more to my honours class at Bangor. It is published now in the hope that it may prove of use not only to specialist students and teachers in universities and sixth forms, but to the wider non-specialist public interested in the practice of politics. For it is primarily a study of politics in action, with more stress on quirks of character and twists of fortune than on those abstract principles or legal theories which in British experience are more often invoked after action than before. It would be no more true to say of the British constitution than of the British empire that it was achieved in a fit of absence of mind, for the objective was always present, however dimly envisaged; but the means whereby it was realized were not only unforeseen, but generally (like the discovery of America) not even appreciated till long after they were accomplished. That is why a study of politics is always out of focus if it confines itself to contemporary practice and ignores history; and the history in this case claims our attention because it brought about what is probably our most distinctive contribution to politics.

Two works of major importance in this field—Professor Ogg's *Reigns of James II and William III* and Professor Walcott's *English Politics in the Early Eighteenth Century*—appeared soon after this book went to press. Had I seen beforehand Dr. Walcott's convincing criticism of the two-party hypothesis, even in the modified form endorsed by Professor Trevelyan and Mr. Feiling (on whom I have largely relied), I might have worded more cautiously some of the conclusions in Chapter VII, and the treatment of George III's political strategy in Chapters VIII and IX might have gained point by a comparison with his analysis of the crisis of 1708 on pp. 43–53 and 58–60. It does not appear, however, that either publication calls for any fundamental revision of the main thesis of this book. Nor again does Dr. Byrum E. Carter's *The Office of Prime Minister* (Princeton, 1956)—a valuable study of existing practice but somewhat outdated on historical origins.

In revising for press I have not always been able to verify references, some of the sources used being out of reach here. I can only trust that no serious inaccuracies have resulted.

New Orleans, 1956   A. H. DODD.

Introduction

Six months after Queen Victoria ascended the throne, Lord Durham was sent as governor-general to Canada. His mission was one of pacification to a colony in open revolt, and twelve months later his proposed remedies were set forth in the classic *Report on the Affairs of British North America*. Foremost among them was the grant of what he claimed to be 'one of the necessary consequences of representative institutions', namely that if the crown 'has to carry on the government in unison with a representative body, it must consent to carry it on by means of those in whom that representative body has confidence'. Such is his definition of responsible government, and he lays much of the blame for Canadian unrest on the flouting of conventions for promoting it which he believes to be firmly rooted in the constitution:—

In England this principle has so long been considered an indisputable and essential part of our constitution that it has really hardly ever been found necessary to inquire into the means by which its observance is enforced. When a ministry ceases to command a majority in Parliament on great questions of policy, its doom is immediately sealed; and it would appear as strange to us to attempt, for any time, to carry on a Government by means of ministers perpetually in a minority, as it would be to pass laws with a majority of votes against them. The ancient constitutional remedies, by an impeach-

ment and a stoppage of the supplies, have never, since the
reign of William III, been brought into operation for the
purpose of removing a ministry. They have never been called
for, because, in fact, it has been the habit of ministers rather
to anticipate the occurrence of an absolutely hostile vote, and
to retire, when supported only by a bare and uncertain
majority.[1]

Lord Durham—'Radical Jack'—was among the more forth-
right and uncompromising of the new whigs who had so
recently saddled the constitution with a novel doctrine of representation in the first reform bill; his views on the implications of
representative government were not necessarily those even of
contemporaries at home, still less of an earlier generation, or of
countries where representation has evolved in a different
political climate. Powers over the executive which he claims to
be 'inherent in a popular legislature' are not exercised to this
day by that of the United States; the Founding Fathers knew
of no such convention in the practice of the British constitution
as they understood it, only half a century before the Durham
Report, nor did its absence strike them as a gap to be filled in
their reformed and transplanted version, preoccupied though
they were with the need for keeping within bounds the power
of the central executive. Lord John Russell as colonial secretary
defined the whig doctrine of responsible government to
Durham's successor in far more guarded and less explicit
terms.[2] Durham himself was under fifty when the Report was
written, and his bland assumption of universal truth for a
convention which hardly went back beyond his own political
lifetime is yet another example of the extraordinary speed with
which novelties, once accepted, can begin to wear what
Archbishop Mathew calls 'that character of the inevitable
which has always such a soothing influence on all those who
possess a tranquil attachment to tradition', and of which he
himself cites a crowning example in the caption from Raleigh's
History of the World: 'Of the last acts of King David: his summoning a Parliament'.[3]

For the plain truth is that while the *aim* of responsible govern-

[1]*Lord Durham's Report*, ed. Sir C. P. Lucas, 1912, ii. 76–7, 278–9.
[2]Ibid., iii. 332.
[3]David Mathew, *The Jacobean Age*, 1938, pp. 222, 14.

ment had been consciously pursued for at least a couple of
centuries before Victoria's accession (and fumblingly long
before that), the devices for securing it which have become so
characteristic of political life in this country were achieved
only in the course of the eighteenth century—some not till the
dawn of the nineteenth, and then in the teeth of opposition
which was often strongest in those most wedded to the end in
view; on the other hand the 'prentice efforts of Stuart con-
stitution-mongers in the same direction nearly all turned out to
be dead ends. It will be the object of the following chapters to
trace this process of trial and error and to examine, so far as
may be, the underlying causes of success and failure.

For such a study the opening years of the seventeenth century
make a natural starting point. It was only then that the demand
of the legislature for some measure of control over administration, as distinct from its own special province of law-making,
began to become vocal; indeed the boundary between the
various provinces of government—legislation, administration,
policy, finance, justice—was then in process of clarification. A
great step forward had been taken under the Tudors; a further
advance was to follow the Restoration, which while sweeping
away the more partisan achievements of the interregnum
consolidated much of what it had accomplished in the field of
administration. While this process was unfolding itself, parliament, like many another victorious host, kept extending its
frontiers as each new gain revealed the outline of further
territory which must be brought under control on pain of
imperilling what had already been won. Legislation, for
example, till the age of the Tudors had meant little more than
the codifying of existing custom after it had been declared by
those best qualified to know. The legislation that brought about
the breach with Rome embodied, under the same innocent
guise, a new departure in national policy; but it was still the
king's policy, on which parliament (as Elizabeth never wearied
of reminding it) was entitled only to a plain 'yes' or 'no' if and
when a plain issue was put before it. Its 'winning of the
initiative' (in Professor Notestein's now classic phrase) belongs to
the early Stuart period.[1]

[1]Wallace Notestein, *The Winning of the Initiative by the House of Commons* (Raleigh
Lecture, British Academy, 1924).

The ancient right of petition had always brought the deliberations of parliament to the fringes of administration and policy; but the grievances aired in petition had been such as members 'brought from their countries'—local complaints to be met by royal promises of investigation and redress or (where necessary)by local bills—until the emergence under the Tudors of those great national issues which, in expanding parliamentary business, gave members a new self-confidence and a sense of common purpose, emboldening them to challenge entry into one field of public policy after another. Even foreign affairs, which had concerned the commons only when they were called on for war supplies, could no longer be sealed off, once the intrusion of the religious factor into this field brought with it the risk that what had been won by legislation might be lost by treaty.

Grievances, however, can be against individuals as well as against policies; here parliament had a handle in its amorphous judicial powers, enabling the commons to impeach an unpopular royal servant at the bar of the lords. This practice, dating from Edward III's reign and used spasmodically during the following century, belongs essentially to the pre-history of the constitution, before there was any recognized line of demarcation between legislation and justice, treason and legitimate opposition, personal vendetta and political difference, legal misdemeanour and error of policy. Yet in a very real sense it was the first approach, if a negative and unconscious one, to the problem of responsible government; for the aim was to make these agents of royal policy amenable to what was then the nearest approach to a dominant public opinion—the views of an aristocratic faction dominant by virtue of its feudal strength. Of this the early Stuart parliaments were dimly aware when they refurbished the weapon of impeachment, in the interests of more developed political concepts, after nearly two centuries of disuse; and the debates provoked by this revival, instructive for the dawning appreciation they reveal of distinctions hitherto blurred, were an important stage in clearing the ground for a firmer statement of the problem of responsible government.[1]

[1]On impeachment see G. W. Keeton, *The Passing of Parliament*, 1952, ch. iv.

The financial powers of parliament, as deeply rooted as those of legislation and justice, like them began to emerge as an instrument for control over policy only with the struggles of the early Stuart period. In the middle ages the main concern had been to establish the principle that a man should not lose his freehold save by his own consent (personally or by proxy) or else by due process of law. As long as the king was expected normally to 'live of his own', and to approach his subjects for money grants only in times of grave national emergency, there could be no serious question of influencing policy by financial pressure. It was the frequent and costly emergencies of Tudor days that removed parliamentary grants from the category of the abnormal to that of the normal; the Tudor invention of the subsidy also did something towards standardizing their incidence, though it was not till after the Restoration that anything like certainty was achieved either in the yield of taxes or in the cost of the services they financed. This left a wide margin of debatable ground, of which Stuart parliaments were not slow to take advantage. It may, as has been suggested,[1] have been through financial ignorance rather than set policy that they kept the crown poor and so amenable to parliamentary interference. But it was with their eyes open that the parliaments of the first James and the first Charles enunciated the principle of 'redress before supply', experimented in the appropriation of these supplies to approved ends, and even attempted to define, limit and control the king's 'own' which he could spend at discretion—efforts reaching a climax in the most loyal of the parliaments of the second Charles.

By Lord Durham's time, as his Report emphasizes, impeachment and stoppage of supplies had been long outdated as means of giving parliament control over policy and policy-makers. Both are of a negative and inherently anarchic character, and both smack of shutting the stable door when the horse has gone. The positive and constructive approach to responsible government could only be by way of first discovering a determinate body of men who could be held accountable for policy, and then finding some means of ensuring that they were the sort of men in whom, or in whose policies, parliament could feel confidence. Otherwise the king

[1] Sir David Keir, *Constitutional History of Modern Britain*, 1948, pp. 248–9.

himself must be brought to book, and that was not only contrary to all accepted constitutional doctrine but destructive (as Oliver Cromwell was to learn) of the very roots of civic stability. The natural place in which to seek out the men responsible for policy was the privy council; but the council was not a body chosen for its opinions, and there was no certainty that any individual councillor had either assented to, or for that matter been consulted on, the policy in question—or even (since the right to seek counsel where he would was a jealously-guarded prerogative of royalty) that the advice had not come from hidden and unacknowledged quarters. Hence the long struggle —foredoomed to failure—against 'favourites' and 'cabals', and the continued efforts to make the council in some way amenable to parliament long after it had ceased to be in any effective sense a supreme organ of government.

These struggles occupied most of the seventeenth century; the century ended with parliament technically supreme in legislation and finance, but the king still in virtually unfettered control of policy and of the agents through whom he carried it out. The compromise worked well enough so long as no great issue arose to put legislation and policy out of harmony with each other, to scuttle parliament into obstructive use of its power of the purse, or to exasperate the crown into openly flaunting those subtle means of 'influence' over the legislature which later and wiser Stuarts had built up as a defence against the humiliations of their predecessors. But when the factors which had plunged Stuart England into revolution began to repeat themselves in the England of George III, the parliamentary opposition found on the one hand that the forces they had to oppose or control were no longer those against which their seventeenth-century forefathers had contended, on the other hand that the new organs of government which had grown up, in the teeth of all opposition, within the framework of the old, could be adapted to their own purposes; and so cabals became cabinets, royal favourites turned into prime ministers, the court party emerged as the government benches, disloyal factions as his majesty's opposition and their leaders as the shadow cabinet. The process was still incomplete at Victoria's accession, but the main features were there, as the Durham Report makes clear, and under the fatherly guidance of 'Lord M', it was in this new whig version of responsible government that the young queen was indoctrinated from her accession. The contemporary constitution had come to birth— a complex of rights and duties which cannot be tabulated or defined because it is the child of history, not of logic.

I

Tudor Heritage

I T is a commonplace of constitutional history that parliament, law courts and privy council all derived from a common matrix—the feudal council to which the mediaeval kings summoned their great tenants-in-chief together with a growing bureaucratic element independent of tenure—the bishops, judges and officers of the king's household. The struggle between the feudal elements, standing for tradition and territorial influence, and the bureaucratic, standing for efficiency and royal control, was a central theme of mediaeval constitutional history, and it cast a protracted shadow into modern times. At the same time parliament was developing out of special sessions of the council for the promulgation of laws and the voting of money grants; this brought in the representative element, which by the close of the middle ages was winning for itself (thanks to financial pressure) recognition as a normal, if not yet an indispensable part of parliament, with a share in most, though not yet all, of parliament's business alongside the lords spiritual, with their independent source of authority, and the lords temporal, now closing their ranks against royal encroachments by turning themselves into a hereditary peerage. The 'bastard' feudalism of the later middle ages made both council and parliament (and at times the crown itself) largely catspaws of aristocratic factions; but when in turn these factions wiped each other out in the Wars of the Roses, the road was clear for the reconstituted monarchy built by the Tudors on Yorkist foundations.

Confronted by what was almost a *tabula rasa*, the Tudors were in a more favourable position to determine the future constitutional development of the land than any previous monarchs since William the Conqueror. Fortunately they had the sense to see that no ruler of an established state ever has a completely blank sheet to write on, and they fully appreciated the strength of the Machiavellian maxim 'Whoever desires to introduce reforms into a state and see them accepted and maintained must retain at least the shadow of the old institutions, so that it may appear to the people that nothing has been altered.' Rather than destroy outdated institutions they shored up the familiar façade and modernized the structure within.

There was, for example, no question of abolishing the historic council, amorphous and overgrown though it was. It never met as a body, but there it was in the background, a sort of reserve of counsellors ready to be called on whenever it suited the king to go outside his more compact and formal body of advisers. Its judicial functions—such as had not been formalized and stabilized in the law courts—were exercised by a select panel meeting at set intervals (but with a more fluid procedure) in the star chamber, to exercise the bulk of the king's discretionary jurisdiction. Another panel, not tied to any set time or place of meeting, formed at once his inner body of counsellors and his chief administrative organ, with residuary powers of summary justice through the right to summon, hear and imprison suspects in time of crisis. Such, in the broadest outline, was the Tudor privy council. The process by which it came into being, and by which in turn it gave place to 'interior councils', is nowhere better described than in a passage written late in the next century by a man who knew politics and administration from the inside:—

Assemblies at first reasonably constituted of a due number and temper for the dispatch of affairs committed to them, by improvident increase come to be formal and troublesome, the certain consequence of multitude, and thereby a new institution becomes necessary: whereupon it is found easier and safer to substitute than to dissolve.[1]

[1]A. F. Pollard in *Eng. Hist. Rev.*, xxxviii. 337–60, 516–39; R. North, *Lives of the Norths*, ed. Jessop, 1890, i. 299.

In selecting this body, the Tudors jealously maintained the utmost freedom of choice, irrespective of tenure or office, and they kept it severely limited, hovering in numbers round a norm of a score or so; only at moments when the monarchy was temporarily weakened did it resort to conciliating powerful interests by swelling the council to a point beyond what made for compactness and competence. On the other hand they never attempted (nor indeed would their resources have allowed it) to emulate the kings of France by turning their council into a secret camarilla of unknown bureaucrats, chosen only for their zeal, efficiency and complete financial dependence on the crown. No English dynasty was ever more aware of the need for public confidence, nor of the way in which confidence is bred in a society with the territorial structure and tradition of that over which they ruled. The right of the feudal magnates to be the crown's exclusive advisers had gone for ever, it is true; 'the Tudors', as Sir David Keir puts it, 'inherited and perpetuated a council emancipated from aristocratic pre-dominance'[1]—but certainly not free from the local influence and prestige attaching to the ownership of land, for that would have undermined public confidence and left the crown dependent for its authority on military and financial resources it did not possess. When the conservative rebels of the Pilgrimage of Grace complained that Henry VIII was filling his council with low-born upstarts, they were expressing standards of gentility that survived in the feudal north after they became outdated in the progressive south and east. The new privy councillors were in the main drawn from the new squirearchy, of gentle birth though not of the older feudal aristocracy, often enough holding old but small estates recently swollen by grant or purchase, and wielding thereby a wide territorial influence over neighbours and dependents for whose dispositions they could answer from intimate knowledge and family connexion; neither nameless bureaucrats nor hangers-on at court.

'Authority', declared Sir William Temple in his apologia for a reconstituted privy council under Charles II, 'is observed much to follow land'; and the duke of Devonshire was echoing the same sentiment when he wrote to Fox nearly a hundred

[1]Keir, op. cit., pp. 18, 114.

years later: 'If the king of England employs those people that the nation have a good opinion of, he will make a great figure; but if he chuses them merely through personal favour, it will never do.'[1] It was in this spirit that the Tudors chose their more intimate counsellors from the rising middle class of agrarian society, which also filled the bulk of the seats in the house of commons and on the county benches. In this way the privy council, so long as it kept its Tudor complexion and authority, remained a vital link with the commons on the one hand and the shires on the other—all the more vital because in neither of these spheres of government could the crown choose its agents with the freedom it enjoyed in selecting its inner counsellors. That both commons and counties not only kept, but enhanced, their place in the scheme of government must be attributed to that same blend of limited material resources with the Tudor gift for tapping the more intangible asset of public confidence.

It is impossible to draw any hard-and-fast line between the advisory and administrative functions of the privy council—its share in the framing of policy and its detailed implementing of that policy. It is in the former field that we know least of its activities and procedure, for naturally what was said on such delicate and inflammable topics was rarely committed to paper except in private letters not meant for the eyes of posterity, or in scraps of court gossip scooped up and passed on by the news-writers. Foreign policy, peace and war, royal marriages or matters arising out of the religious settlement—any of these might be matter for a full-dress debate in council if the sovereign chose to consult it. He might of course prefer to seek the advice of a single trusted councillor or a small inner *coterie* rather than raise what might become a hornet's nest; in either case there was no obligation on him to act upon the proffered advice.

If he did not, it was still the duty of the council, or the minister in whose province it lay, to carry out the policy he had opposed. 'Whether my opinion be seen good or not', wrote Tunstal of Henry VIII, 'I am ready to follow his ordinance and to conform my mind to his most honorable counsel, which I know well seeth further . . . than I do'. Burghley put the

[1]Temple, *Memoirs* (infra, p. 57); *Trans. R.H.S.*, V.i.140.

case more fully in what may be regarded as his political testament to his son:—

> I do hold, and will always, this course in such matters as I differ in opinion from her Majesty. As long as I may be allowed to give advice I will not change my opinion by affirming the contrary, for that were to offend God, to whom I am sworn first; but as a servant I will obey her Majesty's command and no wise contrary the same; presuming that she being God's chief minister here, it shall be God's will to have her commandments obeyed—after that I have performed my duty as a Councillor, and shall in my heart wish her commandments to have such good success as she intendeth. You see I am a mixture of divinity and policy; preferring in policy her Majesty before all others on earth, and in divinity the King of Heaven above all.[1]

This habit of mind made it much easier to maintain some sort of continuity in membership of the council in face of violent changes of policy between one reign and another; it also explains much of the apparent lack of principle on the part of Tudor and Stuart statesmen. To quit the royal service on a matter of opinion was an unworthy piece of 'pettishness' and desertion; to refuse to carry out a policy because one disbelieved in it was sheer treason. There was a long road to travel before a place could be found in the constitution for her majesty's opposition, and Tudor ministers of the crown were far more akin to senior permanent officials of the civil service than to the cabinet minister of today.

An increasingly important phase of the advisory functions of the council brought it into close relations with parliament. It was in council that the decision was made in the first instance to summon a parliament; and before parliament met, the legislative programme to be submitted to it had also been roughed out at the council board. What was still more important, there were privy councillors present in both houses to take the lead in debates with full knowledge (as their fellow-members were well aware) of the royal wishes. If they were peers they had their seats automatically in the upper house; the chancellor and a few

---

[1]Quoted C. Sturge, *Cuthbert Tunstal*, 1938, p. 37, and M. A. S. Hume, *The Great Lord Burghley*, 1898, p. 479n.

other officials sat there as 'assistants' even when they were commoners; but as the complexion of the council grew less aristocratic, privy councillors and ministers who were not peers found it convenient to seek seats in the house of commons. In this way the crown was assured of spokesmen there who could present a well-informed case for government measures and against those obnoxious to it, while to the commons, still in process of finding their feet, there was the obvious advantage of natural leaders with experience of public business and a knowledge of the *arcana* of government. The crown accordingly used its electoral influence to ensure a sufficiency of privy councillors in the house, and the house for its part deferred to their opinions, accorded them as of right seats round the speaker, and expected 'those about the Chair' to take the initiative in debates. The speaker himself, though nominally elected by the house, remained in fact a royal official till well on in the seventeenth century, his name being proposed by a privy councillor (primed beforehand) and automatically accepted. In this liaison lies one of the most potent secrets of the success of the 'popular despotism' of the Tudors. The risk to royal authority of bringing the commons into full partnership was obviated by giving the executive a real but disguised control, never obtruded and freely accepted, over the younger and less experienced branch of the legislature.[1]

'Prominence in the council', it has been said, 'was the best way of obtaining supremacy in the state, and full intelligence of foreign affairs was the best way of securing prominence in the council.'[2] But not all the council were necessarily admitted to the inner secrets of government; the ultimate factor was always possession of the royal confidence and favour, irrespective of the titular office held. Until Wolsey's fall the king's right-hand man was almost automatically the great churchman who held the office of chancellor; it was Wolsey's old servant Thomas Cromwell who first broke with tradition and wielded supreme power under the crown as a mere layman holding none of the great historic offices and, until the eve of his fall, no great territorial dignity. His 'relentless energy' exploited to

[1]Notestein, op. cit.; D. H. Willson, *The Privy Councillors in the House of Commons,* Minnesota U.P., 1940.
[2]F. M. G. Evans (Mrs. Higham), *The Principal Secretary of State,* 1923, p. 56 *et passim.*

the full the intimate access to the king derived from his secular-ized post of confidential secretary, till he almost superseded the privy council, turned what remained of the lords spiritual into royal nominees, 'rigged' the elections to the commons, and in general replaced tradition by ruthless efficiency, eschewing all pomp but brooking no rival near the throne. The aristo-cratic encroachments of the fifteenth century were answered with a vengeance; had Cromwell's rule and system been con-tinued it would have brought England into line with the sort of despotism that Louis XI had planted in France. Yet even Cromwell owed his tenure of power only to the skill with which he showed the king what he wanted and got it done for him. His authority had no roots either in tradition or in public confidence—he was not one of 'those people that the nation have a good opinion of'; and when he overreached himself with the king, not even his carefully packed parliament lifted a finger to save him. After his fall the secretary's office was divided into two (a precaution, perhaps, against another Cromwell with undivided authority), and at the same time removed from the recesses of the palace into the hierarchy of state.

The minority of Edward VI was no time for the development of settled government, and the Marian reaction brought back the traditional sway of a clerical chancellor, with a large, old-fashioned privy council. It was under Elizabeth that the office of secretary came into its own. Up to a point she returned to the Cromwell *régime*, with at first only a single secretary—a man of outstanding ability who was in many ways Cromwell's political heir; but there the likeness ended. The privy council was neither the cipher that Cromwell had tried to make it nor the large and amorphous body that had become a breeding-ground for faction while her brother and her sister ruled; and to balance the pull the secretary enjoyed through his access to confidential papers and the royal closet, there were other able counsellors (or flashy courtiers), often of differing views, whom she did not hesitate to use when it suited her. None ever en-joyed her confidence exclusively or continuously; there was always a temporary favourite in the background to keep her official advisers on their mettle. Even Burghley had long to endure the rivalry of Walsingham (who succeeded him as

secretary when he became treasurer), as well as the royal
flirtations with Leicester and Essex.[1] This balancing of
factions became a stock device of her successors, but none
played it with such success, at least until the days of Charles II.

If the secretary never acquired control of policy he did become the king-pin of administration. Indeed we might regard
him as the link between the deliberative and the executive
phases of the council's work. He it was in the first place who
prepared the business for council, and in Elizabeth's time he
first became something like an *ex officio* member. Through his
hands passed the all-important foreign dispatches, as well as
the endless correspondence with local authorities which came
to form the bulk of the council's written records. As well as
being the council's link with local government, he was also its
principal link with the commons. It came to be an accepted
convention that the secretary, unless a peer (which he seldom
was) sought a seat in the lower house instead of sitting as an
'assistant' in the upper, and acted there as the crown's parliamentary manager.[2] In his office, in fact, was concentrated all
the business of the later departments of state that in course of
time branched out from it; he was the universal joint of government.

[1] *E.H.R.* xxvii. 34.
[2] *History*, xxv. 197.

II

Sowing the Wind

1603–25

THE smooth and effective working of a constitution such
as has been sketched in the last chapter depended in the
last resort on an intimate understanding of the society
that produced and lived under it. Such an understanding the
Tudors had *par excellence*. It is true that they were Welsh, not
English, in origin; but they belonged to a section of Welsh
society that had long been ready to assimilate itself to the
English social and legal system, and more recently to hitch its
wagon to the star of the English court. The founder of the
family fortunes had been rewarded for his services to the last of
the native princes by extensive grants of land held English
fashion, outside the tribal system; a century and a half later
most of his descendants were in the camp of Owain Glyn Dŵr,
himself a Tudor on his mother's side—to the permanent impoverishment of the parent branch; it was a younger son who
sought his fortune at the court, to such good purpose as to take
an English king's widow to wife and to marry his son (who
became Henry VII's father) to a descendant of John of Gaunt.
Henry VII rallied his countrymen to him in his buccaneering
bid for the English throne by an appeal to Welsh sentiment
and bardic prophecy; but it was his set policy—followed to a
successful conclusion by the dynasty he founded, and exploited
to the full by their successors—to merge this sentiment in a

broader British patriotism. And despite the irruption of his grandfather into court circles, the vicissitudes of the Wars of the Roses (as well as his own deeper roots) made Henry a man of the provinces rather than of the court and capital—in close touch with the ambitions and perplexities of the country gentry and the machinery of local government.[1]

Very different was the background of James I. An alien, born to the throne of an independent state proudly conscious of its distinctive legal and social system, he had ruled there for twenty years (preceded by a long minority stretching back to his babyhood) before ever he set foot in his new kingdom. All that he knew of England was what he had picked up from his limited English contacts, read in the light of the practical experiences and abstract theories of a shrewd, learned and observant but opinionated and not very imaginative politician. 'This I may say for Scotland', he told his first parliament,[2]

> and I may truly vaunt it; here I sit, and govern it with my Pen; I write and it is done; and by a Clerk of the Council I govern Scotland now, which others could not do by the sword.

It does not seem to have occurred to him that these were not the words in which to advertise to Englishmen, already nervous for their treasured system of common law, the blessings of closer partnership with a nation where Roman law had triumphed, with all its despotic implications. And parliament might have been even more suspicious had it known the private thoughts about it which he later poured into the ear of the Spanish ambassador:—

> I am surprised that my ancestors should ever have permitted such an institution to come into existence. I am a stranger, and found it here when I arrived so that I am obliged to put up with what I cannot get rid of.[3]

Not that there was anything of the impatient iconoclast about James; he was too indolent and peace-loving for that. He honestly tried to administer the institutions he found to hand;

---

[1] Glyn Roberts in *Trans. Anglesey Antiquarian Society*, 1951, pp. 43–72; A. H. Dodd in *Trans. Cymmrodorion Society*, 1948, pp. 15–16.
[2] *Commons Journals*, i. 362.
[3] Quoted by S. R. Gardiner, *History of England, 1603–42*, 2nd ed., ii. 251.

what remained a sealed book to him was the *spirit* of the constitution and the social order on which it rested. He inherited
from Elizabeth a privy council of fifteen which the Venetian
ambassador described (in a shrewd report on English affairs
written when James's reign was four years old) as the 'ears,
body and voice of the king'—in contrast with parliament, which
the king was said to summon 'out of modesty' on special occasions calling for the 'introduction or amendment of laws, supply,
etc.'[1] James also kept in office Elizabeth's two secretaries of
state: Burghley's son Robert Cecil (soon to become earl of
Salisbury)—the 'little beagle' to whom he was largely indebted
for his peaceful accession, and on whose advice in general he
leaned until his death in 1612; and John Herbert, the South
Wales barrister whom the queen had latterly added as 'second
secretary' (a novel title) on account of his great legal and
linguistic gifts. Herbert, however—a civil servant rather than a
politician—was never consulted on policy; when Salisbury
was not available James turned to any congenial companion—
official councillor or no—who happened to be at hand, and
after his 'beagle's' death he kept the office vacant for four years
rather than promote to it so dry a stick as 'Mr. Secondarie
Herbert'.[2]

Even before Cecil's death a change was becoming apparent
in the king's use of the privy council. To begin with, it grew
rapidly in size—always an ominous symptom, since a swollen
privy council was bound to carry more than its share of what
Clarendon called 'men of great power who will not take the
pains to have great parts', and so clogged and blunted it as an
instrument of policy.[3] The fifteen councillors he inherited from
the last reign grew in four years to twenty-five and by the end
of the reign to thirty-five.[4] The king himself was reluctant to
discuss business in council; even Salisbury had difficulty in
inducing him to attend when the agenda was all routine, and
after his Elizabethan mentor had gone, James's appearances
grew rarer and rarer: he was present only twice in 1618 and

---

[1] Nicolo Molin, 'Report on England', 1607, *Cal.S.P.Ven.*, 1603–7, no. 739, pp.
508–9.
[2] Evans, op. cit., pp. 57–9, 68.
[3] *History*, iii. 54 (Macray's ed. i. 261); cf. the Venetian ambassador's allegation that
Exeter was added to the council in 1627 simply to facilitate the collection of
subsidies in his wide and distant lord lieutenancy (*Cal.S.P.Ven.*, 1626–8, p. 94).
[4] Willson, op. cit., p. 22.

three times (out of seventy-five meetings) in 1622.¹ 'The
Council', wrote the Venetian ambassador, 'spares the King the
trouble of governing . . . he leaves all government to his
Council and thinks of nothing but the chase'.² But foreign
observers do not always see the complete picture. What
James gave over to his council was the day-to-day routine of
administration; policy he kept strictly in his own hands, and
discussed only with his intimate companions—likely enough
on the 'chase' itself, or on other social occasions of which the
ambassador had no inside knowledge. As long as the 'beagle'
remained among these intimates, the advice the king received
at least came from responsible quarters, which is more than
can be said of the *régime* that followed his death; but the discontinuance of the full debates on foreign affairs in the royal
presence that had been a feature of Elizabeth's privy councils
was already beginning to undermine public confidence.

It was primarily in the house of commons that the effects
were felt. When James complained to the Spanish ambassador
(not without reason) that the commons were 'a body without
a head' who 'give their opinions in a disorderly manner' with
nothing but 'cries, shouts, and confusion', he did not realize
how far he was responsible for the fact that the house was
fumbling its way towards replacing the lost leadership of 'those
about the Chair'. If the commons had been satisfied that matters
of high policy had been fully debated and assented to by men
in whom they had confidence and who were on the spot to
explain the royal intentions, they might have been less hasty
over trespassing into these fields themselves. But the resumption by the privy council of the aristocratic complexion it had
shed under the Tudors left few councillors available to sit in
the lower house. Over half of Elizabeth's last council—two-
thirds indeed of those in effective attendance—had been commoners; by 1613 there were actually fewer commoners in a
much larger council, and no great effort was made to find seats
in the commons even for this reduced handful. In the first
parliamentary session of the reign there were only two, and for
part of the time only 'Mr. Secondarie Herbert', who cut no
figure at all in the house. His senior co-secretary had been

¹E. R. Turner in *E.H.R.*, xxxviii. 187–8.
²'Report on England', loc. cit., pp. 508, 513.

called to the lords, and from his new eminence he tried without much success to continue for the new king his services to the late queen as parliamentary manager, by the device of inviting the commons, whenever opposition arose, to send delegates to a conference with the upper house at which he could put the government case. After his death the need to provide government spokesmen in the lower house became more urgent, and by 1621 the number of councillors with seats there had reached nine. Even so no steps were taken towards ensuring their attendance at crucial debates or towards planting there the sort of men who could sway the house, in preference to mere administrators like Herbert. Nor did the king think them important enough to call for his intervention when (as happened to one of them in 1614) the house expelled them for irregular conduct.

Besides all this, the absence of prior debates on policy left these spokesmen often without a brief to speak to. In the higher reaches of policy most of them knew little of the king's views or intentions, and as a body they could seldom speak with one voice; at least one of them deserted to the opposition. Even in the field of legislation they were hampered by the fact that the Elizabethan practice of mapping out a legislative programme before the houses met was in abeyance, except for some minor 'bills of grace' which from time to time the king allowed his councillors to introduce as a sop to appease parliamentary clamours. So that instead of timely intervention on the king's behalf by an experienced parliamentary hand before a crisis blew up, the king's case was presented, too late to have its proper weight, in royal messages of which the effect was blunted by too frequent use.[1]

The root of the trouble seems to have been James's inability to appreciate the importance in English society and politics of the middling range of gentry—the men with no great position at court but with deep roots in the country; he was 'interested', declares a recent critic, 'in the Court, not the Country'. An aristocracy he understood, and his own experiences at home had taught him how necessary it was to keep on terms with it

---

[1]This aspect of the reign, first explored in Notestein's British Academy paper, is examined in detail in Willson's *Privy Councillors in the House of Commons*, from which the foregoing particulars are taken.

and to keep it in dependence on the crown. Where Elizabeth
had made eight new peers, he made sixty, and he did not stint
them of profitable places and honours at court—including, as
we have seen, the lion's share of seats at the council board. But
the English country gentry had no precise counterpart in
Scottish society, and James fatally underestimated their importance. Already faced (if the latest theories be true) with a
declining net revenue from their lands, they now bore the
brunt of the multiplied exactions in purveyance and wardships
by which the king financed the extravagance of his court,
despite the warnings and protests of his 'little beagle'. The
gentry also missed the pickings at sea that had helped to
balance many a tottering budget while the war with Spain
lasted, and this in turn sharpened the edge of their protestant
zeal against a foreign policy that seemed to truckle to Spain,
yoked with a religious policy that threatened to let in the pope
by a back door.[1] A privy council consisting of what the Venetian
ambassador called 'great lords or their dependents', together
with a few colourless civil servants, failed to give confidence
that what the country gentry valued would be upheld in public
policy. It may be doubted whether even the king's lavish hand
with new peerages helped him much; it has been suggested that
too many of the upstart aristocracy were without the influence
in their shires, or in neighbouring parliamentary boroughs,
which might have saved him the uproar raised when in the
elections to the Addled Parliament he tried to use court influences directly and openly—and with conspicuous lack of success.[2]

All the more determined were the gentry that England's
voice should be heard at Westminster. The new temper of the
monarchy found its answer with remarkable speed in the new
temper of parliament. Within a single session it had begun to
find its own leaders from within, to usurp control of disputed
elections and disciplinary powers over its own members, to
sidetrack the speaker (still a royal official) by multiplying committees—especially the new device of committees of the whole
house—where private members presided, and even to develop a
rudimentary machinery of organized opposition. Of this last

[1]H. R. Trevor-Roper, *The Gentry, 1540–1640 (Econ. Hist. Rev.* Suppt., i, 1953,
pp. 35–9).
[2]Notestein, loc. cit., pp. 35–6.

tendency there are signs as early as 1606, when disaffected
members are found meeting in secret to plan their campaign
against the jurisdiction of the Council of Wales over the border
shires, a branch of his prerogative on which the king set great
store.[1] A few years later the tactics of opposition members are
described in detail by a hostile observer who writes of

> . . . secrette and privye Conventicles and Conferences,
> wherein they devised and set down speciall plottes, for the
> carryinge of businesse in the house, accordinge to theyr owne
> humour and dryfte . . . To which purpose yt was devised
> that Syxe of them who had great countenance and dyd beare
> great swaye in the house, shoulde be prepared to speake at
> large . . . and shoulde sett forth all the arguments and
> reasons . . . And that after those theyr speeches the residue
> shoulde be silent, and not to speake any thinge therein at all,
> untille the bylle shoulde be put to the question, and then to
> overthrowe it with a generall, No.[2]

In the circumstances it is not surprising that the new leaders
of the commons should rebuff any attempt in the next parliament to recover the initiative for what might be called the
embryonic treasury bench. Instead of being automatically
included in committees of the house, as had been the general
practice ever since the committee system was instituted, the
privy councillors now began to find themselves pointedly
excluded. Sir James Perrot, the member for Haverfordwest
and one of those who 'had great countenance and dyd beare
great swaye in the house', openly championed the 'indifferent
naming of committees' without regard to 'those about the
Chair'; he paid for his consistent frowardness by being whisked
off to a thankless job in Ireland. When in 1621 the privy
councillors were back in force, it was Sir William Herbert—a
future royalist peer but now the spokesman in the commons of
his kinsman the powerful but disaffected earl of Pembroke—
who voiced the house's resentment at attempts by 'those about
the Chair' to bully the speaker into turning a blind eye to
members unacceptable to court who tried to catch it.[3]

[1]Hist. MSS. Com., *Salisbury*, xviii. 389, 456.
[2]Quoted Willson, op. cit., p. 121.
[3]*C.J.* i. 461, 547; A. H. Dodd in *Trans. Cymmrodorion Soc.*, 1942, pp. 40, 47, 70–1;
  cf. Willson, op. cit., pp. 237–8 and n.

So far, parliament had been on the defensive: its aim had been to free itself from the leading-strings of the royal court and council; but before long there were signs of an itch to carry the war into the enemy's camp by fitting the restricting boot on to the other foot and making the king's men answerable to the legislature. As early as 1614 the king consented to dismiss his chancellor of the duchy of Lancaster when the commons expelled him for an election offence; and the next parliament went a step further by reviving the antiquated weapon of impeachment. It was used in the first instance not against servants of the crown, but against private malefactors whose misdeeds had come to light in the course of an exhaustive inquiry into abuses in high places. Since the matter arose out of an investigation of patents and monopolies granted at the instance of the ruling favourite, Buckingham—and to the enrichment of his family—there lurked in it the germs of a theory of ministerial responsibility, even though at this stage it was not (as was to happen later on) Buckingham's conduct in his public office of lord high admiral that was called in question. But Buckingham wisely listened to the advice of his friend Bishop Williams and dropped his *protégés*; and Buckingham had the last word with the king. So the offenders were punished or fled, the king promised redress, and although by his hasty dissolution of parliament he prevented the measure in which statutory force was given to these promises from reaching the statute book that session, parliament had undoubtedly won the first round.

It had also followed up its initial success. Its persistent inquest on abuses had taken it next to the court of chancery, where they abounded, and which, as a stronghold of prerogative jurisdiction, was always unpopular with the common lawyers in the house. This meant a direct attack on a prominent servant of the crown—though not one who was deeply in the royal confidence, and on charges that were legal, not political. It is unlikely, however, that without a political *arrière pensée* Bacon's conduct as lord chancellor would have been an object of attack, since the charges of corruption levelled against him, (and freely admitted) could have been brought against almost any public official in days when the assumption was that only their working expenses would be met from public sources, while the incomes on which they maintained their families and kept up their private position were provided by fees, presents and hereditary estates. This time the king took alarm, and tried to get the trial removed from the political arena to a special tribunal chosen by him from among the members of the two houses; but once more he found it prudent to give way, and to see his servant dismissed from office and declared unfit for further public employment. The general principle enunciated by the commons in their parting Protestation—'that arduous and urgent affairs concerning the king's state, and the defence of the realm . . . are proper subjects and matter of counsel and debate in parliament' was the last straw. Rather than leave such doctrines on record he tore the page from the journal with his own hand.[1]

It was in the last session of the reign that parliamentary boldness reached its climax, for then the opposition had for a moment what was to give cohesion and courage to Hanoverian opposition parties until at last they were able to stand on their own feet—the support and countenance of a faction at court, including the heir apparent himself. For Prince Charles and Buckingham had just returned from the farcical wooing of the Infanta, smarting under supposed insults and ready to make common cause with the enemies of appeasement. The first object of attack was the lord treasurer, Lionel Cranfield, earl of Middlesex—a business man who had been called in to straighten out the king's finances, and who had no desire to see his good work dissipated in a futile war with a declining power, of which the general opinion of the business community was expressed in the words of James Howell when on a commercial mission there: 'no country is able to do England less hurt, and more good than Spain, considering the large Traffic and Treasure that is to be got thereby'.[2] The gentry in the commons had powerful social as well as political motives for attacking a quondam London apprentice who had climbed through court favour to a high rank in the peerage and a succession of lucrative offices, in one of which—as master of wards—he was responsible for some of their heaviest burdens. Once more it was easy enough to find material for charges of corruption, and

---

[1] G. W. Prothero, *Select Statutes and Constitutional Documents*, 2nd ed., 1898, p. 314.
[2] Howell, *Familiar Letters*, ed. J. Jacobs, 1892, p. 213.

this time the commons proceeded by way of a full-blown impeachment (in contrast with Bacon's case, which had been a unilateral action on the part of the lords to remedy a 'grievance' of the commons); and Middlesex was dismissed and disgraced.

It was the first time for over 170 years that the full battery of impeachment had been turned with success against a minister of the crown, and the farthest step yet taken in the direction of ministerial responsibility. Not that the king admitted any such implication. He saw clearly enough the bearing of the commons' claims, and he warned his son and his favourite (only too prophetically) that they would soon have their 'bellyful of impeachments'. Before ever the storm broke over the lord treasurer, James had made his position clear on the occasion of an abortive attack on Bacon's successor on the woolsack, Bishop Williams. Like Cranfield, Williams had gained the king's ear through the favour of Buckingham, and like him he had boggled at his patron's change of heart about Spain; he was also suspect in the commons as an ecclesiastic, unlearned in the law, who was believed to have stretched the authority of chancery at the expense of the common law. When the first mutterings against him reached the king's ears, James sent a message to the effect that 'if there were any Bill of corruption or bribery preferred against the Lord Keeper they should entertain the same; but he would not meddle with his errors or slips in judgement'. In other words, he would listen to criminal but not to political charges against his servants. Williams had not given any ground for the former, and the matter was reluctantly dropped; the opposition was luckier with Middlesex.[1]

Yet with such powerful support at their backs the commons could not so easily be checked in their career. There was a full-dress debate on foreign affairs—a spectacle to make Queen Elizabeth turn in her grave!—in which the Glamorgan sea-dog Sir Robert Mansell (Buckingham's popular if incompetent vice-admiral) took on himself to put before an enthusiastic house highly optimistic estimates of the men, money and shipping needed for a successful naval war with Spain. Sir

[1]Nat. Lib. of Wales, *Cal. of Wynn (of Gwydir) Papers*, 1926, no. 1198; *C.J.*, i. 688, 785.

James Perrot had evoked equal enthusiasm for the same sentiments (without the statistical backing) in the last parliament;
but now, with the prince and the duke at one with the parliamentary clamour, the ageing king could no longer resist the
demand that he should break with Spain, and parliament for
its part was ready to pay the piper, once it was assured of
some share in calling the tune—or at least calling the piper to
account if he played the wrong tune. With this end in view the
Subsidy Act named as receivers of the subsidy the puritan
ex-lord mayor Sir Thomas Myddelton and seven others whose
names were a pledge of good faith. It was further laid down

> to the end that all the sums of money by this present Act
> granted, . . . may be truly expended for the uses aforesaid
> and not otherwise . . . That the moneys to be received by
> the said treasurers . . . shall be issued . . . to such persons
> and in such manner as by the warrant of . . . ten persons
> his Majesty hath already nominated to be of his council for
> the war, or any five or more of them, whereof two of them to
> be of his Majesty's most honourable Privy Council, . . .
> shall be directed, and not otherwise. And . . . That as well
> the said treasurers as the said persons appointed for the
> council of war . . . shall be answerable . . . to the Commons
> in parliament, when they shall be thereunto required by
> warrant under the hand of the Speaker of the House of
> Commons,

with express provision that if they failed to give satisfaction they
were to be committed to the Tower, or, if peers, to the judgement of the upper house.[1]

The commons were promised categorically that none of the
money voted should be used save by the advice of the council
of war, which included their own Sir Robert Mansell, and
that they themselves should be consulted on future policy—
though not, of course, on strategic plans, which must 'not be
ordered by a multitude'. Even with this obvious reservation it
was a very different tone from what the king had used to Spain
about parliament ten years earlier. James at least knew when
he was beaten, and after forty years of kingcraft he was learning

---

[1] A. H. Dodd, loc. cit., pp. 65–6, 44–5. Terms of Subsidy Act (21 and 22 Jac. I, cap.
xxxiii) in Prothero, *Select Statutes*, pp. 278–80.

the Elizabethan art of climbing down gracefully. Here was something more positive than the revival of an out-of-date procedure to bring to book, under cover of legal misdemeanours, an unpopular minister; it was, as Gardiner says, 'the beginning of a great change'—the recognition 'that certain special officials were to be responsible to Parliament as well as to the Crown'.[1] But how to bring the responsibility home, and above all how to reconcile responsibility to the crown with responsibility to parliament when the two pulled in opposite directions—these were matters still to be resolved, not without dust and heat. But the dust and heat were not for James; within a year he had passed from the scene, leaving the knot to be unpicked by the clumsier fingers of his son.

[1] *Hist. of Eng.*, v. 201–2, vi. 74.

III

Reaping the Whirlwind

1625–42

THE new reign started under promising auspices. It is
true that the twenty-four-year-old king had none of the
popularity of his lamented elder brother, and his self-
confidence had suffered from the invidious comparison, with
the result that he never quite knew the right moment or manner
for asserting himself; but his part in the concluding scenes of
the last reign had shown him both to the country and to himself in a new light. If he was not personally popular (and his
father had never been that) at least he stood (in contrast to
James) for a popular policy, and he seems to have deluded
himself into believing that he had mastered what his father
missed—the knack of managing parliament. James had shrunk
from recalling the houses, as arranged, in the autumn, to
receive reports on the use made of the subsidies voted in May
and to vote the further sums needed to finance the next stage
in the military plans; he knew too well that his diplomatic
manœuvres had not yet reached the stage where he dared
divulge them to parliament, and that only some resounding
success in the military or the diplomatic field could make
palatable to his people the staggering military budget involved
in Buckingham's plans, or the concessions to catholic recusants
which were the price of a French marriage treaty and French
support in the proposed European campaign.

Charles had no such reserves. He was a little dashed, it is true, when Lord Keeper Williams told him that the demise of the crown meant new elections and not just the recall of the parliament in which he had cut so brave a figure. It is true also that he had nothing better to tell members than James would have had to tell their predecessors in the abandoned autumn session. But none of this daunted him. Why should it? Before the old reign ended, the marriage treaty with France had been signed and greeted with joy in the capital, and the strings attached to it could no doubt be explained away, either to parliament (which was bound to dislike them) or to the French court (which had proved unpleasantly insistent) once they had served their turn. Moreover just before parliament met, Buckingham brought home for him his fourteen-year-old French bride, whose personal vivacity and charm—added to the fact that she was the daughter (as she tactfully recalled in this country) of a quondam Huguenot hero—might be trusted to make a sentimental public forget what the marriage involved. Best of all, the navy was quite obviously being put into trim for what the public wanted most—a revival of the glorious and profitable exploits of the Elizabethan sea-dogs. As the new king disarmingly told his parliament when it met within three months of his accession,

> I came into this business willingly, freely, like a young man, and consequently rashly; but it was by your entreaties, your engagements . . . I pray you remember that this being my first action, and begun by your advice and entreaty, what a great dishonour it were both to you and me if this action so begun should fail for that assistance you are able to give me.[1]

So far so good; but when members began to ask awkward questions about the disposal of the last subsidy and the proposed destination of the next, there was no one in the house to answer—partly because there had been no full debates on policy in the privy council as a whole, partly because none of those in a position to speak for the government dared admit the extent to which the country was already committed. A memorandum drawn up for the king on his accession had laid down in clear terms the traditional constitution of the privy council—its

[1]Gardiner, *Hist. of Eng.*, v. 338.

optimum size, mode of summons, powers, procedure and
standing orders, with express provision that 'every Councillor
hath equal vote there' and 'no offence to be taken for any
unfitting advice delivered but as little discourse or repetition
to be used as may be for saving of time'.[1] There is no sign that
the slightest notice was taken; and this was the real root of the
'rashness' for which Charles tried so disingenuously to make
the commons responsible. Pending fuller information, they
voted as an interim measure two subsidies—about a tenth of
what was needed to implement Buckingham's plans—together
with tonnage and poundage for one year only instead of, in the
usual way, for life. It was not till after members, having dis-
patched (they imagined) the main business for which they
were summoned, stampeded in swarms from their seats to
escape the plague then raging in London, that a government
spokesman gave to a very thin house a gross under-estimate
of the further sums needed to finance a strategic plan only
dimly hinted at, but obviously far beyond anything con-
templated when the money was first voted.

Enough had been said to convince the house that the careful
safeguards with which the last parliament had hedged about
its war subsidy had gone for nothing, and that it must not let
the same sort of confidence trick be played on it a second time.
'Counsels and power', declared one member, 'have been mono-
polized'. 'The proper design', complained another, 'no man
holdeth fit should be disclosed to us', and he urged that 'when
his Majesty doth make a war, it may be debated and advised
by his grave council'.[2] This brought Buckingham to his feet in
self-defence. At a joint session of the two houses (now driven by
the plague to Oxford) he delivered his apologia, hinted broadly
that the naval war had first priority and might, if adequately
backed, make the more far-reaching plans unnecessary, and
rebutted the charge of monopoly of power by insisting that both
privy council and council of war had been consulted. It was on
the latter that the commons concentrated, since the Subsidy
Act itself had made its participation and consent an express
condition of the disbursement of the subsidy. Sir Robert
Mansell, the one member of this council who sat in the lower

[1]Printed by Temperley in *E.H.R.*, xxviii. 127–30.
[2]Gardiner, *Hist.*, pp. 410, 414, *Const. Documents of the Puritan Revolution*, p. 1.

house, was closely cross-questioned. Torn between his obligations as a confidential counsellor and as a representative in parliament—faced, in fact, with the fundamental dilemma of responsible government—he maintained at first a stubborn silence; but at last he made the 'bold avouchement' (qualified by perfunctory tributes to the duke's 'good judgment' and 'brave dessigne' and a covering prayer 'that none of his wordes might hurte the Kinge') that Buckingham's plan had been put before the council of war as a *fait accompli* brooking no debate save on details of execution. This brought the focus of the parliamentary searchlight dead on to the favourite himself, and the darling of the last parliament was now more than broadly hinted at as one of 'those that have not parts answerable to their places'. This was too much for the king. In spite of the entreaties of the lord keeper and even of Buckingham himself, the parliament he had so confidently called together was sent about its business with no further vote of supplies, leaving him and his minister to face as best they could commitments hopelessly outmatching their resources.[1]

If this was the mood of members before the war had fairly begun, they were hardly likely to mince their words in the next parliament, called to make what it could of an impossible financial situation after the naval attack on Spain and the half-hearted expedition to the continent had both ended in fiasco, and the French alliance in sterile recriminations. It was clear now that the number of men responsible for the country's plight could be reduced to two: the king and Buckingham. For Charles—even apart from the fundamental maxim that 'the king can do no wrong'—there was still nothing but sympathy; he was a young man, still virtually untried, and from his very good nature open (as he had himself admitted) to rash counsels. There was therefore a widespread determination, couched in terms that significantly recall Sir Winston Churchill's 'One man only' speech on Italy, to bring the favourite to book; but how? Precedents were lacking for an impeachment in which the charges were frankly political. It was in any case difficult to find evidence other than 'common fame' for what had been said and done in secret conclave, and members were still reluctant to base criminal charges on mere 'errors of judge-

[1] Gardiner, *Hist.*, ch. liv, passim; *C.J.*, i. 814-5.

ment'. In the course of debates this distinction, clearly drawn
by James I when Lord Keeper Williams was attacked, was
reiterated more than once by private members—especially
those who had received, or who looked for, favours from the
accused minister; and on this the house as a whole was with
them.[1]

To clinch matters, the king intervened early, both in person
and through Coventry (who had replaced Williams on the
woolsack as a more pliable instrument of the duke) to recall
the commons from their 'unparliamentary inquisition'—or
what Cromwell would have called 'raking into sores'—to the
urgent business of supply. Their novel and half-formed doctrine
of ministerial responsibility he roundly rejected in these uncompromising terms:—

> Some there are . . . that do make inquiry into the proceed-
> ings, not of any ordinary servant, but of one that is most near
> unto me . . . Certain it is that I did command him to do
> what he hath done therein. I would not have the House to
> question my servants, much less one that is so near to me.
> And therefore I hope I shall find justice at your hands to
> punish such as shall offend in that kind.[2]

But the commons were not to be headed off: if necessary
they must rescue their trustful and vulnerable young king from
himself. As trustees, moreover, they were not prepared to dip
again into their constituents' pockets without some more satisfactory guarantee that they were not merely sending good
money after bad; and how could this be, so long as the money
voted was administered by one who had already shown himself
(to put the charge at its mildest) unequal to his job? Yet mere
lack of confidence was no ground for impeachment—this was
indeed its fundamental weakness as an instrument for enforcing
responsibility; so the commons set about the usual unsavoury
business of looking round for grounds on which criminal
charges could be based, and the grounds chosen were (also
as usual) direct or indirect 'pillaging' of the treasures of king
and subject alike for the enrichment of himself and his minions;

[1]See report of debate in MS diary attrib. to Bulstrode Whitelocke, Camb. Univ.
Lib. MSS. Dd. 12.20–22, and cf. *C.J.*, i. 835, *Trans. Cymmr. Soc.*, 1945, pp.
25–8.
[2]Gardiner, *Documents*, pp. 3–6.

into these charges it was easy, without any overt reference to policy as such, to slip allusions to the further squandering of the same treasures in the public discharge of his many offices of state. The case was put clearly and skilfully by Eliot, the unacknowledged 'leader of the opposition' in this house as Phelips had been in the last. There was no intention, he declared, to starve the crown of supplies—very much the reverse; but until these defalcations and misdemeanours had been inquired into and the cause of them removed, there could be in the nation at large neither the will nor the power to underwrite any supplies their representatives might vote. As soon as this basic obstacle should be removed, the commons would feel free to loose the country's purse-strings.[1]

Eliot carried the house with him: whatever difference of opinion there might be about the grounds of accusation, the doctrine implicit in the royal caveat 'I would not have the House to question my servants' was emphatically repudiated in the Remonstrance drawn up by the commons a few weeks later:—

> It hath been the ancient, constant and undoubted Right and Usage of Parliament, to question and complain of all persons of what degree soever, found grievous to the Commonwealth, in abusing the power and trust committed to them by their Sovereign.

And so the charges were formulated and the duke, in spite of his master's specific assumption of responsibility for all he had done, answered them (not ineffectively) line for line; until the king, unable to stand any more of it, ignored the advice of his wiser counsellors and the entreaties of the lords (who wanted him to put himself on stronger ground by awaiting the probable breakdown of the charges), and put a stop to proceedings by dissolving parliament, once more with his wants unsupplied. It was but another example of his fatal propensity, when he did act decisively, to act at the wrong moment.[2]

Before parliament met again, the king's affairs had, almost inevitably, gone from bad to worse. Scorning unpalatable counsels, he had let the quarrel with his French allies drift

[1]Gardiner, *Documents*, pp. 7–22, *Hist. of Eng.*, vi. 80–81.
[2]*Documents*, pp. 6–7, 23–44.

into a futile war; starved of supplies, he had no better success in this than in his Spanish naval venture; and the more ambitious schemes on land had gone by the board. To keep his wars going at all, he had had to find means of supplying himself without parliamentary grants, and these in turn laid his agents and officers open to challenge on the legality of their demands for money, their penalties on those who refused, and all the paraphernalia of mobilization in a state ill-equipped for foreign adventures. The council met frequently: for a time it was in daily session, and was even known to meet twice in a single day; but the raising of money was almost its sole concern, and there were times when so many councillors had gone to their own 'countries' to speed up supplies that none were left to discuss the affairs of the nation. This, however, can have made no substantial difference if (as the Venetian ambassador believed) discussions of policy were stultified by the fact that no one dared oppose any scheme that had the duke's backing— especially with the knowledge that 'what the Council decrees the duke changes to suit his interest'.[1]

Naturally when parliament did meet in 1628 the focus of opposition shifted from the remoter field of European policy (where it was too late to do anything anyway) to grievances that struck nearer home and were more within the recognized competence of parliament. For the moment the novel and thorny question of ministerial responsibility receded into the background, to make way for the more immediate and practical issue of securing the liberty of the subject in the Petition of Right. It was these matters that continued to produce discord between king and parliament, and brought to a stormy end what had been, but for the Petition of Right, another sterile session, with rancours unabated even after the assassin's knife had removed from the scene the man who had been the chief bone of contention ever since the reign began.

The 'Eleven Years' Tyranny' that followed was of course an express repudiation of the very basis of responsible government. The commons had overreached themselves; they were still too hesitant and confused about the whole problem to have done more than lay down the principle without arriving at any clear conception of what it involved. Yet it would be far from true to

[1]*Cal. S.P. Ven.*, 1626–8, pp. 22, 93, 107–8, 118, 128, 195, 530, 558–9, 565, 575.

say that when the issue was raised again in the Long Parliament the intervening eleven years counted for nothing. One lesson at least the king had learnt from the long-drawn crisis: if he could not get on with parliament, all the more necessary was it that he should make a more effective use of the privy council. In many of the debates he had been ill served by spokesmen from the council, because as a body it had never been taken sufficiently into the royal confidence to be able to present anything like a solid front or a concerted case to the opposition, which in turn (as the lord keeper reproachfully recalled) 'suffered the greatest Council of State to be censured and traduced in this house, by men whose years and education cannot attain to that depth'.[1] Indeed there are times when the opposition in the lower house gives every sign of owing some at least of its inspiration to disgruntled councillors in the upper. A notable case is that of the earl of Pembroke, that 'Hamlet of the court of Charles I', as Gardiner calls him,[2] whose sane and balanced counsels cut no ice with the king (though he was too wealthy and influential to be kept out of office), but who lacked the energy and persistence for any sustained political effort. Yet Pembroke's vast estates gave him control over many seats in the commons, and it was from these seats that the voice of opposition was often heard. It is doubtful, for example, whether Mansell's 'bold avouchement' which brought matters to a head in the first parliament, and his still more outspoken criticisms in the second, would ever have been made had he not been a henchman of Pembroke; it was certainly to his patron's backing that he owed his immunity when he was hauled before the council, and stood with equal boldness on his parliamentary privilege.[3]

It was too late now to restore the privy council to its old function of *liaison* with the commons, but at least it could be used as a sheet anchor for public confidence. During the years of personal government, when there was no Buckingham to 'monopolise counsels and power', the privy council recovered something of its old prestige as the hub of policy, and more than its old effectiveness as the hub of administration. The

[1]*Documents*, p. 8.
[2]*Hist. of Eng.*, vii. 133.
[3]Willson, op. cit., p. 200; V. A. Rowe in *E.H.R.*, l. 242–56; A. H. Dodd in *Trans. Cymm. Soc.*, 1943, pp. 69–71.

king himself was assiduous in attendance, debates on policy were frequent, and numbers were kept large and fluid enough to avoid the suggestion of a closed oligarchy, and to throw a cloak of legality over a dictatorial *régime*, without ever getting completely out of hand. Its vigilance over local administration left nothing to be desired from the royal point of view, though from that of the gentry its perpetual demands on them only helped to increase their restiveness.[1] A council of thirty, however, was unlikely to be of one mind on questions of the day on which the country was so sharply divided; and Charles had a pathetic and ill-founded belief in his own capacity to ride the storm by playing off one set of men against another, in domestic as in foreign affairs—a game played with far greater *finesse* by his father and his elder son. Thus the decision to raise supplies by recurrent levies of ship money was one in which the whole council participated, but the half-truth that went out to the country at large—that the ships were to be used to put down piracy and to establish sovereignty over the narrow seas—was all that most councillors knew or accepted as the purpose of the levy; the intention to provide maritime support for Spain against the French and Dutch was communicated only to a limited few known to be without anti-Spanish prejudice.[2]

The inevitable growth of faction in a body the size of the privy council, and the king's exploitation of it for his own ends, were by no means the only factors tending to modify its character and procedure. With the expansion of public business and the growing need for speed and secrecy, especially in foreign affairs, there was bound to develop on the one hand a habit of delegating particular items of business to smaller *ad hoc* bodies, on the other an inner ring of confidential counsellors. As early as 1616 we have glimpses of eleven temporary committees of the privy council, their function being, apparently, to sift and prepare matters referred to them for consideration in full council—what Bacon called 'ripening business'.[3] Charles I made increasing use of such committees, but he also crystallized

---

[1]Clarendon, *History*, i. 149, 158 (Macray's ed., i. 86, 92); Turner in *E.H.R.*, xxxviii. 188; E. M. Lennard, *Early History of English Poor Relief*, 1900, chs. viii and xii.
[2]Gardiner, *History*, vii. 355, 368–9; Clarendon iii. 52 (Macray i. 260–1).
[3]*E.H.R.*, xxxviii. 192; Bacon, *Essays*, 'Of Counsel'.

the practice, foreshadowed in the preceding reign, of setting apart a sort of standing executive for the dispatch, primarily of foreign affairs, but also of any other urgent business on hand. It was already in use in Buckingham's day, though how far it was any check on his supposed 'monopoly' of power it would be hard to say. Just before the duke and the prince returned from Spain, and on the eve of the parliament that put an end to appeasement, an inveterate retailer of court gossip reported

> a whispering that the junta or commission for forain affairs shalbe somwhat abridged in number, for though they be sworn to secresie yet some things are found to be vented and come abroad that were better kept close,

resulting in a general belief that 'there is somwhat abrewing'.[1] After the duke's death the foreign committee became part, if a fluid and fluctuating part, of the normal machinery of government. To the Venetian ambassador it appeared as 'depriving the ordinary Grand Council of all authority, because the number of councillors who received seats as an honorary rank, lessened the security and secrecy of their decisions.'[2]

The proceedings, even the appointment of this inner council, are rarely on record; it had no fixed duties, no fixed composition, not even an accepted nomenclature—all depended on the royal discretion. We know of its existence chiefly through the casual, and often unreliable and inconsistent, allusions of critics and gossip-writers, who sometimes call it 'the foreign committee' (or 'the Scottish committee' when Scotland replaced the continent as the storm centre of politics), sometimes just 'the committee', or 'the Eight' (when that was the number of inner councillors), sometimes by borrowed foreign labels like 'the cabinet council' or 'the juncto'. This very resort to foreign names suggests the belief that there was something foreign to English practice and English ideas in this infant institution; it also tends to distort its true character by suggesting non-existent analogies with French or Spanish practice. The cabinet council was not one of several co-ordinate or concentric councils, each in independent relation with the

---

[1]McClure (ed.), *Letters of John Chamberlain*, 1939, ii. 535.
[2]*Cal. S.P. Ven.*, 1626–8, p. 100.

crown; it always remained technically a subordinate part of the 'one Councell, in which' (as the Spanish ambassador told his government in some surprise) 'all businesses are treated'— however much it might gain in prestige and effective power through its access to information not communicated to the parent body.[1] Its only fixed pivots appear to have been the lord treasurer and one at least of the secretaries of state. In Buckingham's day the lord admiral was naturally a powerful, if not the all-powerful element in its composition, not only because Buckingham held the post, but because the navy then held the centre of the political stage. No one after him—neither Portland nor Wentworth nor Laud—ever dominated the scene to anything like the same degree: archbishops and lord keepers, earls marshal, chancellors of the exchequer and miscellaneous officers of the household appeared and disappeared at the hub of government, sometimes because of the bearing of the office they held on the political situation at the moment, occasionally with an eye to their influence in the country at large, but always in the last resort because the king wanted them near him. It was this fluid and arbitrary character of the 'cabinet council' that made it stink in the nostrils of constitutional purists and delayed so long its evolution into the cabinet as we know it today; for what hope was there of bringing to book a body with no formal existence and no fixed or known composition?[2]

The murder of Buckingham and the lapse of parliament put the question of responsible government into abeyance only, not into oblivion. It resumed its pride of place in the debates of the Long Parliament—not only negatively, by the revival of impeachment, but more positively in demands for the admission of counsellors in the confidence of parliament and for the consultation of the full privy council, instead of mere 'cabals'. Secretary Windebank, who had negotiated with the papal envoy for men and money to crush resistance, and Justice Finch, who was chiefly responsible for the legal enforcement of ship money, fled abroad from the wrath to come as soon as articles of impeachment were drawn up against them; Portland,

---

[1]E. R. Turner, *The Cabinet Council*, 1930, i. 24–5; cf. Bacon 'Of Counsel', North, *Lives of the Norths*, i. 299.
[2]Clarendon, *History*, ii. 61, 99, 118 (Macray, i. 171, 196); Turner, *Cabinet Council*, I., chs. i and ii (esp. pp. 33–8), and in *E.H.R.*, xxxviii. 171–205; E. I. Carlyle in id., xxi. 673–85.

who had had the king's ear during the first six of the eleven years of personal government, was dead; his successors, Laud and Wentworth (now Strafford), faced the music and were put under lock and key while the commons formulated their charges. Laud, as less immediately dangerous, was left to cool his heels in the Tower for three years before he came to trial, and the articles eventually exhibited against him were naturally concerned more with his conduct as primate than as councillor. It was on Strafford that the immediate fury of the house was concentrated; but it proved no easier than usual to translate political distrust into criminal charges—especially capital charges, and his accusers had fully made up their minds that their political objectives were unattainable until this far abler Buckingham was not merely out of office, but 'stone dead'. The long tale of 'oppressions' and 'extortions' which had now become almost common form in such cases yielded nothing that could be construed as treasonable except words alleged (on evidence that was even slenderer than for the lesser charges) to have been spoken in the Scottish committee.

After three weeks of vainly attempting to formulate a case likely to win the desired verdict in the lords, the commons gave it up, and resorted instead to a still more equivocal procedure inherited from the middle ages and last used (ominously enough) to provide Henry VIII with a short and easy way of getting rid of Thomas Cromwell—that of securing a verdict by legislative instead of quasi-judicial procedure, through an Act of Attainder. The same course was followed three years later with Laud; impeachment had again shown its futility as a means of enforcing ministerial responsibility. Yet the Strafford trial did not leave matters where they had stood at the time of the attack on Buckingham; in the novel construction of 'making war on the king' by which the earl's accusers tried to bring his conduct within the four corners of the treason laws, they were in effect using the royal title as a symbol of the community, and castigating obedience to royal commands which ran counter to their conception of national interest as ground, not merely for removal from office, but for charges of high treason. This principle, already implicit in the Triennial Act (with its self-acting machinery for periodic elections with or without the royal mandate), was made explicit twelve months later, on the eve of war, in a parliamentary manifesto which, after duly acknowledging the king as 'the fountain of justice and protection', bluntly declares that

> the acts of justice and protection are not exercised in his person, nor depend upon his pleasure, but by his courts and by his ministers, who must do their duty therein, though the King in his own person should forbid them . . For the King, by his sovereignty, is not enabled to destroy his people, but to protect and defend them; and the High Court of Parliament, and all other His Majesty's officers and ministers, ought to be subservient to that power and authority which the law hath placed in His Majesty to that purpose, though he himself, in his own person, should neglect the same.[1]

This was, of course, the sophistry by which when it came to open war parliament persuaded itself that it was fighting not against but for the king.

Meanwhile the more positive and general approach to the problem of ministerial responsibility was not altogether neglected. In the Ten Propositions sent by both houses to the king six weeks after Strafford's execution they asked not only for the removal of all councillors who had been 'furthering . . . courses contrary to religion, liberty, and good government', but that he should 'take into his Council for managing of the great affairs of this kingdom such officers as his people and Parliament may have just cause to confide in'. The Grand Remonstrance of the following November repeated the demand in more categorical terms as a condition for the granting of supplies, with the further provision 'that all Councillors of State may be sworn to observe those laws which concern the subject in his liberty'; and as a step towards clarifying the distinction between legal and political action against a statesman or minister of the crown, which the Strafford trial had brought to a head, the following tentative formula was offered:

> It may often fall out that the Commons may have just cause to take exceptions at some men for being councillors, and yet not charge these men with crimes, for there be grounds of diffidence which lie not in proof. There are others, which though they may be proved, yet are not legally criminal.

[1]Gardiner, *Documents*, pp. 256–7, cf. pp. 144–55.

To all this the king's reply was clear and uncompromising:—

> It is the undoubted right of the Crown of England to call such persons to our secret counsels, to public employment and our particular service as we shall think fit.[1]

In point of fact Charles had already tried to conciliate the opposition during the Strafford trial by admitting eight of their leaders (all peers) to the privy council. Clarendon, in recounting the incident, analyses with some penetration the weaknesses of the device. The prevailing spirit of faction made the newcomers look on themselves as in some sense mouth-pieces of the parliamentary opposition, and so imported the supercharged atmosphere of the parliament house into what should have been a 'prudent and steady Council' standing *au-dessus de la mêlée* in its 'wisdom, integrity, dignity and reputation'. For while Clarendon reprobated as strongly as any of his then colleagues the domination of the council by a single figure, to the exclusion of all effective discussion, he insisted on what has become the basic principle of modern cabinet government, even in coalitions—the need for unanimity on fundamentals of policy; failing this, as soon appeared, the 'opposition' councillors inevitably found themselves

> not fully trusted, and so became the more incensed with the reproachful distinction at, than obliged with the honourable admission to, that board, where they do not find all persons equally members,

while vital decisions were taken elsewhere. This was the weakness on which parliament fastened when, with the growing practice of the whole reign in mind, it addressed the king early in 1642 against 'Managing and Transacting the Affairs of the Realm in private Cabinet Councils, by men unknown' or by 'unsworn Councillors'—the first of a long chain of protests on this subject.[2]

Faction had now developed far beyond the stage of those 'secrette and privye Conventicles and Conferences' which had alarmed the government thirty years earlier. Eliot, the 'opposition leader' of the last house, had died in prison, the first martyr

---

[1]Gardiner, *Documents*, pp. 164, 231–2; cf. *L.J.*, iv. 431.
[2]Clarendon, *History*, iii. 52–4 (Macray, i. 260–2); *E.H.R.*, xxxviii. 179.

to the parliamentary cause, and in the elections to the Long Parliament it was alleged that his destined successor Pym 'rode about the country to promote the elections of the puritanical brethren'.[1] Pym's leadership in the commons, in close and constant consultation with others of the same mind in both houses, was at first undisputed; so unassailable indeed was his position that on at least three occasions during the early months of 1641 the project was seriously entertained at court of buying him off with office and so knocking the bottom out of the opposition.[2] But after Strafford's execution unanimity vanished, and (as in the session following Buckingham's murder) men who had been ready enough to attack a hated minister shrank from pressing their opposition to the point where it appeared in all its nakedness as directed against the king himself. And so alongside the still dominant opposition there appeared the ghosts of a court party and of a still more important centre party, with Clarendon himself (still plain Mr. Hyde) as one of its leaders. This was the group which, had the king but been able to bring himself to trust and to use it effectively, might yet have rescued him from his *impasse*. But a private undertaking to admit to his inner *juncto* the three leaders of moderate opinion in the commons (at least to the extent of consulting them before making any major decisions on policy) was followed almost at once by the crucial decision to arrest the Five Members—a project to which secrecy was so vital that he dared not confide it to men still jealous for the privileges of their house, and till recently in the confidence of the opposition leaders. The truth is, of course, that public affairs were already moving into the revolutionary phase where force and strategy counted for more than either paper expedients or private undertakings.

The Nineteen Propositions, which embodied the final terms of parliament (or what remained of it at Westminster) before the actual appeal to arms, merely dotted the i's and crossed the t's of their previous expedients in the direction of responsible government. Thus the usual demand for the exclusion of councillors disapproved and the inclusion of those approved by parliament turns into a more specific proposal that no one

[1] Wood, *Athenae Oxonienses* (ed. Bliss, 1813), iii. 73.
[2] *D.N.B.*, xvi. 521–3.

shall sit on the privy council or occupy a principal ministerial
or judicial post without prior approval by both houses, or at
least *ex post facto* approval of an interim appointment in
council to fill a vacancy during a parliamentary recess; and the
protest against 'private Cabinet Councils' develops into a
fumbling attempt to delimit the functions of council and
parliament in such a way as to exclude transaction of public
business anywhere else. Parliament, now claiming to be 'your
Majesty's great and supreme Council', is declared to be the
only proper place for transacting 'such matters as concern the
public', and the council for 'other matters of state'. The distinction corresponds pretty closely with that which was recognized a century and a half later between matters relating to
'the king's service' (that is, loosely speaking, defence and public
order), which were cabinet matters, on which the king was
by then bound to accept ministerial advice or choose another
ministry, and 'the general well-being of the country'—things
desirable but not essential, which lay within the field of parliamentary legislation and were rather the responsibility of
individual ministers; to these the king was still not bound until
they were embodied in acts of parliament.[1] A further provision
of the Nineteen Propositions lays down that the council shall
be limited in numbers to between fifteen and twenty-five,
whose acts shall not be deemed valid unless individually
'attested under their hands'; and this responsibility is to be
further brought home by another recurrent item in the parliamentary programme—the imposition of an official oath drawn
up by parliament.[2]

An interesting feature of the discussions about the final form
of the Nineteen Propositions was the attempt to single out the
principal offices of state over which it was essential to establish
parliamentary control—to determine, in fact, who were the
key men in government. The irreducible minimum, on which
the parliamentary negotiators were instructed not to compromise, naturally included the lord chancellor (or lord keeper),
the lord treasurer and the principal judges; memories of
Buckingham's overweening power and the king's equivocal use
of the navy, and the more recent experience of Strafford's Irish

[1]Pares, *George III and the Politicians*, 1953, pp. 163–6.
[2]Gardiner, *Documents*, pp. 250–1, 253.

intrigues, were responsible for the addition of the offices of lord admiral and lord deputy; while the office of master of wards gave too strong a hold over the fortunes of the gentry to allow of any compromise here.

Seven more offices were included as bargaining counters on the original list, with the instruction that these claims could if necessary be dropped. Five of them were household offices, of considerable dignity but unlikely at the moment to make their holders formidable; the others are more significant. The inclusion in this category of the secretaries of state shows that they were still looked upon as administrators rather than framers of policy; for the outcry which sent Windebank flying overseas was only a part of the general campaign against suspected recusants—the parliamentary leaders were as yet unaware of the direct political dangers to which his intrigues with Rome had exposed them—while his junior colleague Vane was a pliable self-seeker whose son was hand in glove with them. Again, it seems surprising on the face of it that parliament should have dug its heels in over the office of lord admiral and not over that of earl marshal; for a navy cannot be used to overawe a parliament, whereas rumours of the use for that purpose of the army serving under the earl marshal against the Scots covenanters had been a recurrent source of panic as long as it remained under arms, and had indeed been a direct cause of the hardening of hearts against Strafford. But it was from irresponsible knots of officers, not from the cumbrous and creaking military machine, that the danger of 'army plots' arose, and parliament no doubt felt it had made itself secure in this direction by its militia ordinance and its nomination of lords lieutenant, whose control over an essentially local force like the militia was of far greater importance than the dignified but antiquated office of earl marshal.[1] The whole discussion was in any case academic, for the Nineteen Propositions were rather a manifesto of war aims than a serious peace overture. The years of revolution had begun.

[1] *C.J.*, ii. 599, 642.

IV

Revolutionary Interlude
1642–60

A<small>N</small> unsuccessful revolution stands, by its very nature, outside the main stream of constitutional development; yet the period from the outbreak of civil war to the restoration of Charles II cannot be denied a place in this story, not only for the negative reason that for many generations it became in popular tradition a sign and symbol for what was at all costs to be avoided, but also—paradoxically—because the counter-revolution that brought it to a close unconsciously took over so much from the displaced *régime*.

It was a startling enough innovation when, twenty years before this, the commons had first taken on themselves to offer unasked advice on the conduct of a hypothetical foreign war; now they found themselves engaged (with the few peers who stayed at Westminster) in the actual direction of a war at home against the other branches of government, using such parts of the machinery of administration, both central and local, as they had been able to get into their own hands—and all with the object of imposing on the king, before he could return to his capital, the terms he had refused before the final resort to arms. No wonder that in the *Journals* of the house for these early war years the ordinary business of a legislature is swamped by executive details like instructions to armies in the field or to civil officials, audiences to ambassadors or the raising and allocation of supplies. No longer content with attempts to control the executive, the commons are in fact directly taking over its functions, to the neglect of their own. But as prospects of an early settlement receded, both sides settled down to prolonged and systematic campaigning for which these early improvisations were as inappropriate in the civil as in the military field.

In the parliamentary direction of the war a solution was found in the new and characteristic device of government by standing committee. In form, of course, these committees were based upon the normal practice of the commons since Tudor times for putting measures into legislative shape, extended in the next century (as Charles I complained) to the setting up of

> general committees for religion, for Courts of Justice, for trade, and the like . . . to make inquiry on all sorts of men, where complaints of all sorts are entertained, to the unsufferable disturbance and scandal of justice and government.[1]

How much more 'unsufferable' the scandal now that such committees included members of both houses and members of neither, met outside the precincts of parliament, and so far from merely entertaining complaints actually took on themselves the sort of executive functions normally discharged by committees of privy council—subject, however, to the overriding authority, not of the council, but of a parliamentary rump!

At the apex, so long as the war lasted, was the committee of both kingdoms, set up by parliamentary ordinance as a sort of supreme war council soon after the Scots came into the war, and consisting of seven peers, fourteen commoners and the commissioners from the Scots army. Its powers were the result of a compromise after a hot parliamentary debate: in the directing of strategy it had the last word, thereby freeing the legislature from much detailed business for which it was supremely unsuited, and minimizing the dangers of civilian interference in the field which had hampered both armies—as it was later to hamper the armies of the Dutch republic and the initial military efforts of both the French and the Russian revolutions. Even in diplomacy the committee was given a

[1]Gardiner, *Documents*, p. 93.

wide latitude, but dealings with the king or with the Scots allies must all be referred to Westminster; a proposal, moreover, that its proceedings should be protected by an oath of secrecy was vetoed by the lords. Gardiner's suggestion that in this committee we see 'the first germ of the modern Cabinet system' ignores the fact that a far more direct ancestry can be found in the prior evolution of the cabinet council; but the attempt to define in precise terms its responsibility to parliament, even a parliament no longer in any real sense representative, is not without interest in the development of responsible government. So useful was it found that even after the first war was over and the Scots alliance at an end, the English members continued to meet (under the name of the Derby House committee) as a sort of general parliamentary executive.[1] There is a certain irony in the fact that the 'body without a head' so scorned by James I should have been more successful in devising an effective focus of unity for its war effort than James's son, whose councils were always hampered by internal jealousies between civil and military advisers—to say nothing of personal feuds and the endless schemings of the queen.[2]

Financial devolution brought into existence at least three standing committees. Of the committee of twenty-five 'for taking the accounts of the kingdom' we know little beyond its name, since its records are lost; but the committees for the advance of money and for compounding were important collecting bodies which handled vast sums of money, each with its own staff of salaried officials. The first (which eventually swallowed up the second) met twice a week at Haberdashers' Hall from early in the war to hear and determine appeals against the local allocation of the loans and monthly assessments by which parliament financed its campaigns; it consisted initially of five peers and nine commoners. It was for the same purpose of keeping a check on local authorities that the committee for compounding (also including lords and commoners, with a few outsiders) was established at Goldsmiths' Hall, after the war, to replace the various *ad hoc* bodies set up under successive parliamentary ordinances to carry out the policy of 'making the enemy pay'; one of its chief duties was to control

[1]Gardiner, *Civil War*, 1901 ed., i. 304–7, iv. 52.
[2]e.g., Clarendon, *History*, v. 33–5, vi. 240–8 (Macray, ii. 16–18, iii. 192–200).

the county officials and committees that had to carry out the work of spoliation on the spot.[1] Apart from finance and military operations, the other chief field of executive authority delegated by parliament to standing committees was the religious establishment; but here the process had begun long before the war. The committees for 'scandalous ministers' and for 'plundered ministers' were engaged from the early days of the Long Parliament—the one negatively, by deprivation, the other positively, by presentation—in steady encroachments on the royal headship in pursuit of parliament's claim to control the church. These incursions into the executive prepared what remained of the two houses for stepping fully into the breach when the monarchy disappeared. But their effective control of their new executive organs, amid a host of other novel preoccupations, must have been at best spasmodic.

The execution of the king left other administrative gaps to be filled by the triumphant parliamentary rump. Within a fortnight the Derby House committee had been turned into a parliamentary council of state meeting in the same building to replace the privy council. Its membership and powers were determined (like those of the committee of both kingdoms) only after heated parliamentary discussions resulting in a compromise between the doctrinaires who believed that numbers were the best safeguard against tyranny, and pined after a council of a hundred, and political realists like Ireton who had learned from recent history that neither effective government nor effective control could be exercised by so many-headed a body. Even so, the new council (from which Ireton himself was pointedly excluded) was larger than the normal Stuart council and very much larger than what the Nineteen Propositions would have made it; and it was not allowed a permanent president. Its forty members, however, with the exception of three judges and five peers, were all drawn from the house of commons, which limited its tenure of power to a year at a time and laid down in specific terms (as with the committee of both kingdoms) the limits of its authority. Defence, diplomacy and trade were the three branches of government in which it was given plenary powers, including those of summary

[1]Gardiner, op. cit., iii. 198–9; see also introductions to *Calendars* of the two committees.

arrest exercised by the old royal council; otherwise it could only carry out the instructions of parliament or report to it plans 'concerning the good of the Commonwealth'.[1] The programme of the radical wing of Cromwell's army, which 'to the end all officers of state may be certainly accountable', had debarred all councillors and 'placemen' from sitting in the house, was thus emphatically rejected—another victory for the political realists.[2]

The new body was also authorized to follow the practice of the old in delegating specific tasks to sub-committees, and it soon availed itself of this convenient device. For example, ten days after it came into existence the powers of the lord admiral were transferred to it; but these it delegated to a naval committee which acted virtually as an independent department of government until the Protectorate replaced it by a new parliamentary body. Most of the principal offices of state were similarly vested in select bodies of parliamentary commissioners until Cromwell took control.[3] On paper at least the executive in all its branches was responsible to the legislature that appointed and largely manned it; what was lacking, of course, was any sort of public control of the legislature, now consisting of an arbitrary remnant of a single house of parliament which had long since fulfilled its allotted task and ceased to reflect the nation's mood, and yet, under legislation reluctantly sanctioned by the king himself, could no longer be dissolved without its own consent.

When the dissolution that could not be effected legally had been brought about by force, and the self-perpetuating Rump sent, unlamented, about its business, the way was clear—after the short-lived concession to the extremists in Barebone's Parliament—for Ireton and the realists to concoct a constitution which should restore some of those discarded features of the old *régime* most vital to sound administration and public confidence. Once more the government had, what had been so markedly avoided in 1649, a single head. There were safeguards, of course; the protector lacked the power of absolute veto on legislation and the sense of security that comes from

---

[1] Firth and Rait, ii. 2–4; Gardiner, *Commonwealth and Protectorate*, 1913 ed., i. 3–6.
[2] Gardiner, *Documents*, p. 365.
[3] Clowes, *History of the Royal Navy*, 1898, ii. 95; Clarendon, *Continuation of the Life*, 1757, iii. 791 (fo. 417).

hereditary succession; but he had what was far more important, an established revenue based on the normal needs of government (including a standing army) and a far more numerous, more competent and better paid body of professional administrators—even leaving out of account the brief period during which major-generals were set up as district commissioners and the militia kept under arms to support the civil authority. It was from him that all the officers of state, both civil and military, derived their authority. The doctrinaire prejudice against limited executives being for the moment in abeyance, he was given a council of fifteen, to which he might add up to a total of twenty-one, subject to confirmation by parliament when it met; and parliament was also to have a direct voice both in the filling of vacancies and in the removal of councillors guilty of any dereliction of duty. Indeed, while the council, in conjunction with the protector, was given far freer rein during parliamentary recesses than its immediate predecessors, when parliament was sitting almost all it did, and all it had provisionally done before the session began, was subject to parliamentary confirmation.[1]

These parliaments to which the executive was again made responsible were of course far from representative bodies; but at least they were more representative than the discredited Rump. The proscription of those who had actively supported the king was a serious limitation; even more serious were the elastic powers given to the council (and freely used) to scrutinize the credentials of elected members. On the other hand the records of elections show a widespread participation of the country gentry, and prolonged bargainings between the chief local families, that bore the familiar flavour of electioneering in more settled times.[2] The pull always enjoyed in elections by the government in power, whatever it might be, was greatly enhanced for Cromwell's government by its military resources, but this in turn was offset by the enormous increase in county representation—a reform which stood high among the demands of the radicals of George III's reign because of the advantage it gave to the independent voter; and in spite of all precautions, each of Cromwell's parliaments contained a fairly large and

[1]Gardiner, *Documents*, pp. 405–17.
[2]See, e.g., A. H. Dodd, *Studies in Stuart Wales*, pp. 191–3.

vigorous opposition. His first parliament attacked the Instrument of Government under which it had been summoned, and debated a constitutional scheme including (among other checks on the executive) a curious division of power under which 'correspondence with foreign kings, princes and states' lay in the province of the protector in council, but 'no peace shall be concluded but by the consent of parliament' (or, in parliamentary recesses, under limitations previously imposed by it). Cromwell hastily dissolved the house.[1] The amended constitution drawn up by his second parliament in the Humble Petition and Advice increased the protector's powers by giving him the nomination of his successor, but at the same time introduced new safeguards for the independence of parliament and transferred to a body of parliamentary commissioners, acting under rules prescribed in the constitution, the powers of challenging the qualification of members which had been so arbitrarily exercised by the council.[2] The fall of the protectorate after Oliver's death and Richard's resignation made way for a brief return of the doctrinaires and their bogus republic, until they were swept away by the forces that brought the king into his own again.

It is clear that all this constitution-mongering has little direct bearing on the development of responsible government; apart from the fact that reaction against the rule of the Saints involved even their most innocent experiments in lasting obloquy which made it political suicide to attempt to revive them, it may well be doubted whether the desired objective could ever have been reached along these lines. The military prestige and the capital resources of the protectorate, the personality of Cromwell, and the fact that none of the paper constitutions ever got into full working order, enabled it to triumph over the hampering conditions of an executive nominally bound hand and foot by a many-headed assembly; but it would be hard to find examples of a government successfully carried on in this fashion for long on end. It was in more indirect ways that the governments of the interregnum made their contribution towards the solution of this problem of politics.

[1]Gardiner, *Documents,* p. 445, and 427–47, passim.
[2]Ibid., pp. 447–59.

In the first place it was during these years that the foundations were laid of the modern professionalized civil service.
Professionalism was already making considerable strides in
both private and public life before the Puritan Revolution
began;[1] but the wholesale reorganization of government and
the disposal or custody of great blocks of land sequestered or
confiscated from crown, church and 'malignants' called for a
whole army of paid officials. To take a single example: the
committee for the advance of money had under it nearly a
dozen such officials, with salaries ranging (apart from fluctuating perquisites) from £100 to £150 a year, and corresponding
daily and weekly rates. The inital effects were as disorganizing
as might have been expected. It was Milton himself who
deplored, in a classic passage, that

> some who had bin call'd from shops and warehouses without
> other merit to sit in supreme councils and committies, as
> thir breeding was, fell to hucster the common-wealth.[2]

The cleaning up of this Augean stable, and the training of a
school of competent and honest administrators which was
inherited by the restored monarchy, has been claimed as
Cromwell's 'most lasting achievement'. In civil as in military
life he saw in regular and adequate pay the antidote to fili-
bustering. Finance as well as administration benefited, for
apart from the perpetuation after the king's return of new and
more productive means of taxation like the assessment and the
excise, the whole system of revenue collecting was put on a
sounder footing which eventually made possible the distinction
between the king's private and public revenues, the prepara-
tion of a budget bearing some relation to financial realities,
and the appropriation of supplies by parliament.[3]

The Cromwellian bureaucracy was essentially non-political.
Even from his early army days Cromwell had always insisted
that 'the State, in choosing men to serve them, takes no notice
of their opinions'.[4] This had, of course, always been an accepted
maxim of public life; what was novel was its application to a
state riven by faction. And the success of the protectorate lay

---

[1]D. Mathew, *Social Structure in Caroline England*, 1948, ch. v.
[2]*History of Britain*, 1670, bk. iii. (*Works*, Columbia ed., 1932, x. 319–20).
[3]Cunningham, *Growth of English Industry and Commerce*, 1919 ed., ii. 182–4.
[4]*Letters and Speeches*, Letter xx.

in the fact that so long as Oliver lived it did offer the sort of
stability that attracted back into public life not only country
gentry, practising lawyers and episcopal clergy still wedded to
the old order, but the class of minor official more interested in
administration than in politics. The existence of a class of this
sort, providing a permanent backcloth behind the shifting
scenes of politics, is a prerequisite of responsible government;
but before it could attain the detachment characteristic of the
modern civil service there was a long period during which its
service to political stability was rather that of a reserve army
of unquestioning supporters for whatever administration might
be in power. In fact Cromwell's administrators may be looked
on as the remote ancestors of the 'king's friends' of a later age;
at the same time his rule marks the transition between the
courtier and the public servant as minister of state.

Another long-range legacy of this turbulent age was the
opposing but complementary conception of alternative governments as part of the working scheme of politics. The seizure of
the machine of government by an insurgent faction had been
familiar enough in the middle ages; what the interregnum
contributed was the achievement of this sort of *coup d'état* by a
set of men bound together by common theoretical principles.
If for many the principles served as a cloak for personal ambi-
tion, there was nothing novel or exceptional in that; the need for
paying even lip-service to them indicates that party government
was there in embryo. The counter-revolution of 1660 seemed to
have made a clean sweep of the revolutionary expedients it
superseded; in actual fact it had driven them underground, to
be disinterred after 120 years at the crisis of George III's reign.

V

Restoration and Reconstruction
1660–88

THE Restoration brought back not only the monarchy and the church, but the privy council and the country gentry, whose participation in public affairs, far from complete even in the heyday of the protectorate, had fallen off during the brief return of the doctrinaire republic that followed its collapse. It also brought to the helm of government Lord Chancellor Clarendon, the watchdog of the constitution whether in opposition or in office, whether at home or abroad with the exiled court. Clarendon's views on the place of the privy council in the scheme of government have already appeared;[1] from the first he saw to it that it was given its due place in the restored monarchy, with the king in constant attendance—so much so that the office of lord president, which had disappeared during the interregnum, remained superfluous and was not revived until 1679.

Of the reality of the council's debates on high policy, and the activity of the king's participation, we have ample evidence in the notes, still preserved in the Bodleian Library, which passed between Charles and his chancellor at the council table during the early years of the reign.[2] We see in them a readiness on the king's part both to take decisions and to accept advice, which

[1]*Supra*, p. 34.
[2]Bodleian Library, Clarendon MSS. 100–1; facsimile and transcript ed. W. D. Macray for Roxburghe Club, 1896.

had been sorely lacking in the last reign; at the same time they reveal a fund of good humour (not to say frivolity) in which we seem to hear the voice of his French grandfather, together with a vein of indolence which carries us back to his Scottish grand-father; and each of these self-revelations offers some clue to the course of public events that followed. What minister of Charles I would have dared—or needed—to remind his master: 'This debate is worth 3 dinners, I beseech you be not weary of it, but attend it with all patience'? And that such reminders were not wholly idle appears in one of the Merry Monarch's more frivolous notes, when two particularly ponderous councillors were threatening to give tongue: 'If those two learned persons could be sent to supper, we might dispatch it now, but by my Ld of Dorchester's face I feare his speech will be long which will be better for a collation than a supper'. Or again that revealing outburst of his when the regicide trials were under discussion—'I must confesse, that I am weary of hanging except upon new offences'—and his *cri du cœur* about the Presby-terians—'For my part rebell for rebell, I had rather trust a papist rebell then a presbiterian one'—stand in sharp contrast with his father's rigid principles and impenetrable reserve.

Clarendon's objections to a council in which not all coun-cillors are 'equally members'[1] did not blind him to the need for a certain measure of internal caballing, or of precautions against leakage when the business was especially confidential; how could it be otherwise in a council consisting of nine royalist exiles, seven moderate royalists, seven presbyterians and four Cromwellians?[2] Nor could Lord Chancellor Clarendon be expected always to act on the maxims propounded a dozen years earlier by Mr. Hyde as a private citizen. In December, 1660, for example, he advises Charles to have a private talk on Scottish affairs with the high commissioner before bringing them to the council, 'and then it may be they neede not all be called, since some thinges to be directed, may be of secrecy'; or again six months later: 'I do believe it will be necessary to meete privatly upon this businesse of Ireland'. When the sale of Dunkirk is under discussion he recommends 'first declare you have somewhat of importance to propose, and

[1]*Supra*, p. 34.
[2]E. I. Carlyle in *E.H.R.*, xliv. 258.

therefore you will have a Close Councell, and that the Clarke withdraw'. Albemarle's house he condemns as ill-suited to council meetings because 'there are so many Avenues wher woemen and others hearken'; and in other important items of business he urges that those directly responsible should consult beforehand, 'that wee may be of one minde'.

It goes without saying that the practice of dealing in subcommittee with particular items of business was soon revived. Less than a couple of months after the king's return a 'Secrett Committee' of council is meeting at the lord chancellor's for the consideration of 'many thinges of greate moment', among which the king suggests that the appointment of a lord deputy for Ireland might be included. During Clarendon's period of office we catch glimpses of something like fifty temporary committees of the council, and a few more permanent standing committees. Many of them the king attended in person, and there was a feeling among some councillors that those were the only occasions when the committees really got down to business. 'Very constant he is on council-days,' commented Pepys. Foreign affairs, as in the last reign, were dealt with by a select inner body which varied in personnel from time to time. To an advisory committee on trade policy a few merchants outside the council were admitted, little as the chancellor liked this departure from precedent: it was a stage towards the later evolution of an independent department of trade. The navy under the duke of York and the treasury after the death of Southampton went still further in this direction, with a navy board and a treasury commission including several noncouncillors and evolving rapidly as self-contained departments of state which dealt directly with the king and made their own appointments in consultation with him. In all this there was some conscious copying of the businesslike methods evolved during the interregnum. To Clarendon it bore the mark of the Beast, but the king, who lacked his chancellor's reverence for tradition (if indeed he had any bump of reverence at all), was always content *ab hoste doceri* if it made things smoother for him.[1]

The reign of Clarendon came to an end in 1668. He paid the

---

[1] Macray (ed.), *Notes* (Roxburghe Club), p. 5; *E.H.R.*, loc. cit., pp. 251–73 and xxxi. 545–7; Turner in *Amer. Hist. Rev.*, xix. 772–793; Clarendon, *Continuation of the Life*, iii. 790–4 (fos. 416–8); Pepys, *Diary*, 27th Feb., 1665.

G.R.G.—E

penalty of a man who has outlived his generation, who tries to steer a middle course after an age of extremes, and who has to bear the odium of an impoverished *régime* which can neither reward its friends after their own conception of their deserts nor court popularity by a colourful foreign policy. The contrast between Cromwell's high line with the continental powers (which won the chancellor's own reluctant and envious admiration) and the sale for spot cash of Dunkirk, the protector's booty, recalled only too vividly the descent from Elizabethan high adventure to drab Jacobean appeasement, which had started the Stuarts off on the wrong foot. His rigid anglicanism was an offence to the dissenting interest as much as his stiff constitutionalism and conscious moral rectitude were to the younger generation of cavaliers. And finally he was a victim of that rooted prejudice against 'monopoly of power' by a subject against which he was himself forever on his guard. His friend Ormonde urged him to free himself from specialized duties as chancellor so as to devote himself wholly to the general co-ordination of policy and management of parliament as 'first minister', permanently at the king's elbow to counteract the influence of irresponsible courtiers. But Clarendon would have none of it; the post would involve a special grant from a straitened exchequer, and the title itself was 'so newly translated out of French into English that it was not enough understood to be liked'.[1]

Equally conservative was he in his management of parliament. The old 'opposition' member could think of no better way of piloting the king's business through the house than that which had been evolved for purposes of opposition from James I's reign on.[2] Charles II's privy councils were as aristocratic in complexion as James I's had been. They contained few commoners and fewer still who were competent parliamentary hands, so Clarendon had to resort to more indirect methods of securing a compliant house of commons. He tells how he and his colleague Southampton (the lord treasurer), as the king's chief ministers in the lords,

> had every Day Conference with some select Persons in the House of Commons, who had always served the King, and

[1] Clarendon, *Continuation*, ii. 84–92 (46–50 in folio ed.).
[2] *Supra*, p. 15.

upon that Account had great Interest in that Assembly, and in Regard of the Experience they had and their good Parts were hearkened to with Reverence. And with those They consulted in what Method to proceed in disposing the House, sometimes to propose sometimes to consent to what should be most necessary for the Publick; and by them to assign Parts to other Men, whom they found disposed and willing to concur in what was to be desired: and all this without any Noise, or bringing many together to design, which was and ever will be ingrateful to Parliaments, and however it may succeed for a little Time, will in the End be attended with Prejudice.

The idea of organizing a party of 'king's friends' in the commons out of such elements as 'Country Gentlemen of ordinary Condition' and 'the King's menial Servants' (who had flocked into the house in considerable numbers at by-elections as the older members dropped out) ran counter to Clarendon's whole conception of the dignity of politics and his fixed belief 'that great and notorious Meetings and Cabals in Parliament had been always odious' there.[1]

His rivals had none of these scruples, and the king himself, now that he had found his feet, grew weary of the excellent advice which this strait-laced and middle-aged mentor had been pouring into his ears since he was a lad of sixteen. The flow of informal and friendly notes between king and minister, on torn scraps of paper freely decorated with 'doodles', had long since ceased, and Charles was too firmly bent on averting a head-on clash with parliament to interpose any obstacle when, after the treasurer's death had left the chancellor on a solitary pinnacle, a coalition of jealous careerists, disgruntled cavaliers and nostalgic puritans massed forces against him. Not content with the king's complaisance in removing him from office, his opponents exhibited against him articles of impeachment which mark a new departure in that they are avowedly political. No personal crimes or misdemeanours are laid to his charge; apart from some allegations of arbitrary imprisonment, it is his counsels to the king in both home and foreign policy that constitute the ground of impeachment.

[1]Clarendon, loc. cit., pp. 343–5, 351 (fos. 181–2, 184); cf. *supra*, p. 15.

The lords were once again unwilling to convict, but on Charles's advice his minister fled into lifelong exile abroad.

After Clarendon's fall the privy council never regained the primacy he had always tried to give it. Even while he was still in power he had occasion to lament that the king, under the influence of some of the younger courtiers,

> rather esteemed some particular Members of it, than was inclined to believe that the Body of it ought to receive a Reverence from the People, or be looked upon as a vital Part of the Government: In which his Majesty . . . from the ill Principles He had received in France, and the accustomed Liberty of his Bedchamber, was exceedingly and unhappily mistaken. For . . . no King of England can so well secure his own Just Prerogative, or preserve it from Violation, as by a strict defending and supporting the Dignity of his Privy Council.[1]

Numbers in the council soon rose from the original twenty-seven to between thirty and forty, and then soared up towards fifty, and with the revival of faction Charles II resorted to the old balancing tactic of choosing his ministers from opposing factions, in the assurance that they would cancel each other out and leave him *tertius gaudens*. The Cabal ministry, which came into power soon after his fall, stood for the two political extremes between which he had tried to steer a middle course; and in dealing with this ill-matched team the king, like his father before him, admitted to his full confidence only those from whom he feared no serious opposition. He followed the same course in the appointment of secretaries: Bennet (later Lord Arlington), who had held the office in Clarendon's day but intrigued for his fall, was believed to be a Roman Catholic by all 'who did believe that He had any Religion'; he was now given as colleague Sir John Trevor, Hampden's son-in-law, who had sat in Cromwell's parliaments and remained *persona grata* with the dissenting interest (thanks to his presbyterian wife) after the Restoration. To men in the know, however, Bennet seemed in 1668 'the sole guide that the King relies upon' —so much so as to be either 'premier minister . . . or a favourite' (an eminence attributed by others to Buckingham's son, who

[1] Id., iii. 676–7 (fo. 356).

led the opposite faction in the Cabal); Trevor, on the other hand, 'was no further admitted into the secret of affairs than was indispensably necessary from the nature of his office'— in fact a Herbert to Bennet's Cecil.[1]

The tendency to departmental instead of conciliar government which Clarendon had deplored and resisted was now able to make way rapidly. Some attempt to preserve the over-riding authority of the council was made in an order of 1668 that all public business must be discussed first in full council, which should issue the necessary departmental orders after the report from the appropriate sub-committee; but in practice no business could be done on such roundabout lines, and once he felt his hands free the king followed so far as he could the practice of his cousin the French king, and dealt direct with the departmental heads, with the double advantage of speeding up business and evading control.[2] The 'business mind' which had played so large a part in the governments of the interregnum was not to be suppressed by the weight of aristocratic tradition on which Clarendon had tried to base the restored monarchy. It was equally in evidence in the methods of managing parliament which the fallen minister had tried so hard to keep at bay. The younger generation who succeeded him in the royal service were bent on restoring to the court that control over the house of commons which had once been maintained by the privy councillors 'about the Chair', and they were not too squeamish about the means. These could all be summed up under the convenient euphemism Influence, which covered a multitude of political sins and became for the next hundred years and more the principal means of maintaining *liaison* and avoiding deadlocks between executive and legislature.

The method of control was provided by the circumstances of the time. Old cavaliers who had spent their substance in the service of Charles I could not all be compensated after their deserts (certainly not after their own estimate of their deserts) by a direct monetary *quid pro quo*, yet with the growing cost of public life and the rising standard of private expenditure in polite society, something must be done to keep this loyal section

[1]Clarendon, loc. cit., p. 346 (fo. 182); Hist. MSS. Com., 11*th* R., vii. 15; *Cal.S.P. Dom.*, 1667–8, p. 258; Reresby, *Memoirs*, 1734 (ed. Ivatt, 1904), p. 147; Evans, *Principal Sec. of State*, p. 131; cf. *supra*, p. 11.
[2]Keir, *Const. Hist. of Mod. Brit.*, p. 245.

of the community—and indeed the smaller country gentry at large—as a leaven in the house of commons. The answer lay partly in that growth of an incipient civil service, of all grades, to which reference was made in the last chapter—another legacy of the interregnum—partly in the increasing use of secret service pensions as a more direct means of bribery. It was under Arlington and his confidant Clifford, who belonged to the same wing of the cabal and was suspected of the same tendencies in religion, that Influence was systematized and a court party of king's friends organized in the commons. The discovery that Arlington and Clifford had connived in the king's 'popish' intrigues with France (now Spain's successor as the bogy-man of protestant England) engulfed them in a wave of anti-popish fury like that which had destroyed 'appeasement' in 1624, but it did not affect the political system they had established at home, which was continued in full vigour after 1674 by Danby as lord treasurer and Williamson as secretary and 'bribe-master general'.[1]

By this time the reign was moving rapidly towards its crisis. News of the king's intrigues had become public property, and it was news that lost nothing in the telling. The interminable sparring over foreign policy between king and parliament, during the decade after Clarendon's fall, merely echoed the arguments for and against parliamentary control advanced forty or fifty years earlier by Charles I and Buckingham on one side, and Phelips and Eliot on the other; the deadlock was still unbroken.[2] By 1678 the country was in the throes of the 'popish plot' panic—perhaps the most discreditable episode in the history of English politics, and a far more eloquent comment on the breakdown of the contemporary system of government than all the setbacks in war and diplomacy that preceded it. A despotism that makes no pretence of taking the public into its confidence can be tolerated so long as it does its job; so of course can a parliamentary *régime* fully sensitive to public opinion; what is fatal to the health of the body politic is the sort of government where the machinery of consultation has developed just far enough for the public to feel itself in the grip of a policy it fears and detests but cannot, for lack of authentic

[1] A. Browning in *Trans. R.H.S.*, IV. xx. 21–36; *A.H.R.*, xix. 788.
[2] E. R. Turner in *E.H.R.* xxxiv. 176–81.

information, get into clear focus, still less undo. In such an atmosphere rumour flourishes and witch hunts are the order of the day; the popish recusants, whom the king had tried to befriend (from honest hatred of persecution as well as partiality) were the very men on whom his duplicity so tragically rebounded. Before the public panic reached its height, Danby, as minister at the helm, did all he could to allay passions and to restore confidence. He had been brought into power, as a staunch anglican, to counteract the impression created by the manœuvres of the crypto-Romanist wing of the Cabal, and he made a point of showing the country that advice was sought at the top level from men it could trust. Thus in the summer of 1676, just after the king's brother and heir presumptive had avowed himself a Roman catholic, two or three of the most unimpeachably protestant of the bishops were called to special committees of council.[1]

The temper of the time, however, demanded a political scapegoat as well as a religious pogrom, and Danby was too close to the king's ear (though by no means in his full confidence, especially in foreign affairs) to escape attack. Besides, he was more than suspected, for all his careful deference to parliament, of a design to make the crown financially independent. This aim he pursued not only by the very successful development at the treasury of the business methods evolved under Cromwell and resumed when the office was put into commission on Southampton's death, but also (more reluctantly) by concurring in the king's complaisance to his cousin of France on terms of ready cash.[2] By another piece of irony it was Louis himself, incensed at Danby's notoriously anti-French bias, who supplied his accusers (through the English ambassador, who also had a grudge to pay) with incriminating documents on which charges were drawn up representing the lord treasurer as a designer of arbitrary government and a protector of papists. It was not so much to save his minister as to shut down an investigation that might let too many cats out of the bag that the king dissolved his long parliament (dating from the first burst of loyalty that greeted his return), ordered fresh

---

[1] *Cal.S.P.Dom.*, 1676–7, p. 536.
[2] D. Gill in *E.H.R.*, xlvi. 600–22; Keir, *Const. Hist.*, pp. 247–9; A. Browning, *Danby*, 1951, i. 323–5.

elections, and in the meantime issued a full pardon to Danby
but promised his resignation. The new commons, not to be
balked of their prey, put forward the two novel doctrines
(the one legally established in 1701, the other not till ninety
years later) that neither dissolution nor royal pardon could put
a stop to an impeachment; and they proceeded with their
charges. Threatened with attainder, the ex-treasurer (who at the
king's command had gone into hiding) gave himself up and was
committed to the Tower, and there—since the trial was never
completed—he remained for five years, glad to have escaped
the fate of Strafford.[1]

The problem of responsible government was no nearer
solution when Danby fell from power in 1679 than it had been
more than fifty years earlier, when it first became a live issue.
Yet the need for some sort of solution was more urgent than
ever, for both our low prestige abroad and the infamy of the
'popish terror' might have been avoided either by a completely
dictatorial *régime* on the one hand or by an effective system of
responsibility on the other. The first had eluded Charles even
after his French subsidies and Danby's skill at the treasury had
seemed to bring it within sight; as a step, or at least an ostensible
step, towards the second, he now experimented with a reconstituted privy council. The authorship of the reform was claimed
(though the claim has been disputed) by the popular Sir
William Temple, who had won golden opinions as ambassador
to Holland but had hitherto refused to risk his neck or his
reputation by entering politics at home, although he was pressed
repeatedly to save the situation by accepting the secretaryship.
The scheme, announced four days after Danby's committal to
the Tower, involved dismissal of the existing privy council—
which had by this time reached a strength (or should one say
weakness?) of forty-six—and the appointment of a smaller
council of thirty, of whom half should be official and half
parliamentary members—ten lords (two of each grade of the
peerage) and five commoners.

This new model is of interest not because it worked, or could
have worked, or for that matter was seriously meant to work by
anyone but its supposed author (whose knowledge of domestic
politics was slight), but because of the deadlock between legis-

[1]Browning, op. cit., pp. 300–29; W. C. Abbott in *E.H.R.* xxi. 254–85.

lature and executive that it was meant to cure and the grounds on which it was commended. The king himself put part of the case in the farewell message in which he thanks the old privy council

> for all the Good Advices you have given him, which might have been more frequent, If the great Number of this Council had not made it unfit for the Secrecy and dispatch that are necessary in many great Affaires. This forced Him to use a smaller Number of you in a forreigne Committee, and sometimes the Advices of some few among them (upon such occasions) for many years past.

In future, he declared, he was resolved 'to lay aside the Use . . . of . . . private advices, or forreigne Committees' ('to have no Cabinet Council' was a newswriter's summary) and to consult his new council in all things. The 'official' members were to be 'partly out of the officers of the Crown, and partly out of those of the Household'; two bishops ('to take care of the Church') ranked among these—not, strangely enough, among the peers of parliament; the lord chancellor and one chief justice were there 'to inform Him well in what concernes the Lawes', the lord treasurer (or first lord of the treasury) and the chancellor of the exchequer for finance, the lord admiral (or first lord of the admiralty), the master of the ordnance and the master of the horse for military affairs. The lord privy seal and two secretaries were included for administrative purposes, and the office of lord president of the council was revived; the remaining three (and indeed some of those listed above) come under the category of household officials. Something like half the members of the new council had belonged to the old.

Most interesting of all, however, was Temple's comment on the principle of choice:

> One chief regard, necessary to this constitution, was that of the personal riches of this new Council; which, in revenues of land and offices, was found to amount to about three hundred thousand pounds a year; whereas those of a house of commons are seldom found to have exceeded four hundred thousand pounds. And authority is observed much to follow land: and at the worst, such a council might, of their own

stock, and upon a pinch, furnish the king so far as to relieve
some great necessity of the crown.[1]

All this suggests an intention, while leaving parliament supreme
in legislation, to appease its hankerings after control of policy
by admitting to these *arcana* a few select commoners and twice
as many peers; and at the same time to preserve its financial
initiative without permitting it, in the last resort, to hold up
policy by cutting off supplies. It was a scheme such as Clarendon
might have approved, and in that sense a throw-back to early
Restoration politics. He had opposed, for example, the royal
concession of appropriation of supplies because he held that
while it was the commons' right and duty to grant them, their
allocation belonged to the field of policy and therefore of the
council; and the doctrinaire in him refused to see how easily
the limitation could be (and was) evaded. What he would not
have approved was the 'departmentalizing' of the council by
'annexing' membership to particular offices of state, and the
deliberate introduction of an 'opposition' element.[2]

It is true that Temple, who feared and shunned the hurly-
burly of politics, seems to have really believed it possible, in
the heated atmosphere of 1679, to make up the 'parliamentary'
quota of the new council from moderates like himself, 'of most
appearing credit and sway in both houses, without being
thought either principled or interested against the government'; the king was far too good a realist to be under any such
delusion. He knew well enough that neither the twenty-five or
thirty votes he could now command in the lower house,[3] nor
even the more solid and respected block of 'government' peers,
had much 'credit and sway' after the electoral landslides of
that year; so he chose his councillors from both factions, with
the 'opposition' slightly in preponderance and its leader
Shaftesbury (against Temple's urgent representations) in the
office of lord president. Charles's calculation (fully justified by
the event) was that while they were wrangling in council he

[1]*E.H.R.*, xxvii. 684–5; Hist. MSS. Con., *Ormond*, n.s. v. 55–6; Temple *Memoirs*,
iii (*Works*, 1757 ed., ii. 494–544, 553–7); Macaulay, *Essays* (Sir W. Temple).
[2]Clarendon, *Continuation*, iii. 592–612, 698–701 (fos. 312–33). Cf. his observation
that 'the greatest Office in the State, . . . does not qualify the Officer to be
of the Privy Council, before by a new Assignation that Honour is bestowed on
him' (iii. 677, fo. 356). See also Carlyle in *E.H.R.* xliv. 262 and *supra*, p. 49.
[3]G. N. Clarke, *Later Stuarts*, 1934, p. 93.

could be quietly digging himself in with the help of a few
chosen intimates—much as democratic local authorities today
have been known to spend their time on displays of forensic
fireworks for the benefit of the press, leaving the real work of
local government to be done by the town or county clerk or
the director of education. The fundamental difficulty that had
paralysed political effort for fifty years—the impossibility of
dividing legislation from policy or finance from either—
remained untouched; and Charles cannot have seriously
believed that 'secresy and despatch' would be more attainable
among thirty councillors than among forty-six.[1]

And so the old system of government was soon resumed with
a few changes in *personnel*. A committee of intelligence, consisting of 'a fluctuating body of councillors, arbitrarily chosen
by the King, and not reporting to the Privy Council', stepped
into the shoes of the old foreign committee as the most important
and best-informed among many standing committees; Temple
himself helped to knock the bottom out of his scheme by forming
one of a still more select caucus, meeting privately in advance of
sessions of the council; and important decisions like the proro-
gation of parliament were taken without consulting the council
or even the new lord president, who, 'finding himself neither in
confidence with the king nor credit in the council, turned all
his practices and hopes to the house of commons'.[2]

By 1680, when faction had reached boiling-point over the
attempted exclusion of the king's brother from the succession,
and the new party names of whig and tory were being freely
bandied about, Charles was ready to pounce. He had found
an inner ring of ministers more to his taste in young 'chits' ten
years his juniors in contrast with Clarendon, who had been
twenty years his senior or Danby and Temple, his contemporaries); and of these only one—Clarendon's far from strait-
laced son Rochester—was in the 'top secret' of the final deal
with France which gave the king financial independence for
the rest of the reign. Even so, the privy council (which he never
allowed to increase beyond thirty-five) continued in some
slight degree to act as a check on irresponsible government as

[1]Temple, loc. cit., pp. 499–502; Turner loc. cit., p. 269; Godfrey Davies in *E.H.R.*,
xxvii. 685, xxviii. 130–1.
[2]H. W. V. Temperley in *E.H.R.*, xxvii. 685, xxviii. 130–1.

long as he lived.[1] Meanwhile the violence of the opposition leaders both in and out of the two short parliaments that followed the fall of Danby had given him his other chief *desideratum*—a solid body of support among men of 'credit and sway'. After the dissolution of his last parliament in 1681, even the moderate Temple was struck off the council, and of the extremists Shaftesbury and two of his whig colleagues on the council took the fatal plunge from faction into treason; by 1683 all three were dead—one in hiding abroad, one by his own hand and one on the scaffold. Charles was master of the situation.

So, at his accession early in 1685, was his brother James II, whose exclusion from the throne on account of his faith had been so vehemently demanded by the whig opposition and so adroitly sidestepped by Charles. For the first eight months of the reign the same *camarilla* remained at the king's elbow, the same system of government continued, and parliament provided for the king's wants with unprecedented liberality. This was largely due to Sir Dudley North, an able financier (forebear of a much less able premier) who had effected important reforms as a commissioner of the treasury and was found a seat in the commons expressly as king's 'manager' there.[2] Even during these months of harmony, however, the new king showed his intention to jettison the mild checks on despotism which his more realistic brother had accepted to the last. The privy council was watered down to nearly fifty, and the practice of reading there the laws passed in parliament was dropped (to the relief, it was said, of councillors who feared the odium of being held responsible for any exercise of the veto). Then he grew bolder, and began to stretch the prerogative to a point that gave pause to his staunchest supporters, in the interests of a religious policy they feared and abhorred. By the end of the year the weeding out from the privy council of the less compliant of Charles's confidants had begun, and James's loyal parliament, showing signs of restiveness at the new turn of policy, was also dismissed.

Next summer began the infiltration into the council of James's co-religionists—especially such as scorned mere tolera-

[1] *E.H.R.*, xxvii, 685–6 and n.
[2] North, *Lives of the Norths*, i. 340; Macaulay, ch. iv; *infra*, p. 127.

tion and stood for supremacy—culminating in the admission
of his Jesuit confessor, which left even Romanists aghast. By
the middle of 1687 protestant influences had all but vanished
from the hub of government. It was from a council thus
remodelled that James drew the committee charged during the
winter months with the task of bringing municipal government
into line, while the inner cabinet council took measures for a
similar 'purge' in the shires.[1] In both fields James took as his
model his brother's scheme of despotism in the closing years of
the last reign; but whereas Charles's aim had been to weed out
whigs and dissenters, James's hand fell heaviest on tories and
anglicans, the backbone of the monarchy. Alarmed at last by
the spread of opposition, the king tried to neutralize the effects
of what he had done by restoring some of the victims of the
'purge' in the counties and admitting three new privy councillors, one to represent the anglican and two the dissenting
interest.[2] But these moves cut little ice, for none of the new
councillors could be ranked among 'those people that the
nation have a good opinion of': one a notorious double-dealer
of no territorial standing, the second an aspiring lawyer who
held (but seldom visited) a small freehold in Wales, the third
a grandson of one of Charles I's secretaries of state, but the
son of a regicide and in himself a nonentity. In any case the time
had long passed when minor concessions could be of any avail:
James inherited his father's fatal incapacity for knowing when
to act. The chain of events leading to the king's flight and the
crowning of his daughter and her Dutch husband need not
concern us here, for the Glorious Revolution did nothing
directly to advance the cause of responsible government. It
remains therefore to sum up what had been achieved during
these eighty-five years when the privy council was the storm-
centre of politics.

Impeachment as a means of bringing ministers to book had
proved itself again and again a broken reed; yet *faute de mieux*
the commons were reluctant to give it up, and from time to time

[1]Hist. MSS. Com., 12*th R.*, ix. 91; Turner, *Cabinet Council*, i. 442–3.
[2]Lodge's identification of all three with the dissenting interest (*Pol. Hist. of England*,
viii, 1910, p. 283) seems to rest on some confusion between the Sir John
Trevor who was his old solicitor (and his new councillor) and the one who
had been Charles II's secretary (*supra*, p. 52, cf. *Studies in Stuart Wales*, p. 218
and n.).

it was to reappear in political crises, though never again charged
with such significance as in the days of Buckingham or Strafford,
Clarendon or Danby. The crux of the matter lay in the Long
Parliament's doctrine that 'there be grounds of diffidence that
lie not in proof'; but nearly forty years later Charles II brushed
this aside when in the parliament of 1680 he rejected an address
urging him to remove a councillor on the sole ground of his
having advised the premature dissolution of the last parliament,
while promising that neither rank nor office nor royal favour
should protect him from due punishment of any actual crime
proved against him.[1] All attempts at direct control or election
of the executive by the legislature had broken down; and such
expedients as the admission to the executive of selected critics
from the representative assembly resulted either in the buying
off of the critics and the silencing of opposition, or the achievement of such a balance as paralysed action and left the sole
reality of power with the king. Yet dictatorship would not
work either, until the government had at its permanent disposal such assets as Cromwell enjoyed for a time through the
spoliation of monarchy, church and malignants, or Charles II
through his French subsidies.

As we know, a working solution was arrived at in the end
through the combination of a limited political executive drawn
from the dominant group in the legislature, united in a common
policy, and replaced by another when the policy lost support,
with an administrative civil service outside the arena of conflict. The elements of this solution were all present in the
England of 1688; and they were all, with reason, profoundly
distrusted. For limited executives had in practice always meant
arbitrary and irresponsible cabals; party had stood for corruption on the one hand, faction and conspiracy on the other; and
the incipient civil service was a principal means of corruption.
'By 1688', it has been said (perhaps with some exaggeration),
'the cabinet had developed as far as was possible until representative government had taken the place of the personal rule
of the Stuarts'.[2] Party was also in a state of arrested development. The new party nicknames, though firmly repudiated by
the great mass of the independent country gentry, had come to

[1]Lodge, *Pol. Hist.*, p. 175.
[2]Godfrey Davies in *E.H.R.*, xxxvi. 62.

stay, and already there were signs of those characteristic devices of English public life, the political dinner and the political club; but for any more permanent bond we have to look very far into the future. The tories, as the court party, had two solid advantages: the attractive power of government patronage, and the control which could be exercised in the shires through lords lieutenant appointed by the court, and at a pinch dismissible by it. But the lords lieutenant were great territorial magnates, who could not be used as shifting pawns in the political game (as James II found) without undermining the hold of the monarchy over the remoter countryside; and the shrinkage of the court party in the parliaments of 1679–80 shows how little patronage was to be relied on against any great upsurge of feeling in the constituencies.[1]

The nascent civil service, in those days when offices were freeholds and often freeholds for life, gave to politics a modicum of the stability which must be the basis of any form of responsible government; actual dismissals were rare—there was no American 'spoils system'. Yet the more secure the office-holders, the less secure the hold maintained by the executive over the legislature by means of Influence. Professor Browning, after a careful investigation, sums up in these words:

> On the whole, and with some conspicuous exceptions, members of Parliament appear to have spoken and voted much as their previous history and that of their families might lead one to expect. In so far as they were bribed at all they were bribed to be diligent in their business rather than to be false to their convictions.[2]

This suggests that in normal times Influence could serve something of the purpose of a party whip, and prevent politics from descending into an endless succession of deadlocks; but when, as in 1688, issues arose that went to the very roots of politics, the constitution provided no means for resolving the deadlock. The Glorious Revolution was the immediate remedy, but the central problem was left unsolved; it took another century and a half to solve it.

[1] E. Lipson in *E.H.R.*, xxviii. 59–85.
[2] A. Browning in *Trans. R.H.S.*, IV. xxx. 26; cf. E. S. de Beer in *Bulletin of Inst. of Hist. Res.*, xi. 1–23.

VI

Cabinet and Party in Embryo
1688–1714

———————————

DURING the quarter-century following the Revolution of 1688 a certain amount of progress was made towards filling the major gap in the constitution which it had left unfilled; but these developments owed far less to deliberate policy than to sheer pressure of events; in fact they were often accomplished in the teeth of persistent opposition from publicists, partisans and independent country gentlemen. Up to and well beyond the end of the seventeenth century, there was always a strong rallying-point for opposition in the Clarendonian view of the constitution which saw in the privy council 'the greatest Authority in the Government of the State, next the Person of the King himself', resented the delegation of government to irresponsible cabals or departmental heads, and lamented the venality to which politics were exposed when the commons were flooded by what Clarendon called 'the King's menial Servants' and his political heirs called 'placemen'.

The most important single factor in the gradual transformation of politics was undoubtedly the long-drawn continental wars in which the country was involved during all but the last five years of William's reign and the last year of Anne's. They were wars such as England had never known before, in respect of both the scale of operations and the resulting complexity of the problems of diplomacy and strategy, supply and credit,

that were involved. Yet war even on the scale known in the
earlier years of the century had always meant some tightening
up of the machinery of government on the one hand, and on the
other some attempt on the part of the parliament to keep a
check on the money it voted. It was the breach with Spain in
1624 that had begun the continuous history of responsible
government, but Buckingham's assumption of sole control
destroyed both the conciliar organization and the financial
checks imposed when the first subsidies were voted—and thereby started off the chain of events culminating in civil war. That
in turn was directed on parliament's side by what might be
called the prototype of all British war cabinets—the committee
of both kingdoms. Cromwell's Spanish war was managed by the
compact council given him under the Instrument of Government; but he was sufficiently master of the situation to keep
control, especially of war finance, in his own hands, acting (in
Clarendon's words) as 'his own High Treasurer'.[1] Charles II's
Dutch wars, fought entirely at sea, did not involve the same
degree of organization, but they gave Samuel Pepys his chance
to show his qualities as an administrator, and parliament a
loophole for insisting on appropriation and audit.[2]

The wars of William and Anne made cabinet government
inevitable, in face of all prejudice. It is to this period and these
conditions that we may apply with some confidence the conclusion that Roger North drew, prematurely perhaps, about
an earlier age:

> The cabinet council, which at first was but in the nature
> of a private conversation, came to be a formal council, and
> had the direction of most transactions of the Government,
> foreign and domestic.[3]

Whatever its precise relationship to the other committees pro-
liferated by the privy council (some of which survived alongside it), the cabinet is now discharging most of the functions
that once belonged to the parent body: receiving and maintaining correspondence with generals and diplomats, preparing
government measures and statements of policy for parliament

[1]*Continuation*, iii. 791 (fo. 417).
[2]*Supra*, p. 58.
[3]*Lives of the Norths*, i. 299.

G.R.G.—F

(including even drafts of the king's speech), calling before it departmental officials, and examining political suspects in the historic fashion of the 'council board'.[1]

William, coming in as a foreigner, seems to have at first believed that the privy council was the real as it was the formal centre of government; but as the number of councillors had now reached sixty, he felt free for his more secret and intimate transactions to follow the practice of his predecessors by choosing among them at his own discretion, often limiting himself to those whose custody of the essential seals made their concurrence indispensable. After all, it was to extend, not to cramp, his freedom of action on the continent that he had accepted the English throne. A debate in the commons in 1692 makes it clear that the house still felt the old uncertainty about where real responsibility lay; six years later negotiations over the Partition Treaties were carried through in a 'highly informal and irregular way' that laid Lord Chancellor Somers open to a threat of impeachment for his part in them. This, however, was the work of a faction at odds with the substance of the treaties and alert for any weak joint in the armour of those who framed them; it remained accepted doctrine for fully sixty years after this that in foreign emergencies the king could act with a single secretary of state without consulting the cabinet.

The cabinet itself William looked on as a formal body unsuited to discussions of policy or to a direct hand in delicate matters of state, yet one to which it was undesirable to give too great a permanence or fixity. When he went abroad in 1694 he left specific directions that there must be no standing cabinet council—only consultation of the officers of state directly concerned, with 'sometimes one, sometimes another' to assist them. Nor did he consult it much on parliamentary affairs, which he preferred to manage through individual ministers capable of making effective use of the crown's 'influence'. The late Sir William Anson concluded that 'his reign marks a decline in the powers of the privy council, but does not do much to carry forward the development of cabinet government'.[2]

---

[1] Turner, *Cabinet Council*, I, chs. xiv–xvi; cf. Keir, *Const. Hist.*, p. 281n.
[2] Keir, op cit., p. 279; Temperley in *E.H.R.*, xxvii. 682n., 685–6, 689–90; Anson in id., xxix. 63; Foxcroft, *Halifax*, ii. 244.

Under Anne the cabinet, though still looked on askance by many as 'modern and excentrick' (as Defoe puts it), may be said to have become a 'recognized and permanent institution'.[1] It met weekly in her presence on Sundays (as indeed it had done in Charles II's later years), and oftener during parliamentary recesses. But its composition lay within her sole discretion; she was as determined as William had been not to submit her choice to the clamours of party or parliament. What was no longer possible was unrestrained caprice or favouritism.[2] The cabinet must include the principal ministers of state, and the minister must be what Halifax called 'a man of business' who could not only run his department but secure a parliamentary majority for the royal policy. At the same time the older conception of the dignity of a councillor as transcending that of any departmental office, and of the council itself as something more than the combined directorate of a big business concern—in other words, the Clarendonian as distinct from the commonwealth conception of government—died hard, and this traditional aura long clung to the council's offshoot. The result was that early cabinets also included men like the archbishop of Canterbury and the officers of the royal household, who were there by reason of the dignified place they held in the state rather than as departmental heads directly responsible for any specific branch of policy.[3]

This in turn made it necessary—in the interests, as in Charles II's day, of 'secrecy and despatch'—for ministers most directly involved to hold still more private and intimate meetings, often without the queen's presence and always without any set time, place or formal summons. The exact nature of these fluid arrangements, still more their place in the evolution of cabinet government as we know it today, are matters still in dispute. 'Let the form of business', wrote Bolingbroke to Oxford towards the end of the reign, 'be carried on in the Cabinet and the secret of it in your closet'. But what was resolved in the closet would normally need the concurrence of the cabinet, and

---

[1] *E.H.R.*, xxii. 135, xxvii. 690.
[2] Cf. Pitt in 1761 on 'the impossibility of a favourite . . . to be *Minister*' (Namier, *Age of the Amer. Rev.*, p. 168).
[3] Clark, *Later Stuarts*, pp. 244–6; Keir, op cit., p. 281; Trevelyan, *Reign of Queen Anne*, i. 100; Foxcroft, *Halifax*, ii. 495; cf. North, *Lives of the Norths*, 1890, i. 321 (and 300–22 passim).

always that of the queen, before it could be translated into
action. Professor Temperley has compared the contemporary
structure of government to a folding telescope, with sections
fitting inside one another, each giving a closer and sharper view
of policy than the one enclosing it.[1] The metaphor has been
criticized as giving it all too great an air of precision; but at
least it serves to emphasize the 'concentric' character of late
Stuart government; and this character, as well as the lack of
precision, must have helped to perpetuate the initiative of the
crown in politics and to delay the final achievement of party
government. For the sovereign was not inexorably bound to
his or her official advisers in the cabinet, and the removal of a
minister from office did not by any means preclude him from
offering unofficial counsels or the crown from accepting them.
In reserve there was always the antique and ornamental
outer case of the telescope—a privy council whose inflated
numbers now reached eighty, partly because under Anne
dismissal became a rare and extreme measure, no longer
involved in mere disappearance from practical politics or loss
of royal favour.[2] But this very fact made it a valuable reserve
of counsel and rock of stability in the shifting politics of the age;
before the reign ended it was brought into play once more to
break a deadlock.

In so far as royal discretion in choosing the cabinet was
limited, the limitation was not imposed externally but arose
from the character of the job to be done. For example, in war
time it was essential that the cabinet, however divided in
political opinion, should be united in its prosecution or (when
the time came) its termination. This meant abandoning the
principle that resignation was a dereliction of duty and dismissal
a disgrace;[3] a minister might now resign or be dismissed because
of disagreement with the crown or with his colleagues on
immediate practical issues. Both William and Anne preferred,
like their Stuart predecessors, to balance opinions in their
cabinets so as to retain their own independence and superiority
to faction. Even in the first choice of secretaries of state after

---

[1]Temperley, loc. cit., pp. 690, 692–3, and 291–6; Turner, *Cabinet Council*, i. 350–
86, 436, and in *E.H.R.*, xxxii. 192–7; Anson in id., xxix. 61–5, 325–7; Trevelyan,
loc. cit., pp. 288–9n.; Hist. MSS. Com., *Portland*, v. 311.
[2]Clark, op. cit., p. 245; D. Ogg, *James II and William III*, 1955, p. 332.
[3]Cf. *supra*, p. 5.

the Revolution the same balancing principle was observed as Charles II had found so convenient after he dismissed Clarendon. Yet for the sake of unity in prosecuting the war William was impelled in 1696 to give a monopoly of power to the whig 'junto' which was wholly committed to it. For the same reason Anne found herself faced in 1703–4 with the need for shedding from her cabinet extreme tory and defeatist elements that were proving unco-operative with the indispensable architects of victory: Marlborough in the field, and his close ally Godolphin on the home front; a few years later she had to dispense with even the moderate Harley, whom she liked, as the only alternative to losing the generalissimo whom she could not yet do without. 'Is it not very hard' she wrote plaintively to Godolphin when he was pressing on her at this juncture the need for a cabinet appointment on party rather than personal grounds, 'that men of sense and honour will not promote the good of their country, because everything in the world is not done as they desire?' But in 1710, when the time and the country were both ripe for peace, she had the joy of restoring and promoting Harley and dropping the warmongers.[1]

This last change of ministry has many transitional features. It followed traditional lines in that it was brought about, not by a ministerial defeat in the house of commons followed by collective resignation, but by piecemeal dismissal of ministers over a period of five months—a far shorter period, however, than was normal. But it had at least two novel elements which give it an important place in the history of responsible government. The first—that it was almost a clean sweep, not just a partial reconstruction of the ministry—was due neither to Harley nor to the queen, but chiefly to a very 'modern' appreciation by Cowper, the whig lord chancellor (whom she tried hard to retain because he was personally acceptable) that his position in a tory ministry would be impossible. That the lord chancellor should resign when his 'political' colleagues went out was still not an established convention a century later. The second—that many of the higher civil servants who came in with the whigs did not go out with them, nor was there any attempt at a wholesale 'purge' of local government—was the

---

[1]Macaulay, *History*, ch. xxii; Trevelyan, *Queen Anne*, i. 108–11, 200, 213, 274, 335–7, ii. 31–2, 169, 326–8; Keir, op. cit., pp. 277, 281; Davies in *E.H.R.*, lxvi. 246–54.

fruit of Harley's moderation, which thus set an important precedent.

The appeal to the country fully justified *ex post facto* the action of the queen, who might well have claimed with George II (had such an idea occurred to her) to have learned 'to look for the sense of her subjects in another place than in the house of commons';[1] it also justified the measure she took to break down the resistance to the peace in a still whiggish upper house by the creation of eleven new peers at one stroke— another important constitutional precedent. On the other hand, the unexpected extent of the whig landslide at the polls delivered the new lord treasurer into the hands of the extreme wing of his own party, the young bloods of the October Club who were bent on liquidating their political foes for good. Their plan was the painless extinction of dissent through the Schism Act and the limitation of the house of commons to the landed gentry by a new franchise act—legislation which he had reluctantly to support—till at last they were emboldened to call in question the succession to the throne, which had been settled by agreement in the last reign. History abounds in examples of great political leaders hampered at every turn by the diehards, 'ginger groups' or McCarthyites of their own party; one thinks, for example, of Lloyd George in the 1918 election, deflected from a policy of generosity to one of vindictiveness towards defeated Germany by steady pressure from the rear. But it would be hard to find a parallel for the total wreckage in which the rashness of this group of dissidents landed both leader and party.[2]

In a sense there was nothing novel in this conception of the need for basic agreement on policy among the chief ministers of the crown. The older assumption that they were in duty bound to carry out measures they disapproved rather than desert the royal service had gone by the board when fundamental divergences appeared between king and parliament under the earlier Stuarts. Even Clarendon, as we have seen,[3] had assumed that men who did not share the royal aims were no fit councillors to put them into effect. Impeachment and threats

[1] Basil Williams, *Chatham*, 1914, i. 301.
[2] Trevelyan, op cit., iii. 199 and n., 276–307.
[3] *Supra*, p. 34.

of impeachment, by forcing ministers to accept responsibility for royal policy, opened the way to their resignation if the policy had been followed against their advice. The novelty comes in the fact that the real bond of unity between ministers is no longer mere personal loyalty to the crown (though that still counts for much) nor the vagaries of royal favour (though petticoat influence at court played its part first in upholding Marlborough and then in restoring Harley), but a national policy on which crown and parliament are in basic accord.[1] It is also striking that changes in the ministry, though never directly forced upon the crown by parliament, are now sometimes made at the instance of a minister whose presence at the helm of state is vital either in the direct administration of royal policy or in securing the co-operation of parliament. Anne bitterly resented the blow to her prerogative when for this reason she had to part from Harley, but that did not prevent her from still consulting him *sub rosa* with a view to his ultimate return to power. Well over a century later, Victoria felt the same resentment at having to part with 'dear Lord M.'; but by then responsible government had come to stay, and the minister out of power was scrupulous, even at the expense of his personal feelings, to give no appearance of those 'secret whisperings in . . . the back-stairs' that paid such handsome dividends to Harley.[2]

True though it is that no mere adverse vote in the commons could yet bring about the downfall of a minister, it is equally true that a ministry that could not work in harmony with a parliament now in frequent session stood little chance of successfully carrying on the king's or queen's government. For if the Revolution of 1688 had made no direct contribution to responsible government, indirectly it had brought about one of the prime prerequisites by putting on a firm basis the commons' control of finance. The demands of war finance made essential the co-operation of the body that held the nation's purse-strings, and at the same time, by promoting a further reorganization of the treasury and a systematizing of public borrowing through the national debt and the Bank of

[1]Cf. Seeley, *Growth of British Policy*, ii., ch. ii.
[2]Trevelyan, op. cit., i. 186, 337; Turner, op. cit., i. 412; W. T. Morgan, *English Political Parties and Leaders in the Reign of Queen Anne*, 1920, pp. 209, 314–5, 364.

England, they paved the way for more accurate estimates of income and expenditure over the main field of public finance. Even the 'ordinary' revenues (which had once constituted the king's 'own') were now voted in parliament, but these were life revenues, and so not subject to the same inspection and review—with consequences that will appear shortly. The appropriation of supplies and the parliamentary auditing of public accounts, adumbrated in 1624 and conceded (with his tongue in his cheek) by Charles II, now became a reality; so long as the government commanded the confidence of parliament, it could now borrow (as the Roundheads had done during and after the civil war, but without the security of a firmly established government) on the 'public faith' instead of on the word of a slippery monarch.

This could not but affect the relations between parliament and the ministers of the crown. 'The financial powers of the Commons', as Sir David Keir puts it, 'began to draw the Treasury into the parliamentary sphere', with the result that the lord treasurer (or the first lord of the treasury when the office was in commission)—necessarily a key man in the administration—must needs be a competent parliamentary manager.[1] One effect of this is seen in a return to the practice, weakened under the first two Stuarts and almost abandoned after the Restoration, of maintaining a sort of 'treasury bench' in the commons. Somers, the chief legal architect of the Revolution settlement, served the new joint monarchs as their chief legal officer in the commons during the first critical years of the reign; Montagu, its chief financial prop, sat there as a lord of the treasury and chancellor of the exchequer until William's wars were over. Anne's great ministers, Harley and St. John, were in the lower house for most of her reign. None of the ministries of the two reigns was without an effective manager and spokesman in the commons.

The management of parliament involved, of course, the manipulation of Influence. Although we shall find this fruitful source of abuse a constant object of attack from the 'opposition' of the day, those who had to carry on the king's government found that in practice they could not dispense with it. Its source was the 'civil list' granted to the crown for life. At the Revolu-

[1]Keir, op. cit., pp. 274-7, 282; Ogg, op. cit., pp. 340-1.

tion, parliament reverted to the practice of the protectorate and voted for the 'ordinary' needs of government (as distinct from the 'extraordinary' revenue from taxes) a fixed sum for life of £1,200,000—just £100,000 less than Cromwell had received for the same purpose in 1657. At the end of the war with France, however, when the armed forces were placed on a peace footing, the cost of their maintenance (which had accounted for a million of Cromwell's grant) was transferred to the annual estimates, and the crown was given a civil list of £700,000 (later £800,000)—representing Cromwell's £300,000 for 'the support of the government'; this was meant to cover both household expenses and the pensions and salaries of public servants. Even in those days when there were no 'social services' and no paid police force, and the bulk of local administration was on a voluntary basis, this proved inadequate, and from time to time parliament had to grant a lump sum to meet the deficit, but without any detailed knowledge of where the money had gone. This failure to distinguish between the 'private' and 'public' elements in what was still a minor item in the country's budget remained a convenient weakness in public finance until the whole system of Influence was first seriously tackled nearly a hundred years later.[1]

Both William and Anne firmly kept all major appointments in their own hands, and while they might accept advice from ministers they trusted, they would listen to no dictation. Anne never relaxed her vigilance over even minor 'places', partly because she realized that only so long as she retained the power of rewarding her friends and penalizing those who crossed her will would the government really be her government, partly from a genuine hatred of corruption which made her put her foot down firmly on any actual trafficking with places at court. But what with old household offices now turning into sinecures and new junior clerkships in the growing civil service, she could not keep an eye on them all. She trusted Harley, who had a high reputation for financial probity; and long before he became lord treasurer, with an extensive departmental patronage to dispense, his influence behind the scenes carried much weight in appointments.[2]

[1]Gardiner, *Documents*, pp. 452–3; Keir, op. cit., pp. 276, 303–4, 327.
[2]Morgan, op. cit., pp. 136–7, 239, 241, 261–5.

The great patronage departments were the admiralty and above all the treasury, with its army of local revenue officials as well as a substantial establishment of officers and clerks at the centre. Then there was the army, on service for eight years on end under William and still longer under Anne—a startlingly new experience for the country. Its return from active service placed at the disposal of government another swarm of paid public servants in the commissioned officers, while yet another was provided by the inflated staffs of the office of ordnance (with Marlborough himself at the head) and the other branches of the contemporary 'war office'. With the generalissimo an active politician, it was not to be expected that his subordinates would stay out of the game; nor was there any law in force to prevent either them or the civilian 'placemen' from entering it. Here then was potential material in abundance for a parliamentary manager whose job it was to procure majorities in the house for government measures and bills of supply.

As long as William remained at the helm this queer, illogical and delicately poised machinery of government had an effective head, though his absences on campaign made some measure of delegation necessary even to him, especially after the death of his co-sovereign Mary. But the delegation was always to a group of the principal officers of state and household with powers strictly limited and defined under nineteen headings.[1] With the best will in the world, and no lack of appetite for power, Queen Anne had neither the personality nor the brain to fill this rôle in time of prolonged war and acute political strife. She had to have a political manager. The term 'first' or 'prime' or 'premier minister' had been known in politics for a full generation. We have seen how Clarendon rejected it as too 'newly translated out of French' to be acceptable.[2] Yet it crept in, and was used loosely and casually, now of Buckingham or Arlington, rival leaders of the Cabal, now of Sunderland, James II's principal secretary and president of the council. Any such office had of course to stand up to the slings and arrows of an age-long prejudice against 'monopolizing of power' by a subject; but ever since the interregnum there had

---

[1] *E.H.R.*, xxix. 454–5, 459, 461–4.
[2] *Supra*, p. 50; cf. *Times Lit. Supp.*, 27 Feb.–27 March, 1930.

been a body of opinion which stood for 'business methods' and efficiency in government in face of all the majesty of tradition—much as an earlier and more ruthless Cromwell had set about modernizing the government of Henry VIII. Daniel Defoe, with his middle-class dissenting origins and his business interests and contacts, was doubly heir to this heritage. In 1704 he put out a scheme for the complete reorganization of government on these lines,[1] which is worth a brief examination for the same reason as Temple's plan for a reorganized privy council a quarter of a century earlier—not because it was practicable, but because it focused attention on some of the more urgent contemporary problems of government.

It is for its lack of efficiency, not of responsibility, that he attacks the system of his day:

> In matters of war, treatys, embassys, private instructions, expedicions, how many such has the delay, the hesitacions, the ignorance, or something worse, of Privy Councelors overthrown!

Yet how much better was the cabinet as then constituted? 'Cabinets of 10 or 14 are monsters and useless.' The only answer was a 'Prime Ministry'; let it be established and 'the nacion may easily be reconcil'd to it'. And who better fitted to the post than the principal secretary, Defoe's patron Harley, for whom he drew up the memorandum and who was, like him, an ex-dissenter in close touch with business circles, and 'one of the shrewdest political managers the English race has produced'?[2] The secretary's office could become 'an inner Cabinett to the Queen', in fact 'the onely Cabinett' (using the word in its original French rather than its acquired English sense). 'Here all the bussiness of the Crown, the affaires of law onely excepted, will center'; it should have an ample staff of 'able heads, under a secret management', numerous 'agents' and a well-furnished intelligence and statistical service, providing the secretary with bulging files of memoranda on every side of national life. From this 'cabinet' would issue orders needing only formal confirmation by the privy council, with no further discussion.

[1]Printed in *E.H.R.*, xxii. 130 ff.; see also Trevelyan, op. cit. ii. 330–1.
[2]W. T. Morgan in *Essays in Modern English History*, Harvard U.P., 1941, p. 134

Such was Defoe's ultimate ideal. As a temporary expedient he was prepared to admit that the 'conjunccion of the Lord Treasurer' would be useful—temporary, no doubt, because Harley's present good relations with Godolphin, the treasurer, might not (and in fact did not) continue for long.[1] For fully three-quarters of a century the irreducible minimum of counsellors included in the inmost circle of government had been the treasurer and a secretary—the latter primarily for administration, the former for policy.[2] In this respect Defoe's plan follows tradition; but he reverses their rôles and expects his patron's office to come out on top in the end. Meanwhile the treasurer is to be responsible for home affairs and the secretary for the far more important field of foreign policy. On the fringes of this cabinet was to be a sort of outer cabinet consisting of the heads of the law, the army and navy, the church, but they were to be there as expert advisers only; decisions were to rest with the real 'states men', the secretary and (temporarily) the treasurer; and even they were to be above party. Defoe thus follows in general the 'concentric' plan of government with which his age was familiar, but with far greater concentration at the centre, and with a conception of the 'cabinet' that would have precluded the growth of the modern departments of state and the essential principle of collective responsibility.

Even considered in relation to contemporary practice, there are some strange gaps in his scheme. First of all, although by excluding 'affaires of the law' from the secretary's 'cabinet' he leaves a place for parliament in his scheme of government, he has nothing at all to say about its relations with the overgrown State Department of his dreams, and so he shelves the whole question of ministerial responsibility on the one hand and of parliamentary management on the other. In the second place, although he starts by talking in terms of 'secretarys' he soon slides into the singular, and when he remembers the second it is to relegate him to the 'outer' cabinet as an advisory expert. Now it has been suggested that one reason why the need for a prime minister arose, once the monarch had ceased effectively to run his own government, was the existence of two nominally

[1] Morgan, *Pol. Parties and Leaders*, pp. 241–2.
[2] *Supra*, p. 31.

co-equal secretaries; for the allocation since 1689 of the southern department to the senior secretary and the northern to the junior was merely a convenient way of dividing the diplomatic correspondence between them, and did not reflect any distinction in rank or weight—in fact the duality was looked on as a safeguard against excessive concentration of power.[1] As Sir Richard Lodge once observed, if there was to be a leader in the cabinet

> either the task of control must be undertaken by the First Lord of the Treasury, as was done by Walpole . . . or one of the Secretaries must be the predominant partner and his colleague must submit to be little more than a *commis*.[2]

It is clear (though he never expressly says so) that the latter was what Defoe intended. This happened to be one of the periods during which (as in the time of Robert Cecil or Arlington) the secretariat was divided between a politician and an administrator, and Harley's colleague belonged to the second category.[3]

As it has turned out, although the secretariat has profoundly influenced the development of the cabinet by branching out into the various departments of state, it is the treasury that has in practice provided the succession of premiers. Already when Defoe wrote, Harley's colleague Lord Treasurer Godolphin—with the prestige of his historic office, the administrative and financial skill that won him high place under four successive monarchs and made him indispensable to Marlborough in the field, and the wide patronage administered by the treasury—was sometimes referred to as 'prime minister'; for it was he who held the reins in the ministry to the limited extent that the queen relinquished them, and brought his fellow-ministers into line on cabinet policy. But as a peer he had to depend largely on Secretary Harley (who was also Speaker Harley till 1705) to pilot these measures through the commons. The relatively *parvenu* office of secretary had no such prestige and no such patronage, apart from the small staff of clerks—under a dozen between the two of them—paid out of the secretaries' own

[1]Thomson, *Secretaries of State*, 1932, pp. 2–3; cf. *Parl. Hist.*, 1809, v. 7313 (1692).
[2]*Times Lit. Supp.*, 27 March, 1930.
[3]Trevelyan, op. cit., i. 290.

pockets.[1] Defoe's memorandum was no doubt a move in the game of power politics between the two rivals; seven years later, with the war as good as over, the 'warmongers' discredited and the peace to be won, Harley became first lord of the treasury and then, as earl of Oxford, succeeded to the treasurership, 'thereby' (as his brother put it) 'becoming the Primere Minister'.[2] Through the queen's goodwill he had a far freer hand with patronage than his predecessor, but at the same time his peerage robbed his skill as parliamentary manager of half its value; moreover he too had as colleague an ambitious secretary, as ready when the time came to dispute the leadership with him as he had been to steal a march on Godolphin.

Thus the office of prime minister was beginning to take shape —not on Defoe's lines, but with the manipulation of treasury patronage as a principal factor in leadership. Twenty years after Harley became 'primere minister', Walpole as first lord of the treasury, disposing the same patronage under an uninterested alien monarch, and swaying his fellow-commoners with a debating skill that Harley could never boast, was to win a still more decisive round in the contest with the secretariat (in the person of his colleague and former patron Townshend) by putting into effect his determination that the firm should be Walpole and Townshend, not Townshend and Walpole, and packing the recalcitrant secretary off to plant his turnips. But the bitter opposition aroused by the name and office of prime minister in Walpole's day still lay ahead; neither Godolphin nor Harley had the power of regimenting colleagues on the one hand or coercing the crown on the other that belonged to the fully-developed office. It was in Marlborough, that potential Cromwell, that the country gentry saw the old spectre of 'monopoly of power'—the successful general playing a strong hand in politics, and the darling of court and public alike until the queen and his duchess fell out, the public grew war-weary— and the spectre faded.

Cabinet and Influence, however, were objects of frequent attack, from soon after the Revolution, by an opposition which, however variable in composition, stuck doggedly to the task

---

[1] Trevelyan, op. cit., i. 186, 188n., 288, ii. 330; Morgan, op. cit., pp. 238–41; *E.H.R.*, xxix. 65. Even James II had used a commissioner of the treasury as his parliamentary 'manager' in the Commons (*supra*, p. 60).
[2] Hist. MSS. Com., *Portland*, v. 655.

of filling in gaps in the revolutionary settlement. In a debate on the king's speech in 1691, for example, a country member protested that

'Cabinet-Council' is not a word to be found in our Law-books. We knew it not before: we took it for a nick-name. Nothing can fall out more unhappily, than to have a distinction made of the 'Cabinet' and 'Privy-Council' . . . If some of the Privy-Council men be trusted, and some not, to whom must any gentleman apply? Must he ask, 'Who is a Cabinet-Counsellor?' . . . I am sure, these distinctions of some being more trusted than others, have given great dissatisfaction.

The tones are the tones of Clarendon, but the words are those of the poet Waller's quaker son.[1] But cabinets were too elusive a subject for legislation; 'placemen' made a better target, though in practice it proved easier to frame disqualifying legislation against them than to get it past the hostility of ministers, their allies in the lords, and the crown itself—for each of three successive measures in 1692–4 was wrecked on one or other of these rocks. But the opposition had another card up its sleeve: controversial measures could sometimes be secured by 'tacking' them on to others (especially finance bills) that were urgent and non-controversial. By the use of this device a few platoons out of the vast army of revenue officers had been excluded from the house; but this was a mere fleabite.[2]

The opportunity for 'tacking' on a grand scale came with the death in 1700 of the young duke of Gloucester, Princess Anne's only surviving child and the last of the protestant descendants of James II. Unless steps were quickly taken to settle the succession after Anne's death, the door lay wide open for a restoration of the exiled catholic Stuarts—which the king desired as little as his parliament. Rather than see 1688 undone, the king and his ministers accepted further constitutional clauses 'tacked' on to the Act of Settlement, including some they had hitherto kept at bay. One clause gave legal sanction to the claim put forward in Danby's time that a royal

[1]*Parl. Hist.*, v. 731; G. T. Drury, *Poems of Edmund Waller*, 1901, p. lxiii.
[2]Macaulay, *History*, chs. xix–xx; Clark, op. cit., p. 144n.; 11 and 12 Wm. III, cap. 3 (cl–clii), 12 and 13 Wm. III, cap. 10 (lxxix). By 1784 there were 11,500 revenue officers who had votes. (*E.H.R.*, xii. 472).

pardon is no bar to an impeachment. A second virtually repeated one of the Nineteen Propositions tendered to Charles I on the eve of civil war, by laying down that acts done in privy council 'shall be signed by such of the Privy Councillors as shall advise and consent to the same'[1]—a palpable hit at the cabinet.

A third clause had still more radical antecedents; it runs:

> No person who has an Office or Place of Profit under the King shall be capable of serving as a Member of the House of Commons.

The solid country gentry who took this chance to make a clean sweep of the placemen little dreamt that they were borrowing from the Levellers' programme of 1647, which had included an almost identical proposal! Nor is it likely that they saw the implications of their votes, or realized that they were throwing away the baby with the bath water—in other words that in ridding the house of the minor 'placemen' against whom the clause was primarily directed, they were not only striking a blow at corruption; they were also putting out of action the only means then available of avoiding deadlocks between executive and legislature, and at the same time barring the way to any more satisfactory *liaison* by eliminating from the commons the greatest placemen of all—the ministers themselves. Like Defoe's proposals for a 'Prime Ministry', the Act as it stood would have given quite a different twist to our constitutional development; it would have made the commons a far less responsible body than the lords (where ministers could still sit), and it would have forced an approach to the problem of responsible government more in line with modern American practice than with what has become the British way.

From the opposition standpoint the disadvantage of 'tacking' on this occasion was that the 'tacked' clauses were inoperative until the dynastic settlement should come into play on the death of Anne. When she became queen there was a furious struggle, on the one side to remove the mischiefs of the Act before it should be too late, on the other to anticipate the checks it placed on ministers. It was at this point that the lords intervened with a timely reminder that

[1]Grant Robertson, *Select Statutes*, p. 91, cf. Gardiner, *Const. Documents*, pp. 251, 365, and *supra*, p. 36.

to enact that all persons employed and trusted by the Crown shall, for that reason alone, become incapable of being trusted by the people, is in effect to declare that the interests of the Crown and of the People must always remain contrary to each other;

and at last a compromise was arrived at and embodied in a supplement to the Act of Settlement which became law in 1705 and was confirmed in 1707. As soon as the new dynasty came in, holders of all new 'places of profit' created since 1705, and of a few additional categories of existing offices, were to be automatically barred from sitting in the commons; all other placemen (and these would include the ministry) were required only to resign and to submit themselves afresh to the verdict of their constituents. The same measure also repealed the clause of 1701 which had been designed to prevent the growth of the cabinet by revitalizing the privy council.[1]

The compromise had far-reaching consequences, but, as so often in our history, the results were unforeseen and almost accidental. It was accepted, not from any real appreciation of the issues involved, but simply to break a momentary deadlock. The distinction it drew was purely empirical; not till the nineteenth century was the solution arrived at by which the placemen completely excluded from parliament constituted the permanent non-political civil service, while those who merely had to seek re-election were the political heads of departments. Generally speaking, the executive was viewed by the independent country gentleman of Queen Anne's reign in a purely negative light: to him it was something to be prevented from getting into mischief, as it had so often done in the days of his father and his grandfather, whether under a Stuart king or a lord protector. When Sir John Trevor, afterwards Charles II's secretary of state, sat in Cromwell's parliament, he had warned his fellow-members against putting so many restraints on the protector's power to do harm that 'it will be questionable whether he shall be able to do you any good'.[2] The warning still had its relevance.

When something obviously had to be done, the gentry in

[1] 4 Anne c. 8; Grant Robertson, op. cit., pp. 106–7; Trevelyan, *Queen Anne*, ii. 18–19, 94–7.
[2] Burton, *Diary*, ed. T. J. Rutt, 1828, iii. 322.

G.R.G.—G

parliament preferred that if possible it should be done by parliamentary committees like those through which the Long Parliament had run the country till Cromwell came to power, rather than by anything so dangerous as an established government department. It is doubtful whether they appreciated that a continental war against Louis XIV could not be managed on the same lines as the gentlemanly civil war their fathers had fought, or the very limited campaigns of the Buckingham era— with the parliamentary committee that paid the piper calling the tune; members were as determined as their predecessors of Charles I's day to avoid a situation in which they 'gave without seeing the treaties', and King William was as touchy as King Charles about his prerogative in foreign affairs. He was even jealous when parliament tried to regulate war-time trade through one of its committees, and as a counterblast he set up in 1696 a new board of trade and plantations which resumed the work of Charles II's committee of trade, and continued to operate in these two fields till the loss of America.[1] The independent member, for his part, was convinced that his independence hung on keeping at bay an ever-encroaching executive, and foreign observers also came to believe that a supposed separation of powers was the safeguard of English liberties. Fifty years later Montesquieu preached it up as a supreme virtue of our constitution, and both the French Constituent Assembly of 1791 and the architects of the republic of 1848 believed him only too well; both landed themselves in the deadlock against which Mirabeau had warned his fellow-members in 1791, and in both cases the answer to deadlock was dictatorship. The American colonists took the same view of the historic constitution they believed George III to have destroyed, and they made this separation of powers a basic element in their own republican constitution; with a whole continent for elbow-room their posterity managed to avoid serious deadlock between the two branches of government till our own century.

The 'opposition' that from time to time snatched these victories over the ministry must not of course be conceived of in terms of a coherent and continuous body adhering to a formulated policy, but rather as shifting groups, suggestive

[1]Turner in *E.H.R.*, xxxiv. 182; Clark, op. cit., pp. 43, 145, and *Guide to English Commercial Statistics*, R.H.S., 1938, pp. 1–33; *supra*, p. 49.

more of modern French practice than of our own two-party system, yet with an inner core that held together.[1] What is significant is that the idea of legitimate opposition has come to be accepted at all. By the end of Queen Anne's reign she must have been almost the only person in active politics (except Bolingbroke in his 'true-blue' phase) who still believed that opposition to crown policy was disloyal if not treasonable; and even she had not been quite so sure of it while her detested brother-in-law 'Mr. Caliban' was on the throne, for she allowed John Churchill, the brilliant young soldier whose wife was her bosom friend and who was to become the duke of Marlborough, to use her house as a centre for discontented officers and politicians, anticipating in some degree the dealings with the opposition of the Hanoverian princes of Wales.[2] But any hope that when she succeeded she would draw her ministries from the 'opposition' of the last reign proved as illusory as Falstaff's hopes of Prince Hal or whig pipe-dreams about the prince regent. If Marlborough was given high promotion, that was because he was the only man who could do what the country called for; nor was he allowed to cling on to power when the job was finished. The normal expectation that any government measure that was not pure routine would be opposed from some quarter of the house, that on everything of moment there was a ministerial and an opposition standpoint, was an important if unnoticed constitutional development; it meant the edging of the blood feud out of politics. The threatened impeachments, by one set of men, of ministers responsible for the Partition Treaties, by another of the authors of the Treaty of Utrecht, were in fact little more than traditional gestures: neither came to anything, and it is unlikely that either was meant to.

On the other hand systematic opposition, opposition on principle, continued to be reprobated by responsible politicians for another fifty years or more, and party labels were still disliked by the mass of the country gentry. Every parliament of

[1]There is an admirable analysis of the shifting groups that constituted the two 'parties' in the two reigns—their family and professional connexions, their parliamentary followings, their mutual interaction and their views on current issues—in Dr. Robert Walcott's contribution to *Essays in Modern English History*, pp. 81–131 (expanded in *Harvard Hist. Monographs*, xxviii, 1956).

[2]Clark, op. cit., pp. 176, 229; Morgan, op. cit., pp. 40–44; Walcott, loc. cit., pp. 91–2.

Anne's reign had a solid nucleus of 'queen's servants' who refused to call themselves whig or tory but were bound by the queen's personal wishes and could be used against ministers if she fell out with them. Few even of the leaders were good party men, and it was held against them if they were. Godolphin was the typical non-party man, ready to place his great abilities at the service of any government in power. Bolingbroke's literary diatribes against party belong, it is true, to the period when his own party was in political exile, but even as Mr. St. John his initial aim had been to eschew political extremes and to appeal to the solid body of moderate opinion and landed property. Harley was equally impatient of doctrinaire politics and saw 'no difference between a mad Whig and a mad Tory'; he 'disbelieved', it has been said, 'in the whole scheme of party, and would not frame a rigid programme'. Yet each of them found in turn that to carry on the government successfully they needed, as well as the backing of the crown, that of a well-knit body of supporters in the commons and of colleagues united in a broad scheme of policy. And so Harley, in spite of himself, became to all intents and purposes the founder of a party and the head of the first real party ministry; while Bolingbroke, who preached to him the need for party organization and discipline, staked and lost all on a desperate party intrigue that ruined his own political career and sent his and Harley's party for forty years into the wilderness.[1]

Party, then, like cabinet and prime minister, had come to stay, even if the time was still far ahead when there was anything that could be called a 'party system'. In London there were the coffee houses used as headquarters by the rival factions, the Kit-Cat and October Clubs, and (thanks to Harley) the use made of the growing tribe of literary propagandists like Defoe and Swift, with Addison and Steele to answer them. Defoe was also the indefatigable agent who kept Harley in touch with local groups up and down the country. It has been claimed that, like party organization in modern America, this development contributed to national unity by gradually substituting national policy for local and personal feuds as electioneering issues, important and even decisive as these often

---

[1]Feiling, *History of the Tory Party*, 1924, pp. 385-8; Morgan, op cit., pp. 248, 303, 398-9; Hist. MSS. Com., *Portland*, v. 311; Trevelyan, op. cit., i. 213.

remained in the remoter countryside for many years to come. It speaks volumes for the wide diffusion of political interest that Swift sold 11,000 copies of his *Conduct of the Allies* in a month.[1] The fact that at the end of the seventeenth century it would still be hard to relate either of the party labels to any consistent body of principles is really beside the point: to the outsider (and even to many Americans) it would be equally hard to arrive at any hard-and-fast theoretic definition of the principles behind the two major American parties today! What matters is the existence of a recognizable body of men united enough to be called in by the head of the state to take over the government when public opinion seems to call for a change; and that state of affairs was at least well on its way in the England of Queen Anne.

This was not always clear to contemporaries who inveighed against party, dwelt on the 'mighty difference between the politics before and since the Revolution' (which had settled, on terms acceptable to both parties, the issues that first gave rise to them), and recognized 'no other distinction, but for or against the government'. Bolingbroke, the ablest exponent of this view, saw no further than his less brilliant contemporaries the implications of party government, nor did he ever squarely face the alternatives.[2] 'Party', says Professor Trevelyan, 'is the real secret of the step upwards from Cabal to Cabinet':

> Without the party bond we should have had Ministers . . . allying themselves with the Crown or the mob against their colleagues. Thanks to the party bond, the Whig Junta was sufficiently united and powerful to win the war in Queen Anne's reign and to make the Union with Scotland. Thanks to the party bond, the Tories under Oxford and Bolingbroke adhered together long enough in office to force through the difficult and indispensable Peace of Utrecht.[3]

And even if Macaulay did over-rationalize the conflict and over-sharpen the picture, it would be idle to deny some measure of genuine common principle, other than the bare 'for or

---

[1] Trevelyan, op. cit., i. 196; iii. 193; Morgan, op. cit., pp. 398–9; cf. Dodd, *Studies in Stuart Wales*, pp. 214–5.

[2] Feiling, op. cit., p. 430; Bolingbroke, *Dissertation upon Parties*, 1735; H. N. Fieldhouse in *History*, xxiii. 41–56. Hume, writing only six or seven years later, gives a far more balanced view than Bolingbroke (*Essays*, I, ix; II, xiv).

[3] *The Two-Party System in English Political History*, Romanes Lecture, 1926, p. 11; cf. Keir, op. cit., p. 272n.

against the government', to these incipient parties, whether we lay the stress on differences of political, religious or economic outlook.

In view of the traditional structure of English society, where the provinces have counted for so much more in politics than in a centralized country like France, an understanding of party must begin with an understanding of the prejudices and attachments of the country gentleman,[1] as we see him in Addison's Sir Roger de Coverley or Steele's Tory Foxhunter or Fielding's Squire Western: devoted to throne and altar but suspicious of courts and capitals; a Little Englander and an isolationist, but fiercely jingo when his country's independence or its chosen way of life seems threatened, and equally touchy about his own independence and what was due to his order; contemptuous of foreigners and papists, traders and dissenters; in fact the true John Bull—for the John Bull created and christened in Arbuthnot's pamphlet of 1712 is a townsman and a trader. 'We supposed the Tory party', wrote Bolingbroke in 1717, 'to be the bulk of the landed interest', while in their rivals he saw

> the remains of a party formed against the ill designs of the Court under King Charles II, nursed up into strength and applied to contrary uses by King William III, and yet still so weak as to lean for support on the Presbyterians and the other sectaries, on the Bank and the other corporations, on the Dutch and the other Allies.[2]

It is of course a partisan estimate, but it brings out the essential truth that at the end of the seventeenth century whiggism stood for something new and sectional (might we even borrow Senator MacCarthy's thunder and say 'for un-English activities'?), toryism for what was established and traditional. What mattered to the country voter was these values, not the party label which might or might not conceal them; and how he voted depended on the quarter from which at any moment he believed them to be threatened. The task of the new pamphleteers and party organizers was to persuade him that his guarantee lay in the party ticket.

[1]Cf. *supra*, pp. 13–14.
[2]*Letter to Sir William Wyndham*, 1753.

The division is naturally not peculiar to English politics; it has its analogy, for example, in the cleavage between France of the Revolution and France of the *roi très chrétien*. Fortunately the cleavage in British politics, real though it was, was neither so deep nor so fundamental. Both parties stood by the Revolution settlement, though they might not agree about all its implications; both stood for the protestant ascendancy, though one might think of it primarily in terms of dogma, tradition and ceremony, the other in terms of freedom and independence; both supported war with France, although the tories were fain to stop it at the point where its continuance might change the balance of society in favour of the military and moneyed interests—much as Lord Lansdowne would have stopped the first World War in 1917 before it brought about the social disruption he foresaw. But although this prospect was less alarming to the whigs—backers of Marlborough and creators of the Bank of England and the National Debt—they were no less convinced than the tories that land was the ultimate foundation of national prosperity and the only proper passport to political power; party was not a mere expression of class. It is perhaps typical of the better side of English party politics that 'the most loveable portrait in literature of a Tory country gentleman was drawn by a Whig'.[1] This was what made it possible to comprehend both parties within a single constitution without bringing it to a standstill, and to evolve the principle of constitutional opposition, England's great contribution to the practice of politics in this age.

The crisis in which the reign ended threatened to put a stop to this peaceful development, to re-open fundamental issues and so to put the clock back to the age of Danby and Shaftesbury, if not that of Strafford and Pym. It all began with a struggle for leadership in the tory party after it had swept the polls at the elections of 1710 and 1713 and seemed assured of a long tenure of power under the open favour of the queen. Bolingbroke—as Henry St. John—had first entered ministerial office with Harley (who had persuaded the queen to accept him) in the coalition of 1704; he was now secretary in his all-tory administration, but he was impatient of the older man's leadership and thought he saw a chance of displacing him by

[1] Trevelyan, *Queen Anne,* iii. 107.

appealing to the strong wave of true-blue tory sentiment that swept the country when the tory government put an end to what had become the whig war and the threatened sway of the warmongers and financiers. Oxford, 'vacillating and cautious', suspect to the 'ultras' for his dissenting origins, his trading connexions and his known moderation, was at a great disadvantage against his younger, bolder and completely unprincipled rival. There are some points of resemblance to the struggle for power between Walpole and Townshend in 1730, and even to that between Asquith and Lloyd George in 1916; but the issues at stake were made far more critical by two major occurrences of 1714: the queen was stricken with what proved to be mortal illness, and her destined Hanoverian successor, the popular Electress Sophia, died, leaving an unattractive son (heartily disliked by Anne) as heir presumptive to the British throne. The Elector George was suspected of being hand-in-glove with the whig opposition, and known to have shared their disgust with the tories for bringing to an end England's part in a war which Hanover would have fought to a finish. And the queen did not make things easier for her ministers by the fact that she was as touchy about any mention of her successor as the great Elizabeth had been.

The analogy of Elizabeth's closing years suggests itself in other ways too: the main concern of the tory ministers now, like that of the Elizabethan recusants, was 'not so much to oppose the entrance of the . . . king . . . but only that . . . they would know on what conditions his Majesty would receive them'.[1] For now that politics had suddenly returned to the 'neck-or-nothing' phase of the later years of Charles II, there was no telling what rod the foreign king and his whig associates might not have in pickle for the men who forced the peace and betrayed the allies. What both parties failed to realize (with perhaps typical insularity) was that to this unadaptable and very German despot, with no sentiments save for his beloved Hanover, English politics meant nothing and England herself was no more than a pawn in the game of German politics. There followed an orgy of intrigue and counter-intrigue with the Hanoverian court and with those of France and Lorraine (where the Stuart pretender successively took refuge), in which

[1]Parsons to Garnet, etc., 6 July 1603, quoted J. Gerard in *The Month*, 1896, p. 181.

neither of the rivals came out well, but Bolingbroke, the gambler, committed himself much farther than the hesitant lord treasurer. He had his brief hour of triumph; Oxford was dismissed, and for two days his rival was nominal head of the ministry, but the queen drew the line at Bolingbroke as treasurer. Then, with a superb effort, she roused herself from the lethargy of approaching death to avert the civil war she saw approaching just as surely—even though she knew she would not live to see it herself. Summoning the privy council, as a body beyond party and superior to the cabinet, on its advice she handed the treasurer's white staff with her dying hands to the duke of Shrewsbury, a non-party magnate who had been among the emissaries to William of Orange in 1688 and was known to favour the Hanoverian succession. She died, George I was proclaimed, and a new era opened in British politics.[1] Anne may have been wrong in her judgement; it may be, as Sir Charles Petrie has tried to show, that James III would have made a better job of it than George I;[2] but at least it was a crowning act of heroism in an undistinguished and unhappy life, and in itself goes far to justify Professor Trevelyan's eulogy of her as 'for all her simplicity the wisest and most triumphant of her race'.

It was also the swan-song of the privy council in high politics. The council was brought in then to break a deadlock which had begun as the familiar game of political tennis between two skilled players, but ended by casting the crown into the hazard; it was one which neither cabinet nor parliament could break, and with the queen herself *in extremis*, some accepted authority must act at once on pain of national catastrophe. The occasion never rose again, and the council sank back into the routine which had become its normal function since 1688. The last effective council debate on policy of which we have record had taken place in 1695. The attempt in 1701 to checkmate the cabinet by restoring the non-party council as the supreme organ of policy was, as we have seen, the snap success of a faction, and the clause was repealed before ever it came into action. When in 1713 some councillors tried to have the Treaty of Utrecht

---

[1]Trevelyan, op. cit., III, ch. xvii; Feiling, op. cit., pp. 451–83; Clark, op cit.,
   pp. 232–8; *E.H.R.*, xxvii. 686–7; Keir, op. cit., p. 288.
[2]*The Jacobite Movement*, 1932, ch. iv.

debated in full council as the sale of Dunkirk had been in 1662, they found that they were called together only to give formal sanction to a *fait accompli*. The judicial functions the council had lost in 1641 (which did not include its appellate jurisdiction in ecclesiastical and overseas suits, represented today by the work of the judicial committee) were never restored, and their disappearance, it has been pointed out, removed 'an important motive for retaining a corporate form of council'.[1]

For that reason the routine and administrative duties were taken over by other bodies nominally subordinate to it but in practice (like the cabinet) superseding it, and leaving it to meet only on rare and solemn occasions—and then never in full strength: out of a total of eighty only twenty-eight were there to register the Treaty of Utrecht, and twenty-three at Anne's deathbed. Correspondence with local authorities, once so important a part of the council's activities, was now mostly relegated to obscure clerks in the secretarial offices, leaving country gentry resentful at the disappearance of the more personal relationship of their fathers' day—burdensome as that generation had often found it. Plantation affairs went to the autonomous board of trade and plantations; formal business and dealings with Ireland and the Channel Islands—as well as a good deal of internal correspondence—were dealt with in a sort of standing executive which gradually absorbed most of the other committees of council and came to be known comprehensively as 'the committee', without further qualification. For most purposes, other than judicial affairs and public policy, this committee was already superseding the council before the Hanoverians arrived, but it was they who gave it formal sanction.[2]

This did not prevent official directories like Chamberlayne's (the prototype of Whittaker) from continuing as late as George II's reign to speak of the council—with the truly Clarendonian ring appropriate to the first edition, which appeared just after the chancellor's fall—as 'The *Primum Mobile* of Civil Government, from which all the inferior Orbs derive their motion'; or from describing its procedure much as Sir Julius Caesar

[1] *E.H.R.*, xxvii. 685–7; *History*, xxii. 242; Gneist, *History of the English Constitution*, 1885, p. 590.
[2] *Supra*, p. 29; *A.H.R.*, xvii. 762.

described it in 1625, and its function and purpose in those terms of 'Secrecy and Expedition', 'Matters of Complaint and sudden Emergencies', which Charles II had used to excuse his resort to more intimate counsels.[1] The next fifty years in the growth of the constitution were to be a running commentary on this contrast of form with fact.

[1] John Chamberlayne, *Magnae Britanniae Notitia, or, The Present State of Great Britain*, 1737. The first edition (1669) was published by his father Edw. Chamberlayne, tutor to Charles II's natural son the duke of Grafton and to Queen Anne's consort Prince George. *Cf. supra*, pp. 22–3.

VII

The Monstrous Regiment of Whigs
1714–60

IT had taken a revolution to put Dutch William on the throne, but it was what would nowadays be called a bi-partisan revolution, and William was in any case too proud to rule as king of a party, and too wise to foster political cleavages in a nation whose united strength was what he wanted for his struggle with France. And so in a surprisingly short time the 'principles of 1688' passed into national mythology with Magna Carta as an object of general veneration, not just a party cry. How different with George I! His accession had needed no departure from the normal machinery of the constitution; even if there were fifty-seven more direct heirs, no one had ever disputed the right of the crown-in-parliament to vary the succession within the royal house, nor could there be any cavil at the credentials of the parliament that passed the Act of Settlement or of the public officials who put it into effect on the demise of the crown. And yet George did rule as a party king, and his accession, so far from fostering unity, brought back into politics that principle of *vae victis* that had seemed to be yielding to a more civilized give-and-take. In many respects the Hanoverian succession was a set-back to orderly constitutional development.

The initial fault cannot be laid at the door of the new king, who had been studiously correct in his dealings with English parties while he was still in Germany; nor of the earl of Oxford, who had striven for a settlement of the succession on a national instead of a party basis, and had resisted the clamour of his followers for a wholesale share-out of the spoils of office when they triumphed at the polls; nor yet of the whig opposition, which had been quite ready for the obvious course of a coalition government to hold the fort for the Hanoverian king-designate. It was Bolingbroke's dangerous and irresponsible game, Oxford's vacillation and weakness in countering it, and finally the tactical use made of their errors by the triumphant whigs, that made politics take this turn for the worse. When on the queen's death the seals were broken on the lists sent from Hanover (in accordance with the Regency Act supplementing the Act of Settlement) of those who were to serve with the principal officers of state on the regency council till the king's arrival, they revealed a solid phalanx of whigs. One of their first acts was to get rid of Bolingbroke (who as secretary would have had far too much control over the coming election), leaving the king on his arrival to complete arrangements for what was in effect an all-whig ministry; for the few minor posts offered to tories were so few and so minor that they were generally declined.[1]

Early the next year writs were issued for a new parliament. An injudicious pronouncement by the pretender on the one hand, and a highly tendentious election proclamation from the throne on the other, produced, with the help of the usual pull (financial and otherwise) of the government in power, an overwhelming whig majority, after a campaign rivalling in violence those of Queen Anne's last two elections. The new parliament promptly showed its temper by reprimanding through the speaker a member who dared to criticize the election proclamation, and it proceeded to prepare articles of impeachment against Bolingbroke, Oxford and others among the fallen tory leaders.[2] It seemed that another era of political proscription had set in; but 'kindly old England', in Professor Trevelyan's phrase, 'has always in the long run revolted against

---

[1]Trevelyan, op. cit. iii. 299; Michael, *England under George I*, i. 57, 66–7; W. T. Morgan in *Essays in Mod. Eng. Hist.*, pp. 135–6.

[2]Michael, op. cit., i. 90–102, 114–16, 120–2. There is an admirable analysis of the electioneering of 1715 and its results by W. T. Morgan, loc. cit., pp. 133–76. See also Feiling, *Second Tory Party*, 1938, pp. 14–15.

"fascist" exponents of the penal suppression of "the other side"'.[1] Bolingbroke, to the relief of the prosecution, fled to the pretender in France; Oxford, less accommodating, stood his ground, and was committed to the Tower, where he remained in far from close confinement for two years, in constant touch with tories and Jacobites, before he was brought to trial. By then heats had abated and the trial was allowed, with a sigh of relief, to fizzle out. But Oxford, though continuing to play the Jacobite and to put in appearances in the house of lords, no longer counted in politics; his ambitions were now satisfied by building up the great Harleian library which, housed in the British Museum, has done far more for British scholarship than its owner ever accomplished for British politics.[2] At last even Bolingbroke was pardoned and (having quarrelled with the pretender) returned to England; and though his attainder prevented him from joining Oxford in the lords it did not prevent him from becoming a focal point for opposition and arresting the drift to single-party government. At any rate the long history of political impeachment was at an end. Better ways had at last been found of bringing ministers to book for 'errors of judgment', and the procedure was henceforth reserved for grosser and more palpable misdemeanours in public life.

Yet if there was little 'penal suppression', even after the armed risings of 1715 and 1745, political proscription of a milder order there certainly was. Whatever may have been the original intention, the miscalculations of the chief tory leaders had now given ample pretext for the exclusion of the whole party from office as tarred with the Jacobite brush. And so there followed the long whig monopoly, not only of the principal offices of state, but of all the minor jobs and sinecures in both central and local administration through which parliamentary majorities were maintained.[3] The outbreak of 1715 also gave an excuse for the parliament then sitting to avoid the risks of an early election and to prolong its own existence (and that of future parliaments) from the statutory three years to seven. The repeal of the Septennial Act became

[1] Loc. cit., p. 96.
[2] Michael, i. 126–30, ii. 21–4.
[3] Feiling, p. 16.

for the rest of the century a stock item first of tory, then of radical propaganda; but the act withstood all assaults until the present century because, long before its repeal, other ways had been found of preventing parliaments from getting out of touch with the trends of opinion. Fortunately for the health of politics, a split soon appeared in the ranks of the monopolists themselves; within three years there was an opposition again, within ten it had in Bolingbroke a formidable leader, even though outside parliament, and within twelve a pungent literary organ in *The Craftsman*. Yet the fundamental mischief remained: politics became a pure game of ins-and-outs between rival groups within an exclusive circle of whig families, united only in a determination to keep it exclusive; and this exclusiveness was maintained, to the great impoverishment of politics, long after all shred of its original pretext had vanished[1]—much as the protestant ascendancy battened for two centuries and more after the Armada and Gunpowder Plot on the fiction that every papist was a potential Guy Fawkes or fifth-columnist.

The vicious principle that made every change of administration an excuse for a reshuffle of minor offices cut short the development towards a stable and expert civil service, divorced from party politics, which had begun before the change of dynasty—so much so that when the long ascendancy was broken by George III he found that civil servants left in office still felt politically bound to their old patrons, and had to be bundled out as spies in the camp.[2] When the basic job of governing was overshadowed by the scramble for office so completely as it was during this age, it was fortunate that the age was a static one, mercifully free from social upheavals within or military threats from without. In the army there was some check on the practice of assigning commands as a reward for political service, or cashiering for political opposition, in the fact that 'the Hanoverian dynasty . . . retained a strong German predilection for the parade-ground, which it would not unreservedly sacrifice to the parliamentary arena'; and the navy board always managed to keep a good deal of independence from treasury control in its finances and therefore in its

[1] F. S. Oliver, *The Endless Adventure*, 1930, i. 265–8.
[2] Namier, *England in the Age of the American Revolution*, pp. 480–1.

appointments. But in colonial administration jobbery was
screened by the broad Atlantic—until its effects came home to
roost in the American Revolution.[1]

The department of government that worked only too
smoothly was the manipulation of parliament. There were no
unresolved deadlocks between executive and legislature,
because Influence was now reduced to à fine art and the
commons rashly abandoned the practice developed during the
last two reigns of ordering accounts of public income and
expenditure—doubtless because once the whig ministers controlled patronage (and therefore the commons) such checks
were no longer considered by them to be necessary or desirable.[2] Unlike William and even Anne, the first two Hanoverians
took little direct interest in patronage, except where the army
was concerned; it soon became an accepted convention that
the bulk of the treasury patronage was at the disposal of the
first lord, to assist him in managing on the king's behalf both
elections themselves and the parliaments elected.[3] Not that the
'management' of elections was solely or even mainly a matter of
finance; the minister's first duty was to be knowledgeable about
constituencies and candidates, and to let the government's
preferences be known to the people who counted locally—no
light task even when the world of politics and society was so
much smaller and more compassable than today.

After George I, whose ignorance of the language made
county society and politics a sealed book to him, the crown
began to take some hand in this, but always on the advice of a
minister with the requisite inside knowledge and contacts. By
the middle of the century it had come to be looked on as a
piece of 'insolence' for electors to brush such directives aside
merely because they were 'independent gentlemen' with 'no
places, no employments'. Still, places and employments
generally went a long way towards securing compliance when
less tangible hints had failed, and they had the great advantage
that many of them cost the government nothing, since payment

[1]Namier, *Age of Amer. Rev.*, p. 181n., and *Structure of Politics at the Accession of George III*, 1929, i. 37, 42; Keir, op. cit., p. 303. George III followed awhile, but soon dropped, the whig practice of political 'purges' in the army (Dobrée, *Letters of King George III*, 1935, viii (pp. 23–4), xiii (p. 26); M. S. Guttmacher, *America's Last King*, N.Y., 1941, pp. 68, 89n.).
[2]*E.H.R.*, lxii. 491n.
[3]Michael, i. 101; Namier, *Age of Amer. Rev.*, pp. 145, 155, 163.

was by fees. The rest could be left to its friends in the constituency—except of course in boroughs where a government department like the treasury or the admiralty had direct nomination. The cruder use in elections of secret service money was greatly exaggerated in popular rumour, as Sir Lewis Namier has so effectively shown; where crown or public funds were used in this way it was to serve the purpose of the party fund today—to enable a poor but well-affected candidate to meet the often crippling costs of a contest—and the results were not impressive.[1] Above all it must be borne in mind that the 'carpet bagger' was still *rara avis* in politics outside the smaller and more corrupt boroughs; the choice of candidates was between local families of weight and standing, and the fact that one candidate might have the imprimatur of the government did not necessarily destroy his broadly representative character, any more than the 'coupon' of a modern party headquarters.

Inside the house Influence was used much as it had always been used since it was first organized under Charles II: a lavish distribution of 'places' as rewards for past or prospective services, and a more sparing use of public funds to enable impecunious supporters to keep afloat. It was the contemporary equivalent of our payment of members—with the important reservation that eighteenth-century M.P.s were paid not just for being there, but for voting the right way. On the other hand there was no system of piece-rates or payment by results; the largesse was distributed not on particular divisions but for the session or for life—which still left the recipient a good deal of latitude in voting. By the middle of the century nearly half the house was in government pay in some shape or form. Normally the system enabled ministers to carry through their programmes, not without opposition, but without deadlock, and it is hard to see how any other system could have done so before party discipline became effective. An experienced parliamentarian who was also an author of distinction defended the old system when it was on its last legs by pointing out that

---

[1]Michael, i. 115; Namier, *Age of Amer. Rev.*, p. 129, and *Structure of Politics*, i. 238, 243–62, ii. 519–78; A. S. Foord in *E.H.R.*, lxii. 489–91. Walpole is said to have spent a million and a half of secret service money during his last ten years; how much of it went on elections can never be known (Feiling, *Second Tory Party*, p. 32).

G.R.G.—H

a Minister . . . must be possessed of some attractive influence, to enable him to draw together these discordant particles, and unite them in a firm and solid majority, without which he can pursue no measures of public utility with steadiness or success. An independent House of Commons is no part of the English constitution.[1]

The last phrase, of course, overstates the case. Whatever its normal state of dependence, the house of commons could and did take the bit between its teeth and go its own way in defiance of ministers when its feelings were strongly roused; so, for that matter, could the electorate. Indeed supporters of the government were in some sense freer to vote against it on particular issues—even important ones—in days when a government defeat did not necessarily involve the dislocation (and the possible diversion of the loaves and fishes) implicit in a change of ministry.[2]

The operating of this vast and complex machine of Influence called for a peculiar combination of qualities and tastes: boundless industry and patience, a prodigious memory for detail, a wide circle of acquaintances, a tough skin and a sheer love of manipulation, bustle and intrigue. Rarely have these qualities been combined to such effect as in the duke of Newcastle, the prototype of all political 'bosses' and the prop of the whig ascendancy from Walpole's ministry to the accession of George III. His fabulous wealth, which he spent lavishly in the cause, and his direct territorial sway in at least four counties and seven boroughs (with a still wider indirect influence through allies and connexions) made him a formidable figure at elections even before he had any government money or patronage to handle; and when to that was added an intense delight and *expertise* in electoral strategy, it was inevitable that he should be accepted as the honest broker who could be trusted to make the best political use of any patronage, public or private, handed over to his care. For thirty years ministries came and ministries

---

[1]Quoted Namier, *Structure of Politics*, i. 265; see also ibid., p. 12, and *Age of Amer. Rev.*, pp. 123, 257. Similar sentiments are expressed in Hume's essay 'Of the Independency of Parliament' (*Essays*, I, vi, 1741–2); cf. also the bolder assertion of Rigby, a notorious trafficker in the system: 'Without influence and what is called undue influence too, this government could not subsist' (1768; Feiling, op. cit., p. 103).

[2]For examples of defeats of North's government by its own supporters see Feiling, p. 116, and cf. *infra*, p. 193.

went but Newcastle as secretary of state went on for ever, because none of them could hold together and maintain their majorities without him. At last he even slipped into the habit of talking of his elaborately classified election lists as 'choosing the parliament'—which was not so wildly at variance with the facts. On the other hand, responsibility frightened him and policy left him floundering, so his two short spells at the treasury were an anti-climax; his experience and his talents cut him out for a party whip, not a premier—least of all a war premier.[1]

Whatever the benefits of what we may call the Newcastle system in preventing friction between executive and legislature, it certainly gave politics an air of unreality. Economic forces were already driving a wedge between the great territorial magnate and the small squire or freeholder who could no longer afford the expense of candidature or representation unless as a government pensioner; and those who scorned (or failed to land) these prizes, and stayed at home, looked on the game of politics at Westminster with indifference or contempt. For if in the house tories were in a permanent minority (though always a substantial one when important issues arose), the political tradition for which they stood was very much alive in the country, as the literature of the age amply bears out. Even after fifty years of Newcastle's system, elections at the beginning of George III's reign showed that in the constituencies least amenable to gerrymandering about half the voters were still tory in outlook.[2] This gulf between the politicians and the country had many unhappy results. While enhancing the irresponsibility of those in power, it made criticism (which could never be turned into action) captious and unconstructive, and the country squire, secure in his own little kingdom, more determined than ever to run it as he chose, without direction from above. It was well for the country that, with all his ineptitudes and petty tyrannies, he ran it as well and conscientiously as he did; but the economic transitions of the age might have been accomplished with less violent dislocation and more sense of common direction and purpose had 'the

[1]Basil Williams, *The Whig Supremacy*, 1939, pp. 27–9, 353–4 and ch. xii, and in *E.H.R.*, xii. 448–88; Namier, *Age of Amer. Rev.*, pp. 76, 145, 154, 399, *Structure of Politics*, p. 260.
[2]Namier, *Age of Amer. Rev.*, p. 257; Feiling, ch. i.

government' not become something remote, olympian and more than suspect to the local communities.

Yet even in this age of maximum irresponsibility there were a few long-term gains for responsible government. It was under the first two Georges that the cabinet and the office of first minister began to take on a clearer outline; at the same time the conception of a constitutional opposition gains ground and there is even some progress towards the separation of the civil service from politics. Initially, it is true, the Hanoverian succession was a set-back to genuine cabinet government. The king had his Hanoverian as well as his English ministers; the Act of Settlement debarred them from office in the English government, but the king would have been lost without them, so for some years there was a sort of dual cabinet, and who was to say which minister was responsible for any act of state? Opinion here was that it was the Hanoverian ministers who had first access to important documents and to the king's private ear; nor is it to be wondered at if he preferred to speak in his own tongue to fellow-countrymen on matters he understood rather than wrestle with unfamiliar ideas in French or dog Latin (since English remained as incomprehensible to him as German to all but one of his English ministers). If anyone was chief minister to George I during the first five years of his reign it was the Hanoverian Bernstorff. None of the English ministers could rival him in knowledge of Europe except perhaps Stanhope, and he was inexperienced in office. The filling of so weighty and invidious a place as that of lord treasurer had been evaded (on Hanoverian advice) by putting it into commission again—for good this time—and the office of first lord, important as it was financially and therefore in the management of parliament, did not yet carry anything like the same automatic prestige or primacy.[1]

It was the conviction that Bernstorff and his colleagues were running England in the interests of Hanover that provoked the first ministerial crisis in 1717, when Secretary Townshend was dismissed and his brother-in-law Walpole, the first lord of the treasury, insisted on going with him—much to the chagrin of the king, who could ill spare so able a financier and parliamentary manager. The split was made more serious by the

[1]Michael, i. 103, 106–7, 327–31, ii. 270–2; Basil Williams, *Stanhope*, 1932, p. 153.

king's quarrel with the prince of Wales, which gave the new opposition a ready-made *point d'appui*; and the Hanoverian ministers were not above taking a hand, for their own ends, in the game of English domestic politics. But two years later Stanhope, by first scoring off Bernstorff in the diplomatic field, and then negotiating a reconciliation between king and prince and the return of the disgruntled whigs to the ministry, completely spiked the Hanoverian guns and made himself master in his own house. The whig reunion also destroyed any immediate prospect of a tory return to power, even as a wing of a coalition; henceforth the whig ascendancy was unchallenged, surviving numerous later 'splits' for another forty years. Stanhope himself died in the moment of triumph; but the cabinet had come to life again.[1] In 1721 Robert Walpole, who had returned to the ministry in a minor capacity, was again made first lord of the treasury as the only man capable of rescuing the country from the disastrous effects of the bursting of the South Sea Bubble. He held the post for twenty years, and in that time he left a lasting mark on the character and leadership of the cabinet.

The cabinet had never ceased to have a formal existence, and for the first few years the king normally presided there in person. His first absence in Hanover, during the second half of 1716, made new arrangements necessary. He took Stanhope and Bernstorff with him, leaving the prince of Wales as 'Guardian of the Realm', but with powers so restricted that in practice everything of moment had to be referred to Hanover—a source of great weakness and friction in British policy during each of the occasions when this situation was repeated. The cabinet continued to meet, with the prince presiding, but its deliberations were confined to relatively minor domestic affairs and formal ratifications: major decisions were made in Hanover by the king and his 'inner' cabinet. This remained henceforth the general pattern of government whether the king was at home or abroad, but with one important difference: the prince drops out of the picture. George I was far too jealous of his son, who was slightly more fluent in English and slightly more at ease in English society, to place him where he might steal some of the not too effective paternal thunder; yet he

[1]Michael, ii. 302–8; Williams, *Stanhope*, pp. 370–2, 419–24.

himself found cabinet meetings irksome because he understood
so little of what was going on and set no great store by it anyway. So the cabinet continued its regular and formal meetings
under the chairmanship of a minister deputed by the king and
reporting to him in writing; while foreign affairs, the branch
of policy that really interested him, could be discussed in con-
scientious French with the small group of ministers directly
concerned. This system had the advantage that it needed little
modification when the king went off on his periodic trips to
Hanover. For the rest of George I's reign the cabinet served
during these absences as a regency council with the curious
title (a legacy of William III's reign) 'the lords justices of
England'; but one at least of the secretaries went with him
(sometimes both, since each was jealous that the other might
steal a march on him), so that the informal but all-important
ministerial colloquies could be carried on in Hanover. Under
George II his very competent queen, so long as she was alive,
acted as regent when he was abroad, but after her death the
cabinet was once more used as a regency council on these
occasions.

Walpole made no formal changes in what had now become
the accepted practice. Cabinet meetings continued to be
formal and to include purely 'honorific' elements not directly
concerned with policy; so he too preferred more limited and
informal ministerial consultations. Yet just because he was so
long at the helm, trusted by the king to give a common direction
to the team of colleagues chosen for him (though increasingly
on his advice), and to pilot their agreed policy through parliament, the initiative was gradually passing from crown to
minister.[1] During the concluding years of his ministry the onset
of war had its usual effect of tightening up administration, and
so giving a more definite and settled form to the 'inner' cabinet.
Consisting as a rule of five members (with others called in for
occasional consultation), it met more frequently—usually in
Walpole's own house—and reported its findings formally
to the king, especially during his absences in Hanover. It was
these absences that had first given legal standing to the full

---

[1] On the matter of this and the preceding paragraph see Michael, op. cit., i. 106–7,
ii. 24; B. Williams, *Whig Supremacy*, pp. 37–41; Turner in *E.H.R.*, xxix. 456–9,
465–76.

cabinet when it served as a regency council, so that when a dozen years after Walpole's fall doubts were expressed in a lords' debate whether the collective acts of the cabinet, as distinct from what ministers did in their individual capacities, were valid in law, a full and effective answer could be given. And it was the same conditions that were now finding for that airy nothing the inner cabinet a local habitation and even a name. For the latter the classical taste of the age suggested *conciliabulum*, or little council, which Newcastle thought a 'silly term' and George III could not spell; yet it served for as long as the institution itself remained distinct.[1] The situation about 1740 has been well summed up in the words:

> The cabinet, unknown to law under its own name, was legalized. The inner cabinet, not only unknown to law but unrecognized by the constitution, was regularized.[2]

The very existence of a 'double' cabinet was for long, however, a brake on the development of responsible government, as Burke was to proclaim at a later date (though with no very clear idea of remedy or disease); for on the one hand the crown could with complete constitutional propriety use the outer body, which included members with no direct concern in policy, as a check on the working inner cabinet when it happened to be at odds with it, while on the other hand cabinet ministers could and did evade responsibility by declaring in parliament when cabinet policy was under fire (as did the duke of Argyll in 1740) that the decision in question had been taken at an inner conclave to which they were not admitted.[3] It was not till the time of the younger Pitt, as will appear later, that these confusions were cleared up and the 'honorific' members ceased to attend or to be called to cabinet meetings, leaving only—as had been urged as far back as William III's day— those with 'a right to enter there by their employments';[4] in other words the 'outer' cabinet melted back into the privy

---

[1]Turner, *Cabinet Council*, ii. 314–5.
[2]R. R. Sedgwick in *E.H.R.*, xxxiv. 301, and 290–302, *passim*; Temperley in id., xxvii. 691; Turner in *A.H.R.*, xix. 27–43, and *Cabinet Council*, ii, *passim*.
[3]Turner, *Cab. Council*, i. 392–4, ii. 309; Anson in *E.H.R.*, xxix. 75–7, and in *Law and Custom of the Constitution*, II, ch. iii (3).
[4]Anson, *Law and Custom*, 2nd ed., ii. 111.

council, leaving the inner core as the body which could be held collectively responsible for policy.

This collective responsibility still lay far ahead, but collective consciousness arose directly out of the royal attachment to Hanover—much as Cœur de Lion's attachment to the Holy Land, more than 500 years earlier, had given his barons the taste of collective action that prepared them for extorting Magna Carta from his successor. For while the king was away, and especially while George II was campaigning in Germany, real control tended more and more to centre in the group of ministers in London. Almost to the end of his reign George II occasionally presided at cabinet meetings when he was at home, but the practice was coming to be regarded as unusual, and what made it so was not primarily the language difficulty—a very much smaller problem for George II than it had been for his father—but rather the discovery that ministers were no longer at sea (as Pepys had found privy council committees in Charles II's day) when the king was not there to take charge. A century earlier the commons had learned to manage their debates without a lead from 'those about the Chair'; now the king's counsellors in their turn were learning in his absence to run the country as a self-acting team, even in time of war. Stuart parliaments and Hanoverian cabinets both bungled the job at first; both learned through a collective experience which became itself a bond of union.[1]

Yet this cohesion could never have come about had there not been a dominant will to consolidate the cabinet, and to answer for it to the king on the one hand and to parliament on the other. This was the achievement of Sir Robert Walpole. Apart from the length of his sway, and the ascendancy in parliament and in the royal closet which it both betokened and fostered, there is no reason why he should so long have gone down in history as our first prime minister—a title he repudiated as firmly as Clarendon had done two generations earlier, and which was first fastened on him by the malice of his enemies. Still less ground is there for dating his reign as prime minister from 1730, when he became really supreme in the cabinet, as is done in the Royal Historical Society's *Handbook of British Chronology*. For if the criterion of a prime minister is that he

[1]Turner, op. cit., ii. 96–8; Temperley in *E.H.R.* xxvii. 693; *supra*, p. 49.

should be unquestioned master in the cabinet, then very few of Walpole's successors for the next half-century would pass the test, and the end of his own tenure of power should be dated 1739, when his mastery was at an end. Indeed very few of the criteria of cabinet or premier as we know them today would be applicable at all to Walpolean practice. He did not choose his colleagues, though his suggestions went far with the crown (as, for that matter, Harley's had with Queen Anne); they did not all necessarily speak with the same voice in the house—least of all before 1730; it was they who pushed the first lord (very much against his better judgement) into war with Spain in 1739, yet he still clung on to power; and when the next general election showed that the country had turned against him, it was not this 'swing of the pendulum', nor yet defeat on a major issue in the house, but just a snap vote, that forced at last his resignation; even then, his colleagues did not all go out with him, but they were content with a re-shuffle after the fashion of modern French cabinets.[1]

And yet, as so often happens, popular tradition has the root of the matter in it, for the age of Walpole did mark a decisive stage in the growth of cabinet government and of the office of prime minister. His power was based ultimately on the fact that no one else—least of all the king in whose name it was carried on—could hold the administration together and steer its policy through parliament. No one achieved anything like his dominance for many years to come; but what he had shown was that unless the king could do the job for himself then one of his ministers, under whatever name and in whatever office, must take the lead in the cabinet. And the obvious man for the job, if he was capable, was the head of the treasury. 'Great men', wrote Edward Wortley Montagu (a junior treasury commissioner himself before Walpole's rise to power) 'have generally been of the Treasury, and when a Commissioner of the Treasury has equal favour with any of the other Ministers, he will be First Minister.'[2] But there were still many exceptions.

[1] Trevor Williams in *History*, xxii, 245; the whole 'revision' (pp. 240–52) is still the best summary of evidence on the growth of the cabinet, with a valuable bibliography of the principal books and articles, which have not been substantially increased since it was written eighteen years ago. See also Basil Williams, *Whig Supremacy*, ch. vii.
[2] Quoted Michael, i. 163.

The only man of weight in the ministry that succeeded Walpole's was Carteret, and he resumed the office of secretary of state he had once held under Walpole, because it would give him control of foreign policy—his only political interest—the treasury going to a political nonentity. There followed the safe but timid Pelham ministry, in which Newcastle stuck to the secretaryship he had held since Walpole's day, leaving the treasury and the leadership of the commons to his more capable brother Henry Pelham so long as he lived, and then himself trying his hand (somewhat disastrously) as first lord and nominal head of the ministry.

The elder Pitt, who succeeded him as chief minister, took the southern secretaryship, leaving the treasury to the great whig magnate the duke of Devonshire; but with all his gifts of statesmanship he could not get on without Newcastle's patronage machine, so the great political boss was brought back to the treasury while Pitt retained the real direction of the ministry and the war. So too, in the next reign, with the coalition ministry Pitt formed just after the Stamp Act had brought trouble to a head in America: here the treasury, so far from being the key post, was turned down by Pitt's brother-in-law Lord Temple on the ground that it would leave him 'a great cipher at the head of Treasury, surrounded by other ciphers, all named by Mr. Pitt'. For himself Pitt at first proposed a new secretaryship for American affairs, so that the head of the ministry should be at the storm centre of politics. It would have been an interesting development constitutionally, and in view of his immense popularity across the Atlantic it might at an earlier stage (before he lost grip) have been decisive politically. But when an American secretaryship was in fact established two years later it went to a junior minister; and in his own ministry Pitt eventually took the sinecure office of lord privy seal and (in an ill-advised moment) a peerage. His throwing of the reins, in face of broken health and hampering honours, to an ill-assorted and mettlesome team, proved the tragic anti-climax of a great career. But Chatham can no more be fitted into any orderly scheme of constitutional development than Cromwell, whom in some ways he resembles. He was far too great an individualist to set much store by the 'collectivity' of his cabinets, and his own leadership in them depended, not on any constitutional convention, but on sheer dæmonic force of personality.[1]

In assigning primacy to the treasury in the passage quoted above, Wortley Montagu makes the important reservation of 'equal favour'—favour, that is, of the crown, which was just as necessary in Walpole's day as in Harley's. In fact it was generally assumed that when the prince of Wales became George II, Walpole would have to give place to the disgruntled whigs out of office who had frequented the prince's levées. That this did not happen was due to the sound sense and political acumen of Queen Caroline. Yet the character of royal 'favour' had changed radically in the course of a century. It was not for such qualities as had given Buckingham his 'monopoly of power' under Charles I that the two Georges kept Walpole in office; it was rather because he was 'the most consummate manager of the House of Commons that has ever been'. And it was not because the crown no longer wanted him that he fell from power—on the contrary, George II insisted (most unconstitutionally by later standards) on consulting him out of office, as Queen Anne had done with Harley;[2] it was because the commons had turned against him. That ascendancy over the house of commons was what made Walpole's ministry unique. Because the sources of his strength lay there, his successors gradually came to realize that if the ministry was led by a peer, then his cabinet must contain a commoner of sufficient standing both in the house and among his colleagues to enable him to expound and defend government policy there, as 'those about the Chair' had done in the days of Elizabeth. Newcastle, with his unbounded faith in his own system, was slow to learn that it was no longer possible to manage the house of commons by what Professor Pares calls 'remote control'; it was Pitt and Henry Fox who, after a running fight with Newcastle and then Bute, at last won recognition for the position of leader of the house, or 'His Majesty's Minister in the House of Commons'.[3]

[1]B. Williams, *Chatham*, ii. 208–9, 124n.; E. R. Ritcheson in *A.H.R.*, lvii. 376–83; W. S. Taylor and J. H. Pringle, *Chatham Correspondence*, 1839–40, ii. 468–9; Namier, *Age of Amer. Rev.*, p. 181 and n.; R. Pares, *Geo. III and the Politicians*, 1953, pp. 166n., 177.
[2]B. Williams, *Stanhope*, p. 253, *Whig Supremacy*, p. 17.
[3]Pares, op. cit., pp. 42–8; Namier, *Age of Amer. Rev.*, p. 415.

Inevitably the growing power of the cabinet and the first minister meant that to that extent the stock of the monarchy was declining. The cabinet dutifully submits its conclusions to the crown, but the crown grows more and more out of touch with the processes of discussion by which the conclusions are arrived at. Signs of decline are already perceptible during the last two decades of George II's reign, when his queen's death and Walpole's retirement left him dependent on his own very limited resources of mind, will and character to meet the demands of an age when politics were passing once more out of the static phase. Carteret (whom Newcastle had bullied the king into dismissing) summed him up by saying that he had 'not sufficient courage or activity or sufficient knowledge of the country or perhaps of mankind'. The result is seen in his feeble protest that in choosing who were to serve him, 'so far from an option he was not even allowed a negative'. Walpole, it has been maintained, had always 'acted on the Commons in the interests of the court, whereas Henry Pelham acted rather upon the court in the interests of an aggregation of groups in the Commons'.[1] The process of encroachment on the political initiative of the crown bears some analogy to the development of collective bargaining in the later world of trade unionism. The first stage, corresponding to that in which it ceases to be a penal offence for an individual workman to 'withdraw his labour' if he is dissatisfied with the term of service, had already been reached when it was no longer held reprehensible for an individual minister to resign on a point of policy. The collective resignation of a ministry, of which the first clear example comes in 1746, is the counterpart of a collective withdrawal of labour; but long before it was put into action it had existed as an unspoken threat, the more effective as it became less possible for the king to find alternative ministries strong enough to put essential measures through the house—much as the mere legalizing of trade unions advanced the principle of collective bargaining even when it was still impossible to strike without getting on the wrong side of the law.

In both fields of human co-operation collective strength is equally liable to be abused: vexatious and irresponsible strikes in furtherance of no rational or accepted scheme of industrial

[1]Pares, op. cit., pp. 97, 176; Winstanley, *Personal and Party Government*, 1910, p. 9.

policy have their political analogue in petty acts of coercion—
whether to force in a minister uncongenial to the crown or to
force out a congenial one unacceptable to his colleagues—such
as George II had to put up with at the hands of Newcastle,
and George III so firmly refused to tolerate until at last the
sons of Zeruiah proved too hard for him. Often enough this
coercion was irresponsibly exercised, not to enforce a policy,
but simply in the interests of an exclusive family clique determined to stick together. Yet in this mere team spirit, even
without any party principle to give it content or party organization to give it coherence and continuity, lay the germ of a
cabinet collectively responsible for a common policy, and
resigning collectively when the policy is held up by either royal
or parliamentary obstruction.[1]

Opposition to government measures remains almost entirely
negative and factious, and consistent or 'formed' opposition is
therefore generally reprobated—with some reason—as disloyal and obstructive. To make itself respectable it has to
look for patronage in the royal household, nor does it look in
vain. For George II found himself hoist with his own petard
when his son Frederick—father of the future George III—
turned his house into another cave of Adullam for whigs in
revolt from Walpole and tories bent on a return to power.
Until after the minister's downfall it was Bolingbroke who
remained the brains of the movement, though for the best part
of eight years he exercised the remotest of remote control from
his snug retreat in Touraine. Twice over the opposition seemed
on the brink of triumph—first when the country revolted
against Walpole's excise scheme of 1733 and its author saved
himself only by ignominious retreat, and then again in 1741,
when the mismanagement of a war he had never believed in
laid him open to damaging attack; but each time opposition
was flattened out by the combined effects of the bulldozer of
Influence and the weighty prejudice (soon to be reinforced by
the second Jacobite revolt) that opposition is next-door-
neighbour to treason. The general election that followed, held
in an atmosphere of war fever and bread riots following a
wretched harvest, narrowed Walpole's majority below the
safety level, and brought about his resignation soon after the

[1]Turner, loc. cit., pp. 277-9; *E.H.R.*, xxvii. 699; Pares, op. cit., pp. 61-4, 95-6.

new parliament met in 1742; but perhaps even this electoral victory owed less to pressure of public opinion than to the fact that the touchy Newcastle, feeling himself neglected by his chief, was then sulking in his tent.[1]

The 'arch-corrupter' had gone, but the system remained. Attempts to purify the electoral system and to repeal the Septennial Act broke down. A motion for inquiry into the fallen minister's conduct of affairs for the past twenty years (as a condition of supplies) was lost by two votes; a pensions bill which passed the commons was rejected by the lords. All that was achieved by the new parliament was a minor act excluding from the commons—among other officials—deputies and clerks in a number of government departments, but allowing each principal secretary one under-secretary eligible for election. This still left the main body of civil servants open to the manipulation of political bosses; even in the last quarter of the century some 500 places of profit under the crown could still be held with a seat in the commons. Its importance lay in the implicit distinction (which became an accepted convention in the next century) between the parliamentary under-secretary, a politician changing with changing governments, and the permanent under-secretary, a civil servant outside politics.[2]

With so thin a crop of wool to show for so loud a cry, it is not surprising that agitation against the 'system' should continue. Parliament had hardly got down to work before members were pursued by 'instructions' from their constituents. Following the example of London and Westminster, as many as a score of large and small boroughs and well over a dozen counties adopted this novel practice; and the rejection of the chief proposals for reform only intensified the bombardment, which continued right through 1742. There is a strong family resemblance about most of the 'instructions', suggestive of a common inspiration: attacks on standing armies (combined with demands for the vigorous prosecution of the war), on parties, placemen, bribery, 'management' of elections, the Septennial Act, the excise (sometimes even the land tax), the neglect of trade—above all on Walpole himself—these were the usual

[1]Pares, op. cit., p. 50; Oliver, op. cit., i. 336–7.
[2]Cobbett's *Parl. Hist.*, 1812, xii. 428–532; Grant Robertson, *Statutes and Documents*, pp. 125–6; *E.H.R.*, xlix. 310–11, lxii. 498.

stock-in-trade. Sometimes a few local grievances are added; the most violent advices (such as the impeachment of ministers or the refusal of supplies) usually came from borough constituencies.[1] Members, when they replied at all, were at pains to remind their constituents politely of their own independence;[2] and correspondents of the *Gentleman's Magazine* shook their heads over this unprecedented interference with members' liberty of action (except one who—significantly enough—found his precedents in the seventeenth century). It was also pointed out that the body issuing the instructions had no constitutional standing:

> In one Place 'tis a solemn Act under a Public Seal, in another a common Letter written after Dinner. Here, a regular Assembly is summoned for that Purpose, and there it suffices if a few People meet at a Tavern;

and the charge is substantiated by the occasional repudiation of 'instructions' from one set of electors by a second lot meeting independently.[3]

Nothing came of it all. Bolingbroke, except for flying visits in 1742 and the next year, remained in France; Wyndham, who would have made the tories a far saner and steadier leader, was dead; and no one else could give coherence and a constructive policy to the discordant and impracticable groups of tory politicians and discontented country gentry. When in 1744 Bolingbroke—back for good at last—opened negotiations with Pelham for an all-party administration to include tories as well as malcontent whigs, on the basis of measures for effectively reducing Influence by the disfranchisement of revenue officers and the eradication of party from local government, it was in the end only the whig wing of the coalition that benefited, and nothing more was said about the elimination of Influence. As a last attempt to bring to bear on the government the tory influences still so strong in the shires, a 'plan for the counties' was drawn up under which a 'great council' of fifteen (eleven from the shires and four from cities and boroughs) was to make effective the real voice of the country by keeping

[1]*Gent. Mag.*, pp. 29, 96–7, 159–61, 216–7, 274, 486–7.
[2]Ibid., p. 596, cf. Pares, op. cit., p. 51n.
[3]Ibid., pp. 583, 594–5, 648, 650; see also Cobbett, *Parl. Hist.*, xii. (1741–3), 416–27.

in touch with local clubs of 'independent electors' on the one
hand and M.P.s on the other. The original mode of appointment was left comfortably vague, except for a romantic
suggestion that the ancient heptarchy should provide the basis
of representation; but it was to be kept going by co-optation.
Next year the second Jacobite revolt still further discredited
the name of tory, and left the triumphant whigs and the Newcastle system more firmly entrenched than ever.[1]

For all his superficial brilliance, Bolingbroke was too bankrupt of character and principle to lead a movement of regenera-
tion in politics; he was never able to live down his own past. It
is even possible that by overshadowing the less showy gifts of
Wyndham he stood in the way of the recuperation and enrichment of public life by the return to it of the Hanoverian tories.
His slogan of a patriot king banishing party from politics and
corruption from patronage, whatever momentary appeal it
might have for politically 'displaced persons' who from time to
time resorted to his camp, savoured too much of sour grapes,
and ignored too blandly the teaching of experience that the
only alternatives to government by patronage or party are
deadlock or dictatorship. Disraeli's claim for him as one of the
'three greatest of English statesmen' must be dismissed as a
mere *jeu d'esprit*—part of his appeal from the new to the old
tories—for in his lifetime Bolingbroke was never more than a
stormy petrel of politics. His importance lies in the use made of
his ideas after his day. Both the elder Pitt and George III took
a leaf out of his book, and the explosive issues they imported
into politics provoked a new appeal to political first principles.[2]
It was as one of the anti-Walpole group of whigs that Pitt the
elder entered the orbit of Bolingbroke and absorbed some of his
notions. His opposition cost him his army commission and
delayed his political advancement, for his views on foreign
policy were no less offensive to Carteret and the king than his
earlier diatribes against the ministry had been to Walpole. He
was not even brought in with his fellow-dissidents to the 'broad
bottom' administration of 1744, and when at last Newcastle
tried to appease him with minor office he was equally critical

---

[1] R. W. Greaves, in *E.H.R.*, xlviii. 630–8; Feiling, ch. iv.
[2] Oliver, *The Endless Adventure*, i. 265, 283–9, 323–30, 342–64; H. N. Fieldhouse in
History, xxiii. 41–56; Disraeli, *Sybil*, ch. iii.

of the great political 'boss' as a war minister. But his impatience with jobbery, his personal incorruptibility in office, and his burning and disinterested patriotism gave him a hold on popular imagination that no previous statesman of the century had enjoyed, and made his leadership inescapable.

There was no doubt something of the charlatan in Chatham as well as in Bolingbroke, though in the one it arose from cynicism and in the other from a *penchant* for self-dramatization. It is also true too that neither was anything like a clear-headed or consistent political thinker, though Bolingbroke had the skill to give his clap-trap the air of a dispassionate philosophy and Chatham's confusions and sophistries were charmed away by the magic of his oratory. What mattered, however, was that between them they put into currency a set of dynamic ideas destined after their time to give some reality to the party politics they both repudiated. The Patriot King element in Bolingbroke's political thought—the idea of a king, independent of party, crusading against corruption and choosing his ministers for merit only—had a special appeal for one like Pitt whose connexion with the great whig families of the Revolution was of the slenderest, and it continued to attract him long after his irresponsible salad days as a 'boy patriot' in opposition; but he never held to it consistently. His scorn for whig family 'connections' did not extend to the head of the great patrician clan to which he was allied by marriage, the unpopular and dictatorial Lord Temple, who with no other qualification for politics than that (in his own words) he 'loved fraction and had a great deal of money to spare', became the nigger in the woodpile every time his brother-in-law's stubborn family pride insisted on dragging him in as a ministerial colleague. That Pitt also found himself compelled to compromise with Newcastle was no more than a reluctant recognition that until the system was smashed he must abide by the rules of the game. The side of Bolingbroke's propaganda to which he clung longest and with most conviction was the conception of the crown as the people's champion against a corrupt and unrepresentative oligarchy. Hatred of corruption made him also a critic of the rotten boroughs and to that extent a mild parliamentary reformer. The Great Commoner had of course as great an ascendancy over the commons as Walpole, and until his own fatal acceptance of a peerage he had to use his difficult brother-in-law as mouthpiece in the lords; but he was always acutely aware of and sensitive to a wider public opinion beyond. It was this that made him a champion of civil rights, a free press and the reporting of parliamentary debates, and impelled him (like Canning after him) to give his foreign policy a popular and patriotic appeal, in contrast with the chilly and aloof 'Hanoverianism' of Stanhope or Carteret.[1]

Events of the next reign were to undermine his faith in a patriot king and to modify his views on party. While still eschewing organized opposition, reiterating his wish 'if it were possible . . . to abolish all distinction' [of party] and insisting that 'no single man's private friendships or connections . . . are sufficient of themselves either to form or to overturn an administration', he no longer applied this rule to 'that honourable connection which arises from a disinterested concurrence in opinion upon public measures'. He went so far as to maintain that

> there are some distinctions which are inherent in the nature of things. There is a distinction between right and wrong—between Whig and Tory;

and he now even justified a certain natural leadership in the great whig families of the Revolution on whom the new king was turning his back, like some French or Spanish Bourbon of the Restoration cold-shouldering a Napoleonic veteran. But all this made it no easier in practice for him to co-operate with whig groups guilty (by his standards) of having betrayed their country's liberties in the Wilkes case or her honour by a craven peace with France. His own principles—a throw-back to the age when whiggery had been a creed and not just a system—proved too unaccommodating for any joint 'platform'; party was to him, in fact, a set of principles held with the uncompromising fervour of a Hebrew prophet, rather than a set of men ready to compromise for the achievement of an immediate practical programme.

For this if for no other reason, Chatham could never have made a good party premier. What he did for domestic politics (as distinct from his achievements overseas) was to bring back

[1] Basil Williams, *Chatham*, ii. 272, 292.

the fire of conviction by a return to the bellicose anti-French traditions of the Restoration and Revolution whigs, and to their championship of civil and religious liberty—above all by his personal integrity and his ruthless disregard (like some Beaverbrook before his time) of all obstructions, human or institutional, in the way of the national war effort. In these ways he laid the foundations for the new and more genuine two-party system that came to life after the French Revolution. His name became a legend not only among tory country gentry, whose hearts warmed to his militia schemes and his trouncing of the acquisitive whig magnates for their muzzling of critics, but equally among shopkeepers and city merchants bred in puritan and Cromwellian traditions of overseas trade and settlement, of zeal for reform and for administrative efficiency.[1] Herein lay his ultimate services to responsible government.

At the end of George II's reign the initiative in politics was still with the crown, but there were signs of decline. The growing self-confidence and corporate sense of the cabinet—in particular of the inner cabinet, the real mainspring of policy— was gradually fitting it to take over control; and although it was still a body chosen by the king, in fact as well as in name, with only the limitation that it must have a leader with sufficient control over the commons to ensure the necessary supplies and legislation, in practice he was becoming subject to increasing pressure from political groups in his choice of ministers. This loss of power was not so much inherent in the change of dynasty as due to the incompetence or lack of interest of the kings themselves: much of it had taken place as recently as the last dozen years of George II's reign, since Newcastle became such a power in politics, and might therefore be as easily undone by a king of greater acumen and application.

And there was every sign that such an attempt would have popular backing, for the power to which the Hanoverians had had to yield was a narrow and exclusive clique—a 'Venetian oligarchy', as Disraeli was later to call it. The oligarchs had rendered great service to the country in promoting tranquillity

[1]Taylor and Pringle, op. cit., iv. 17–18n, ; Lecky, op. cit., iii. 358–62; Pares, op. cit., pp. 54–7; Winstanley, *Lord Chatham and the Whig Opposition*, 1912, p. 346; G. H. Gutteridge in *Univ. of California Publications in History*, xliv, 1952, pp. 35–6; Namier, *Age of Amer. Rev.*, pp. 134, 165.

and stability, security and prosperity, after the long period of political uncertainty and upheaval; but they had done it at a heavy cost, of which the country was now increasingly aware. Tranquillity meant winking at abuses lest attempts at reform should arouse slumbering passions; stability meant the avoidance of government defeats in parliament or at the polls by the elaborate and almost watertight Newcastle system of corruption; security meant the maintenance of the dynasty, at home by giving a permanent lease of power to the faction that had brought it in, abroad by diplomatic manœuvres which had given us the name in Europe of 'perfidious Albion'; prosperity meant the avoidance of public expenditure on schemes of domestic development or imperial expansion so as to let the money 'fructify in the pockets of the people'—that is, the people whose political support was important. Reaction against this now discredited *régime* of corruption and 'safety first' was what made Pitt a national hero and his name a myth in Europe and America as well as at home. Thus there were already present the elements that were to put an end to the age of tranquillity and to restore to politics a sense of reality, urgency and responsibility.[1]

[1]Feiling, ch. v.

VIII

The Patriot King in Action
1760–83

———————

G EORGE III had not attained his majority much more than a year when he ascended the throne. His father, the prince of Wales, had died when he was thirteen, leaving him heir not only to the throne of England but to the Hanoverian dynastic tradition of hostility to the reigning monarch. Brought up in this atmosphere, he imbibed a hatred of his grandfather, George II, that was little short of pathological, and a hero-worship of his mother's favourite and his own tutor, the earl of Bute, that has been rightly called 'maudlin'.[1] So his great aim was to rescue the monarchy from the family cliques to which he believed his grandfather to have sold out, and to restore to it something of the dignity and independence embodied in that idea of a Patriot King which had long been an accepted slogan of the prince's disgruntled crew at Leicester House; and the heaven-sent instrument for the purpose was his 'dearest friend' Bute, a Scotsman and a courtier so completely aloof from the ruling set that for the past twenty years he had not even been chosen as one of the representative Scottish peers for a seat in the lords.

The time has long passed when historians could speak of George III as if he were another Charles I; to him as to every other responsible politician of his age the Revolution of 1688

[1]Pares, op. cit., p. 101.

remained the polestar of English polity. Yet there are some
suggestive points of similarity in character and circumstance
between the two kings, and a brief consideration of these may
help to put the crises of the reign in perspective. Both came to
the throne without any proper apprenticeship to the work of
government—Charles because as younger son he was not
destined for it, George through the incurable jealousy of
Hanoverian kings for their heirs and successors. By the same
token neither had come much into public notice, but what
little was known about each stood in his favour; for each had his
full share of the domestic virtues, and found a substitute for the
dissipation of courts in cultivating, the one his artistic sensibilities, the other a boundless curiosity that made him a great
book collector and an assiduous patron of astronomy and
exploration.[1] Each enjoyed the initial advantage of being
popularly identified with reaction from an unpopular policy—
appeasement, in the one case, the Newcastle system in the other;
but with the important difference that Buckingham's early
popularity as champion of an 'active' foreign policy shed some
reflected glory on his royal patron and intimate, whereas Pitt,
who held the same position (with better reason) at the beginning of George's reign, was to the king simply 'that mad
Pitt' who must be got rid of as soon as it could safely be done.[2]
The deep-rooted national distrust of 'alien' kings also stood
to the advantage of both; for Charles had left Scotland when
he was three, and George, the first of the Hanoverians to be
born here, was a known enemy to the 'Hanoverian' foreign
policy of his predecessors. But when he announced that he
'gloried in the name of Britain' the patriotic appeal was marred
by a suspicion that 'Britain' had been substituted for 'England'
out of deference to Bute; for even after half a century of
legislative union a Scots 'favourite' was still looked on with no
friendlier an eye than the 'famished cattle' who had followed
James I to his new kingdom from his old.

   Charles's devotion to Buckingham had its counterpart in
that of the equally inexperienced and self-distrustful George to
his 'dearest friend'; and when once the prop was removed
(by assassination in the one case, more gradually in the other

[1]Pares, p. 66, cf. Fortescue, *British Statesmen of the Great War*, 1911, pp. 18–19.
[2]Pares, p. 102n.

as the king outgrew him and found his own feet), neither ever gave his complete confidence to another. Yet the underlying lack of self-reliance revealed itself in both in fits of unreasoning stubbornness on the one hand and a love of intrigue on the other; and neither was prepared to impute any but dishonourable motives to those who opposed him: hence, for example, the violent oscillations of sentiment expressed in George III's letters to or about the Pitts and even North, reflecting the degree of concurrence in his plans. But while Charles's intrigues were always feeble and blundering, landing him as a rule in worse tangles than those he tried to shuffle off, George learned to be an extremely shrewd political tactician—partly at least because, unlike Charles, he also learned to shake off his natural indolence and to master detail. Above all he shared, as his predecessor had never done, the prejudices of the great mass of his subjects; in other words, he understood—or at least grew to understand—the country over which he ruled, and often to understand it better than the politicians who claimed to represent it and resented his 'intrusions'.

The ministry he found in power was the one led by Newcastle (at the head of the treasury) as party manager and Pitt (southern secretary) as organizer of victory. For a war ministry, it was a singularly ill-matched team, for while Pitt kept looking for more worlds to conquer, his jealous and timid colleague longed only for a return to the more tractable and less exacting sort of political world where he knew his way about. For these leaders, George was bent on substituting Bute, who depended on and was devoted to himself alone; but he was prepared to bide his time. Bute's existing office in the royal household introduced him into the outer cabinet, and after five months he was brought into the *conciliabulum* itself as the somewhat reluctant successor to Pitt's undistinguished colleague the northern secretary. All this was done with the full concurrence of Newcastle as nominal head of the ministry, but without consulting Pitt. But Newcastle himself saw his precious patronage slip away as more and more appointments were taken over by the crown direct, and a tighter control kept on the secret service funds; and he was not without grounds for believing that he was being played off against Pitt and Pitt against him. Yet he had been in power too long to be ready to relinquish it without a struggle. He was blissfully unaware that the king had already confided to Bute his intention to replace the duke by 'a man devoid of his dirty arts who will think of mine and his country's good, not of jobs'—in plain words, of course, Bute himself. Twelve months after the reign began, Pitt found himself outvoted in the cabinet in his own field of foreign policy, and resigned; but it was Bute, not Newcastle, who stood to gain. By the summer of 1763 the whig 'boss' had at last come to realize that his position was untenable, and he relinquished the treasury to Bute, who now became head of the ministry in name as well as in fact, with a clean sweep throughout the country of the officials appointed by Newcastle, and even some steps towards a political purge of the army.[1]

In order to vindicate beyond cavil the sovereign's complete freedom of choice in selecting his servants, the king had chosen as his instrument a man so far outside the ranks of the politicians that he was not even a member of either house, and so far from enjoying the compensation (for what it was worth) of extra-parliamentary support that he was hated throughout England as an intrusive Scot. It was a real *tour de force* to have placed at the head of the ministry, within three years of his accession, one who manifestly owed his position neither to the support of the whig cliques nor to a popularity like that of Pitt, but solely to the royal favour, and to have maintained him there long enough to wind up a glorious war, on terms denounced by the idolized architect of victory. But a mere display of power was by no means all the young king wanted. Six months after Bute took over the treasury, when he was already beginning to find he had bitten off more than he could chew, his royal pupil spurred him on with talk of a great crusade:

I own I had flattered myself when peace was once established that my D. Friend would have assisted me in purging out corruption, and in those measures that no man but he that hath the Prince's real affection can go through; then when we were both dead our memories would have been respected and esteemed to the end of time.[2]

[1]Winstanley in *E.H.R.*, xvii. 678–91; Namier, *Age of Amer. Rev.*, pp. 468–83; Dobrée (ed.) *Letters of King George III*, pp. 21, 23–4, 26.
[2]Quoted Pares, p. 104n., Dobrée, op. cit. p. 24.

It was a generous dream, but a very naïve one, such as could have appealed only to two people very inexperienced in English politics. Bute was the first to come to earth; it was he who had to run the gauntlet of the politicians, and it boded ill for the proposed crusade that in order to 'manage' the commons during the debates on the conclusion of peace he had to bring in as leader of the house the most corrupt and unprincipled politician of the day, Henry Fox. After twelve months of it, Bute threw his hand in and advised the king to find a new first lord among the experienced politicians. So first positions were perforce abandoned. The purification of politics was postponed *sine die*—in fact, when some seventeen years later the whigs were driven by their own experiences to take up the campaign themselves, the chief opposition came from the king and his minions. Once more a comparison with Charles I suggests itself: for he too began with the ideal of a monarchy that stood for national interests, overriding special privileges, sectional advantage, factions and sects, yet found himself driven to fill his coffers by selling offices, ranks and patents to the injury of the common weal. The claim that the monarch is as free in choosing his servants as any private gentleman had also to be abandoned as unworkable. It was perhaps George's only departure from the principles of 1688, implying as it did a return to the rule of favourites and to the most arbitrary practices of Charles; for neither William nor Anne had claimed so complete a *carte blanche* in the choice of their chief advisers or so complete an assimilation of their public office to their private whims. George Grenville aptly called it 'arming his favour against his authority'.[1] The blunder arose from his complete devotion to Bute and his extreme lack of experience of public affairs. Both handicaps were overcome within a few years, and by about 1765 it was George who was teaching his old tutor the limits of constitutional propriety.

What the king came to understand with surprising speed, as he shook off the leading-strings of Bute, was that politics as practised in eighteenth-century England were a game of skill, to be played according to the rules like cricket or the chase or the 'fancy', or any of those other sports to which the English aristocracy and their dependents were becoming so much

[1] Quoted Feiling, op. cit., pp. 240–1; cf. *supra*, pp. 68–9.

addicted. It was no more derogatory to the monarchy to pit its skill at the game against that of subjects than it was for Lord John Sackville to play cricket for Kent under the captaincy of the gardener at Knole; and there were still many tricks and turns of wrist by which monarchy, once it had learnt the technique, could score heavily even against experts at the game without ever departing from the letter of the rules. And although the king warmly repudiated 'men of less principle and honesty than I pretend to' who 'look on public measures and policy as a game', his own unacknowledged relish in the game is always peeping out in his letters.[1]

The rules, as he understood them, included as a matter of course the legislative and financial supremacy of parliament as established in 1688. For example, although he regarded the royal veto on legislation (which had been dormant since Queen Anne's time) as a vital reserve weapon of the royal prerogative, he had the wisdom never to brandish it, preferring to achieve his ends by less open and invidious means.[2] Nor did he ever attempt to raise money outside the authorized parliamentary channels. He even began his reign by surrendering his hereditary revenues to parliament in return for a fixed 'civil list', but he found himself in practice unable to live within this income and he resented no less than his predecessors any parliamentary inquiry into the causes of the deficit—especially as it was often due to the exigencies of secret service abroad, which could not be met from so public a source as parliamentary grants.[3] But he also accepted the conventions of a chief minister and a cabinet which had grown up since the Revolution. The chief minister he acknowledged as 'by rights, the king's chief confidant, whose opinions and convenience, in a parliamentary monarchy, must be studied'; but he never regarded this convention as binding him to confide in no one else, or to accept the minister's opinions and his choice of colleagues as a condition of his service, nor did he ever pledge himself to 'put his personal influence and connexions unreservedly at the disposal of his official servants'. Above all, he clung through every crisis to the principle that 'the executive

[1]Trevelyan, *English Social History*, 1942, p. 408; Dobrée, p. 122.
[2]Dobrée, pp. 103, 183; A. Aspinall in *Proceedings of Brit. Acad.*, xxxviii. 238.
[3]Keir, op. cit., p. 304; Dobrée, p. 85.

power is vested in the Crown, and not to be infringed by the Commons'.[1]

Thus although Bute went out of office in 1763, it was he who arranged the cabinet that was to succeed his, and for perhaps a couple of years he continued to have access to the king's closet much as Harley had advised Queen Anne while out of office. Unfortunately Bute remained a sort of skeleton in the closet long after he had ceased to haunt it in the flesh, and belief in his 'backstairs' influence lingered on to poison politics when in fact the king had found his own feet and needed no such secret props. There was much talk of a group of young office holders attached to Bute whose votes he was supposed to have placed at the king's personal disposal to be used, when it suited him, against measures proposed by the ministry of the day but disliked by the king. Such groups of 'king's friends' and 'queen's friends', as we know, were an old established feature of the political landscape; but there seems no sufficient reason to doubt the king's good faith when he denied having used them to undermine the policy of his own ministers.[2] If each of Bute's successors, until the king found Lord North, had only a year or two of power, the reason must be sought rather in the instability of political groups than in 'backstairs' royal intrigues. Although they were chosen from the necessities of the political game rather than from personal predilections, the king seems to have 'played the game' by them as he understood the rules; Horace Walpole at least declared in 1769 that he 'never interfered with his Ministers', but 'seemed to resign himself entirely to their conduct for the time.'[3] But it took him over twenty years to live down the Bute episode; he had started the reign on the wrong foot.

Another set of rules related to the cabinet. Here too some conventions were deeply enough rooted for the king to accept them as binding; others amounted to no more than claims, too recent to be universally accepted, which he felt free to flout at will. To the latter category belonged the demand that the chief minister should have the sole choice of his own colleagues, and

[1]Pares, pp. 176, 108–9; Dobrée, p. 183.
[2]Pares, pp. 107–8.
[3]*Memoirs*, quoted Namier, *Monarchy and the Party System*, 1952, p. 5; cf. Pares, op. cit., pp. 173–4. On the substance of the foregoing paragraphs see Pares, ch. iv, Guttmacher, *America's Last King*, chs. iv–ix.

George would have none of it; yet he soon came to recognize
that the man who was to captain his team must have a good
deal of latitude in balancing interests and blending qualities
if he was to produce results, even though that meant bringing
in players uncongenial to the crown. In compensation it was
only reasonable that the king should have at least some members
personally devoted to him to keep his end up in the cabinet.
The formal outer or 'nominal' cabinet had by now become, in
Sir Lewis Namier's words,

> a Council of State rather than an Administration; it repre-
> sented the Church, the Law, the Court, the Services, and (at
> the tail-end) the chief departments of State.

It still met (with the king presiding) on formal occasions, such
as the reading of the king's speech at the beginning and end of
a parliamentary session, or to advise on the exercise of the
prerogative of mercy in capital sentences at the Old Bailey;
but as an organ of policy it had now almost abdicated in favour
of the 'efficient cabinet' of working departmental heads, where
the royal presence, though still not quite a thing of the past,
was now confined to rare and critical junctures. Perhaps a more
important distinction, now that the outer cabinet was fading
away, was that between informal meetings of departmental
ministers (not necessarily all of them) to concert measures for
mutual convenience, for which they were individually responsible, and a formal cabinet meeting called to offer formal and
collective advice to the crown on a point submitted to it, and
on which it assumed collective responsibility.[1]

All the more necessary was it, if the king was to keep his hand
on policy at all, that he should have in the cabinet a friendly
informant to keep him in touch with cabinet discussions without waiting for the formal minute incorporating the final
decision. It was precisely the loss of this living contact that had
been the most serious result of the drift of the first two Hanoverians away from cabinet meetings, and the third was determined to make good the loss.[2] For another unwritten rule that
he accepted was that once a formal minute had reached him
on a point of policy referred by him to the cabinet, he was

[1]Pares, pp. 168–9; Namier, *In the Margin of History*, 1939, pp. 105–10.
[2]Aspinall, loc. cit., p. 195 (1793).

bound to act on it or else take the risk of dismissing the ministry and looking for another. His aim therefore—especially when he had felt compelled to call in a prime minister he did not wholly trust—was in the first place, in forming the cabinet, to avoid commitments on points of policy where he differed from his ministers, and then to foster dissension such as might keep at bay the collective memorandum of advice which he could not ignore, or at least mar its effectiveness by written 'dissents' from the majority view. Moreover, until after the succession of crises culminating in 1783 it remained a convention that, while the cabinet might discuss informally any matter it chose, a formal minute to the king should only be on a matter specifically referred to it—much as Elizabeth's commons were expected, on pain of her high displeasure, to stick to the text she set them. George III puts the point clearly in a letter of 1781:

It is quite new for business to be laid before the Cabinet and consequently advice offered to the Crown unasked; the Minister of the Department always used to ask the permission of the King to lay such a point before the Cabinet.[1]

There is little enough in all this to justify Burke's fanciful picture of a sinister secret cabinet of the king's creatures meeting to undermine or to undo the work of his official advisers; yet there did lurk a real danger to parliamentary and responsible government in the fact that most cabinets and all ministries contained members who took pride in being administrators and royal servants rather than politicians. Their very experience and skill as administrators made it difficult, and their freedom from party ties unnecessary, to sacrifice them when a cabinet resigned or was dismissed, so that they often became semi-permanent ministers, attached only to the crown.[2] This stability may have been a gain to efficient government; but while the crown (which was permanent) went on resuming patronage from ministers (who were ephemeral), while ministers themselves became increasingly dependent on skilled and experienced administrators to cope with the growing

---

[1]Aspinall, loc. cit., p. 175n. On the conventions of the eighteenth-century constitution see also Holdsworth in *Iowa Law Review*, xvii. 161–80.
[2]Namier, *Monarchy and the Party System*, pp. 12–16.

complexities of government, and while the bureaucracy remained in politics, the danger kept growing that the country would in fact be run by experts concerned only to 'carry on the king's government', and resembling but too closely the efficient non-party bureaucrats whom Cromwell had attracted to his service. This was perhaps the reality behind Burke's nightmare of an 'interior cabinet'[1]—none the less menacing because it had neither the coherence nor the conscious purpose with which he endowed it; to that extent it gives support to his classic defence of party.

For party was never one of the rules of the game that George III accepted—any more than did Chatham, or the mass of the independent country gentry, or the great civil servants of the age. Refusal to attend a cabinet meeting on the ground of inability to co-operate with others whom the king had summoned was a form of defiance he would not tolerate. Early in the reign so influential a magnate as the duke of Devonshire was for this reason struck off the privy council—a practice abandoned, as we have seen, by Anne. It was a disciplinary weapon that George never relinquished, though later victims (like Fox) gave more solid grounds for exclusion. None of the ministries of George III, so long as he remained in effective control, was framed on party principles—or indeed, with one exception, on any principle at all save that of carrying on the king's government by a working balance between different pressure-groups; the exception was Chatham's ministry, which was a deliberate (and unsuccessful) attempt at an all-party coalition to handle the American crisis. If George had had to abandon his rôle of slayer of the dragon of corruption for the humbler one of taming it in the interests of monarchy—and a monarchy not quite so free from external pressure as he had hoped—he did not yet despair of slaying the dragon of party; and there is no room for doubt that at this stage the bulk of his subjects would have applauded his success, even though—as Burke rightly saw and as even Hume had been dimly aware—it would have postponed indefinitely the dawn of responsible government.[2] He came nearest to success when after the succession of short, unstable ministries that followed the

---

[1]*Present Discontents, Works*, 1837, 1. 136–40.
[2]*Supra*, pp. 68, 106; Hume, *Essays*, I, vi, and II, xiv.

resignation of Bute, he found in 1770 the minister after his own heart in Lord North, who combined the advantages of a skilful debater, popular in the commons and sprung from an old, distinguished and unimpeachably English family—all the qualities Bute had lacked—with Bute's freedom from party ties and his readiness to regard himself as purely and simply the agent and mouthpiece of the king. The result was a ministry that lasted longer than any since Walpole's time, and bade fair to consolidate the rule of the Patriot King.

That in the end, after a dozen years of it, even North had to 'desert' his master and leave him once more a prey to contending factions was due in part to unforeseen weaknesses in his own character and constitution, but more to the pressure of external events. For North proved only too pliable and self-effacing. So completely did he dissociate himself from the Walpolean idea of a prime minister that he would take responsibility only for his own department of the treasury, leaving the other departmental ministers to deal quite independently with the crown and to answer individually to parliament for their departments. This was the so-called 'departmental system' which used to be attributed to the machinations of George III, but which was rather the result of North's constitutional indolence and indecision. He admitted this himself when it was all over:

> In this country some one man or some body of men like a Cabinet should govern the whole and direct every measure. However, the Government of Departments was not brought about by me . . . I found it so, and I am ready to confess that I had not vigour or resolution to put an end to it.[1]

Actually, as we have seen, the king also believed in cabinets, and liked his chief minister to take general responsibility under him for policy, even while insisting that ministers 'should hold of him [the king] and not of one another or of the first [minister]'.[2]

It may well be, however, that the 'collectivity' of cabinets had begun to weaken under Chatham—an unrepentant 'departmentalist'—and his successor Grafton, who was as

[1]Quoted Aspinall, loc. cit. p. 214 (misquoted in Lecky, *Eighteenth Century*, v. 213).
[2]Quoted Pares, p. 117n.

indolent as his own successor North. It is during these years, at any rate, that the king begins to interfere in administrative details and in cabinet management to an extent he had never thought necessary before, and in doing so formed permanent contacts with that group of 'hard-working and intelligent "men of business"' which from Bute's time had been working its way upwards from junior posts in the administration, at once laying the foundations of a modernized civil service and (as M.P.s in daily contact with the ministry) providing the king with what Fox called his 'trained bands'. They were Bute's permanent legacy to politics—non-party men whose contribution lay in the field of administrative reform. The dangers inherent in this situation are obvious, nor did the undermining of responsibility go unperceived at the time; but it was North's indolence, rather than any sinister scheme of the king's, that led George to use agents whose main care was for getting things done, with the intent not so much of going behind his own official advisers in any question of policy as of infusing some energy into a paralytic administration.[1]

What really put the royal experiment in jeopardy was the emergence of national issues which turned politics into something more vital than a game of cricket with its gentlemanly rules, and brought into play again that incipient public opinion which in the heyday of the elder Pitt had at times proved too much even for Newcastle's party bulldozer—till the very country gentry began to doubt whether support for the throne and contempt for faction were really the be-all and end-all of politics. It all began before ever North came into power, while Bute's short-lived successors were still trying to keep their end up. Indeed it was hatred of Bute that produced the first rumblings, although he had retired from office before the storm broke. Nothing else would have made a popular hero out of a bankrupt and profligate demagogue like Wilkes—with little to recommend him beyond reckless courage and a ready wit, an easy charm of manner and a vitriolic pen—but the fact that he pilloried the royal favourite and played down to the popular prejudice against Bute's countrymen by calling

[1]Pares, pp. 174–5, and n.; *D.N.B.*, xvii. 253, xxix. 309, xlix. 46; *E.H.R.*, lxx. 463; Butterfield, *George III, Lord North and the People*, 1949, pp. 149, 164; Feiling, pp. 102–5; L. Sutherland, *The East India Company in Eighteenth Century Politics*, 1952, p. 205 and chs. viii–xiii, *passim*; Guttmacher, p. 132; *supra*, p. 106.

his paper the *North Briton*; it is doubtful whether anything but a scurrilous attack on the favourite would have precipitated his master into the fatal error of treating as a personal attack a libel on the king's speech at the opening of parliament, instead of leaving the responsible ministers (who were only too willing) to burn their fingers over it. Devotion to his 'dearest friend' had blinded him to one of the fundamental rules of the political game, and placed him in the position of Charles I when he took personal responsibility for the misdeeds of Buckingham or Charles II of Danby—and after all even Charles II had declared, in lighter vein, that his deeds were his ministers'!

Once having implicitly renounced the protection of the doctrine that the king can do no wrong, George brought the monarchy back into the open arena of politics, and heavily he paid for it. 'Influence' still saved the government from actual defeat, but only by the skin of its teeth. A stormy and prolonged debate in February 1764, on the measures used against Wilkes (and through him against the liberty of the subject), not only united for once all sections of the whig opposition—including even Pitt, with his strong bias against a 'formed opposition'— but ended in a division in which the usual three-figure majority of the government was reduced to a bare fourteen. What is even more significant is that the minority included a substantial number of independent country gentlemen as well as dis-gruntled politicians; in fact the great bulk of those representing the older tory tradition voted against the government (and therefore against the crown)—not, of course, from any love of Wilkes, but because, as one of them put it, they thought it

a strange infatuation that for the sake of punishing one impu-dent worthless fellow, persons that have a grain of under-standing or honesty left, should be desirous of throwing down all the fences of their liberties which the wisdom and courage of their ancestors had provided.[1]

It was an ironical outcome to three years of the Patriot King that the assault on party should have produced an opposition momentarily more strongly united and more solidly based on principle than any since the days of Queen Anne, and that the

[1]Winstanley, *Personal and Party Government*, pp. 158–66, 191–5; Namier, *Age of Amer. Rev.*, pp. 231–3, *Structure of Politics*, i. 182–7; Feiling, p. 83.

freeholders of England, whom the crown was to have rescued from the corrupt politicians, should now, through their representatives at Westminster, be bent on tarring both, in effect, with the same brush.

The opposition, however, failed to push its advantage, and soon disintegrated again—largely through the chronic inability of the elder Pitt to co-operate; it was internal disruption rather than external pressure that brought to grief successively the next three ministries. When Wilkes returned four years later from his flight to France to re-enter parliament, king and commons were at one in ignoring all the rules of the game to expel him from the house, nor could all the eloquence of Chatham (as he now was) dissuade the lords from joining in the chase. This time the government majority was nearly six times as great, and as the vote was now directly on Wilkes himself (whose character few could approve) and only indirectly on a general principle, the independent members were almost evenly divided between support and opposition for the motion.[1] The executive had resumed its sway over the legislature; the danger to the king's government now lay farther afield. Since redress of grievances could no longer be hoped for from parliament, agitation spread gradually to the cities and towns (which had been Pitt's great backers against Newcastle and the party politicians in the days of the war with France) and eventually to the shires themselves.

That discontent and rioting should be rife in the unruly London mob, which idolized Wilkes, was only to be expected, nor was it surprising that strongly-worded petitions should pour in from the traditionally turbulent city of Westminster, or from the county of Middlesex, from which he had been forcibly unseated. But now subversive rumour began to spread to the peaceful countryside, in such guise as appears in a letter of 1769 from Cowper's friend the Rev. John Newton, curate at Olney in Buckinghamshire, in which he writes of his parishioners to Lord Dartmouth (an ex-minister politically attached to his brother-in-law Lord North):

A few months ago I heard that some of them in their prayers at home had been much engaged for the welfare of Mr.

---

[1] Namier, *Structure of Politics*, i. 189–90.

Wilkes. As the whole town of Olney is remarkably loyal and peaceable with regard to the government I was rather surprised that gentleman should have partisans amongst our serious people. Upon enquiry I found that they had just heard of his name and that he was in prison; comparing the imperfect account they had of him with what they read in their Bibles they took it for granted that a person so treated must of necessity be a minister of the Gospel, and under that character they prayed earnestly that he might be supported and enlarged.[1]

Wilkes found support in surprising quarters, but perhaps none more surprising than this! But there were more dangerous symptoms afoot than the prayers of ignorant villagers. It was customary at the spring assizes, especially in times of war or domestic crisis, for the government to receive loyal addresses from the assembled gentry and freeholders at the prompting of the judges, sheriffs and lords lieutenant, who were all government nominees subject to degrees of pressure which varied from the judges, holding office during good behaviour but unwilling to put promotion in jeopardy, down to the sheriffs, whose annual appointment was one of the means by which governments tried to keep their hand on elections. Lords lieutenant generally held office for life, and the fact that several of them had latterly been removed for political opposition was yet another feature of the reign that recalled the critical days of Charles II and James II.[2] In spite of this, the attempt to procure loyal addresses from the shires in the spring of 1769, while the Wilkes trouble was at its height, fell singularly flat, except in Scotland, which had not yet forgiven the insults to the nation embodied in attacks on Bute. Three of the home counties, with Shropshire, Bristol, Liverpool, Coventry and the two universities, were (with some difficulty) persuaded to repudiate the sentiments of London, Westminster and Middlesex; but they did so in such terms that those who shared these sentiments felt bound in self-defence, after the final vote against Wilkes had been given in the house in May, to petition in the opposite sense. As many as seventeen shires took this step, some

---

[1]Hist. MSS. Com., 15th R., i. 191.
[2]Feiling, pp. 78, 82, 136; cf. *supra*, p. 63.

(notably Yorkshire) calling on the crown to dissolve parliament and to appeal to the constituencies whose liberties it had betrayed, others more cautiously confining themselves to the conventional prayer for the removal of evil councillors.

A total of 60,000 signatures was claimed for these petitions, and Chatham alleged that they represented in population and wealth more than half the electorate; but such numerical estimates are neither reliable nor particularly relevant. The posse of gentry and freeholders at the assizes was probably the best index available of extra-parliamentary opinion; and it boded ill for the monarchy when loyal addresses could not be extracted from this quarter, where (as the *Annual Register* commented)

> moderate men, even when far from being satisfied with the measures of government, will seldom hazard a refusal, which, however unjustly, the party that happen then to be warm in outward professions of loyalty, will always construe into an instance of disaffection.[1]

Not less ominous was the gulf that was revealed between opinion in and out of parliament. It is significant that Wilkes himself, even when he sat in parliament, seldom spoke there, finding a more responsive audience in readers of the *North Briton*. Political pamphlets and periodicals had of course been familiar since the days of Swift and Defoe; but a new phenomenon appeared when the newspapers themselves became a platform for political controversy. It is impossible to compare the circulation of the letters of Junius, whose vitriolic campaign against the king and his ministers sent the circulation of the *Public Advertiser* rocketing for three years from 1769, with that of (for example) Swift's *Conduct of the Allies*, because so many other papers pirated them—which is itself eloquent of the state of public feeling.[2]

What the king and his ministers were doing in effect was to create a new basis of political consciousness, and to re-awaken the Fourth Estate. Hitherto John Bull, though emphatically a social animal, had not normally been a political one, at least as politics are understood today. When he elected his repre-

[1] *Annual Register*, 1770, pp. 56–8; Lecky, v. 315–43.
[2] Winstanley, op. cit., p. 159; Lecky, iii. 445–89.

sentatives to parliament, he was not particularly interested in their opinions. Legislation was still a very minor part of the business of parliament, and what law-making there was was chiefly of a local character. So what the country elector wanted was a man who stood well in the neighbourhood and would keep his constituents' end up at Westminster, supporting the king's government, but keeping a wary eye on its use of the nation's money in the common interest. Gentlemen's agreements for an equitable share-out of two county seats, or of shire and borough seat, between two rival interests or factions, were a common seventeenth-century device which lasted well on into the eighteenth. They saved untold expense (to the grief of the venal voter) and safeguarded what was called 'the peace of the county', without in the least detracting from the representative character of the members; rather the contrary.[1] For except in the larger boroughs (where political feeling tended to run high and had ready-made organs of expression which Cromwell and his two Stuart successors had all tried in vain to silence), a candidate's opinions counted only when a crisis arose in which public feelings were deeply engaged.

Even elections to the Long Parliament had not as a rule been fought on political lines, and if candidates' political records were freely canvassed in those of the interregnum, that was because the state was being run by a party. When the course of events in Charles II's reign provoked a widespread panic that the country was being sold out to Rome, opinion once more played its part in parliamentary elections for a few critical years, but against strong prejudice on the part of old-fashioned people who thought it 'monstrous' that 'political partisanship should override local and personal obligations'.[2] The recovery of the monarchy from 1681 brought things back to normal until the Revolution, which was fought out in the main outside parliament; this once more stabilized the electoral system and politics generally until, late in Anne's reign, the reappearance of the dynastic question and the cry of 'The Church in danger' threw another massive stone into the pool. The Newcastle system and the substitution of septennial for

[1]Feiling, p. 6.
[2]Mrs. Eric George in *E.H.R.*, xlv. 554 and later examples in *Trans. R.H.S.* IV. xxi. 156; cf. A. H. Dodd, *Studies in Stuart Wales*, pp. 201–8.

triennial elections were designed to secure the new dynasty and its hereditary props and to restore electoral stability; in a large measure they succeeded, but succeeded at the expense of the responsiveness of the electoral machinery to strong movements of feeling and opinion. The sudden proliferation of 'instructions' to members in 1742, to which reference has already been made, was an attempt (perhaps not quite so spontaneous as it appeared) to break through these shackles. The object, however, was not to influence elections—except by long-range threats of what might happen in an indefinite future to a member who failed to come up to scratch—but rather to indicate the conduct expected of members already elected; and in the absence of published debates and division lists this could not be tested except by overt acts like acceptance of office, for which a few M.P.s were rapped over the knuckles by their constituents. The whole movement was a flash in the pan, and an attempt to revive it in 1769 fell singularly flat outside London, Middlesex and Norwich.[1]

That is why, when political passions boiled up again in George III's reign, they had to find outlets outside the electoral system, and the ordinary unpolitical John Bull found he could not discharge his ordinary county duties without finding himself pursued by political petitions and resolutions, nor open his daily newspaper without being confronted with fierce political diatribes or unauthorized (and indeed illegal) reports of debates in the house. It all contributed towards the creation of an active and informed public opinion, an obvious *sine quâ non* of responsible government. What Wilkes had begun (and later continued by his struggles for legalizing the reporting of parliamentary debates) was brought to a head by the disasters of the American war. The quarrel with America began while the Wilkes trouble was in its early stages; Chatham hoped, but failed, to heal it in his all-party ministry, and it was left to North to mismanage the war. At the outset independent opinion was more divided over America than over Wilkes. Emigration had slackened off for some time, and personal contact with the colonies had in consequence been reduced to a minimum. The country gentry, and even Junius, saw little to object to in the Stamp Act; it was among the trading interests in the bigger

[1]*Supra*, pp. 110–11; *Gent. Mag.*, xii. 581, xxxix. 51, 73–8, 161.

towns—dreading a loss of profitable markets—and the closely allied dissenting interest, with its New England contacts, that criticism of government policy was most vocal.[1]

When war actually broke out and fears became facts, indignation at the plight in which the government had placed the country became more widespread, although in the house itself no motion for accommodation with the rebels stood the slightest chance of success. The first effect of the war—even before the colonists began finding allies in the old world—was to reduce our total annual exports from 17 to 14 million pounds,[2] and as some of our most stable and widespread industries (notably textiles) were hit at a very critical period of their growth, the dislocation was correspondingly severe. The most vivid picture of the state of mind of the country within a few months of the outbreak of war comes in a letter written by John Wesley from Haverfordwest to Lord Dartmouth in August 1775; and as Wesley probably knew the country better than any man then alive, and was by no means predisposed either towards the colonists or against the crown, the passage is worth quoting at length.

In every part of England where I have been (and I have been East, West, North and South within these two years) trade in general is exceedingly decayed, and thousands of people are quite unemployed. Some I know to have perished for want of bread; others, I have seen creeping up and down like walking shadows. I except three or four manufacturing towns which have suffered less than others . . . The people in general all over the nation, are . . . far more deeply dissatisfied than they appear to have been even a year or two before the Great Rebellion, and far more dangerously dissatisfied. The bulk of the people in every city, town, and village where I have been, do not so much aim at the ministry, as they usually did in the last century, but at the king himself. He is the object of their anger, contempt and malice. They heartily despise his majesty; and hate him with a perfect hatred. They wish to imbrue their hands in his blood; they are full of the spirit of murder and rebellion, and I am per-

[1]Namier, *Structure of Politics*, i. 188–9; Junius, Letter i (1769).
[2]The statistics, published in 1812 by the chief clerk to the board of trade, are taken from G. L. Craik, *History of British Commerce*, 1844, iii. 67.

suaded, should any occasion offer, thousands would be ready to act what they now speak. It is as much as ever I can do, and sometimes more than I can do, to keep this plague from infecting my own friends. And nineteen [of]¹ twenty to whom I speak in defence of the king, seem never to have heard a word spoken for him before . . . Even where I was last, in the West Riding of Yorkshire, a tenant of Lord Dartmouth was telling me 'Sir, our tradesmen are breaking all round me, so that I know not what the end will be'. Even in Leeds I had appointed to dine at a merchant's; but before I came, the bailiffs were in possession of the house. Upon my saying 'I thought Mr. —— had been in good circumstances' I was answered, 'He *was* so: but the American war has ruined him.'²

The wide extent of dislocation, in days when industry was still widely dispersed, is confirmed from other sources: for example a traveller in remote Merioneth a few weeks later found manufacturers in the insignificant local cloth trade 'excessively anxious about affairs in America'.³ But the concentration of wrath on the king personally was the inevitable effect of his open appearance in politics in the Wilkes case and the propagandist use made of it by writers like Wilkes himself and Junius. As the war spread, so did popular discontent. The entry of France in 1778 brought exports down to 12 millions, and after temporary recoveries, the total had sunk by 1781 (after the Dutch had joined our enemies and the northern powers had formed an Armed Neutrality to the injury of our trade) to 11 millions.⁴ Even more serious was the loss of sea power. In the late summer of 1779, and again two years later, the Channel was dominated by the two powers we had so soundly beaten twenty years earlier; 'for the first time since 1690', says Lecky, 'England saw a vast hostile fleet commanding her seas, and threatening and insulting her shores'. The depredations of Paul Jones and other American privateers also recalled conditions of ninety years back, for never since had 'our shipping [been] so much damaged, or our

¹'or' in H.M.C. transcript.
²Hist. MSS. Com., 15*th R.*, i. 220.
³Sir Thomas Cullum, Sept. 1775 (*Y Cymmrodor*, xxxviii. 58).
⁴Craik, loc. cit.

traffic so far driven from its usual channels'. The mischief had begun even before France came in to batten on our misfortunes, and it brought these misfortunes home to the length and breadth of our coasts; in 1777, for example, a Chester paper announces the presence of three American privateers hovering in the neighbourhood and their capture of 'several vessels . . . one of which it is feared has the Bishop of Bangor's furniture on board'.[1]

Administrative breakdown (which is virtually what had happened here) signalized by humiliation abroad and accompanied by heavy economic pressure at home, in a country of proud tradition and unabated energy—these are the factors that most surely breed a sense of frustration finding its outlet in revolution; and to make matters worse, after Chatham's death in 1778 there was not a politician whom the public trusted. How near England was to revolution in 1780 is still in dispute. There was certainly no lack of what even Professor Pares admits to have been 'portents', even though he rejects Professor Butterfield's view that they spelled anything like revolution.[2] Foremost among the 'portents' was the so-called freeholders' movement which began in Middlesex in 1779, was captured by Yorkshire (with Christopher Wyvill as leading prophet), and soon spread like wildfire. The regions which took the lead were those that had been foremost in the petitioning movement of a decade earlier, and often in the *furore* for issuing 'instructions' to M.P.s forty years back. But there were some striking differences. Earlier movements of revolt had nearly all been urban in character and inspiration, the country (so far as it participated at all) taking its cue from the towns; for example it was not the county of York but the city (where politics were unusually free and vigorous)[3] that had distinguished itself in 1741 by the extreme courses it urged on its members. But the movement of 1780 was a revolt of the independent country gentry and the freeholders who had been accustomed to follow their lead but had latterly been squeezed out of active politics (as we have seen)[4] by economic pressure. When in so many counties the 'great preponderance of pro-

---

[1]Lecky, v. 9, 84; Craik iii. 68; *Chester Chronicle*, 25 July, 1777.
[2]Pares, p. 199, and in *E.H.R.*, lxv. 526–9.
[3]*Trans. R.H.S.*, IV. xxi. 155.
[4]*Supra*, p. 99.

perty' supported the petitioning movement; when seventeenth-century controversial literature could be ransacked afresh for arguments; when an ex-sheriff could urge his fellow-freeholders through the local press, in a solidly tory country like Wales, to warn the king in its petition of the 'ignominious exile' in store for him if he did not banish evil counsellors from his presence—there was some ground for believing that revolution was at hand.[1]

The Middlesex gentry had originally planned to make electoral reform the point of attack, but they fell in with their Yorkshire allies in substituting a general plea for economy, which was bound to catch on in a time of financial stringency, and under cover of which the whole system of corruption could be attacked. The particular point of attack in the petitions, however, was a minor consideration, for few expected them (in view of previous experiences) to be taken seriously in a house of commons constituted as at present or by a monarchy now in league with it. The attitude of at least the more violent of the promoters resembled that of one wing of the catholic conspiracy of James I's reign which eventually took shape in Gunpowder Plot: then too a petition was to be organized for presentation in parliament, and failing acceptance, 'which' (declared an informant) 'they neither expect nor much care', resort was to be had to demonstrations of a more forcible kind.[2] Naturally little was said at this stage about ulterior measures, but it was urged that the counties sending petitions should form 'associations', with standing committees to watch over the progress of the petitions, and the advice was widely followed. The original county meetings had won a surprising measure of support among the more substantial gentry, but the committees naturally fell into the hands of the more radical type of agitator, and a wide range of reform proposals, going far beyond the mere 'economy' programme that formed the original basis of union, produced growing divisions between shire and shire on the one hand and between radical agitators, opposition whigs and independent country gentry on the other. In March, 1780, delegates from twelve county committees (out of the twenty-

[1]Lecky, v. 95; *Chester Chronicle*, 2 July 1780. Cromwell's speech dismissing the Rump had been used as propaganda against a corrupt parliament in the Wilkes case (Feiling, p. 108).
[2]*E.H.R.*, liii. 643-4.

eight that petitioned), and four boroughs, met in London to form a central association in which some of the more rabid promoters of the movement saw the germ of an 'anti-parliament' ready to replace the effete body at Westminster should it fail to reform itself; before breaking up it produced a radical programme of electoral reform to be used locally as 'instructions' for candidates in the forthcoming elections.[1]

Naturally the programme won only limited support in the shires, and whatever unity of purpose the movement had possessed soon evaporated. The resemblance to the tory 'plan for the counties' drawn up nearly forty years earlier is very striking; but the Jacobite *débâcle* that followed this had frightened off the country gentry from schemes that might land them in treason, and more recently the lesson had been driven home by the American revolt, with its central congress and its 'committees of correspondence', and nearer home by the Irish volunteer movement that owed so much to America's example. Thanks to George III, what had been a tory programme in 1744 had now become a radical plan of campaign; the transition may be seen in similar proposals put out by the Society of Supporters of the Bill of Rights (a by-product of the Wilkes agitation), which were also designed as 'instructions' for M.P.s.[2]

The agitation was not without its effects at Westminster. It had now become clear to the whig opposition that any hope they might have of sailing back into power on the strong reaction in the country against the king's personal government must depend on their renouncing the system of Influence by which they had maintained themselves in power till 1762, but which had since been used with such deadly effect against them. Strange irony that it should have fallen to Newcastle's political heir, Lord Rockingham, to urge on his fellow-freeholders of Yorkshire, and to Rockingham's follower Edmund Burke to propose in the house, a political programme that cut at the very roots of the Newcastle system! It was a programme on which all sections of the whig opposition could for the moment unite, with strong support from the non-party country gentry who had been hot on the trail of corruption since Dutch William's day—with the result that it was only by the narrowest

[1]Butterfield, op. cit., and in *Trans. R.H.S.*, IV. xxix. 69–91.
[2]*Supra*, pp. 111–2; Feiling, pp. 112–3.

of majorities that some of the crucial bills for 'economical reform' were fended off by the government. Not only so, but while the freeholders' 'Plan of Association' was still under heated discussion, John Dunning contrived by a snap vote, in the course of debates on the county petitions, to win a majority of eighteen for his historic motion 'That the power of the crown has increased, is increasing and ought to be diminished'.

The whig opposition was too disunited to follow up this spectacular victory by any constructive plan. A proposal to move the crown not to dissolve parliament until the grievances aired in the county petitions should have been redressed smacked too much of the Long Parliament to carry the house. A reduction of the power of the crown through party government and the gradual elimination of Influence was as far as the Rockingham whigs would go: they were strenuously opposed to the proposals for shorter parliaments, an increase in county representation and some extension of the franchise, which the central 'association' was trying to foist on the county committees, with the support of the party led by Lord Shelburne. This group in turn, on which the mantle of Chatham had fallen, inherited his rooted distrust of party and belief in the independence of the crown; while Henry Fox's son Charles, a convert to the opposition since his dismissal from the ministry in 1774, used his brilliant debating talents in a bid for leadership on a programme combining the Rockingham doctrine of party government with the Shelburne addiction to electoral reform.[1]

The upshot was that when in July 1780 the king suddenly dissolved parliament with one of its seven years still to run, the elections found the whig factions at sixes and sevens once more —though with divisions of principle rapidly encroaching on the older tie of family 'connection'; the independent gentry, already hanging back, were finally scared off by the revelation in the Gordon Riots of May of the unchecked anarchy to which mass petitions to parliament could lead. Influence, more strenuously exerted than ever,[2] resumed its electoral sway, and

---

[1]Butterfield, op. cit., ch. vii.

[2]*Trans. R.H.S.*, IV. xxi. 156–7; Lecky, v. 98. In fact expenditure on elections from the privy purse had begun to rise when in 1777 George decided to devote £12,000 a year to that purpose. From 1779–82 £100,000 of public money went down this bottomless pit, two-fifths of it from the royal coffers. (*E.H.R.* lxii. 490 and n.; Feiling, op. cit., p. 103).

the government found itself in a stronger position after the election than before. The bills for 'economical reform' were rejected by far larger majorities, though North threw an unappreciated sop to the opposition by appointing a commission of extra-parliamentary experts with wide powers to investigate the public accounts; it sat for six years, and its fifteen reports provided his successors with material for farreaching reforms vital to the achievement of responsible government.[1] For petitions that still came in from belated shires there was short shrift. Yet these pyrrhic victories brought small comfort to North, for the dismal tale of failures abroad was unabated, and he was now conducting a war policy in which he had ceased to believe, simply because a sense of personal obligation forbade him to leave his master in the lurch. But the surrender at Yorktown fifteen months after the election, followed by a vote in the commons against continuing the war, decided him early in 1782 to 'desert' his post, leaving the king to the tender mercies of the whig factions. What is more, the whole cabinet resigned with him, excepting only Lord Chancellor Thurlow, whose post was still regarded as judicial, and therefore not subject to the vicissitudes of politics even though the holder was an active politician—and as such a brake on collective responsibility in successive cabinets till Pitt got rid of him in 1792.

After threatening abdication, George accepted with a wry face a ministry in which Rockingham had the treasury and the two secretaryships went to Shelburne (who took what had become the home and colonial department, and so had the job of negotiating with the colonists), and Charles Fox (with foreign affairs as his province). Internal differences among the ministers enabled the king to retain some of the initiative and independence of the crown by playing the old game of *divide et imperá*, and treating Shelburne (through whom he had formed the ministry) as equal in status and patronage with Rockingham.[2] But it was no longer possible to dam back the flood of 'economical reform'—indeed Rockingham had made it a condition of taking up office, and the king had no option but to accept. Government contractors were excluded from the house of

---

[1] D. L. Keir in *Law Quart. Rev.*, l. 374–5.
[2] Pares, p. 123n.

commons by one measure; a second disfranchised the vast army of revenue officers, constituting at least a tenth (some said a fifth) of the electorate, and one of the chief strongholds of Influence; a third abolished a number of sinecures and reduced the secret service funds. At last the king had to admit the principle of parliamentary inquiry into the civil list, which even George II had successfully fended off when investigation was threatened into Walpole's use of the secret service money; all that remained of his 'own' was now his privy purse. It was a clear victory for the Rockinghamites over Shelburne, who fully sympathized with the king's reluctance to expose this *arcanum* of prerogative; on the other hand Shelburne would have gone further than his colleagues in resuming the detailed control over departmental, as distinct from royal, expenditure which the commons had so unwarily abandoned in 1714.[1]

These measures, combined with the recovery of sea power in 1782, and of trade with remarkable speed once peace was signed in 1783, removed the more urgent causes of popular discontent and helped the country to swallow the humiliation of American independence. The flow of county petitions had never quite ceased until North's resignation; only a few days before he went, a county meeting in Caernarvonshire (whose remoteness from the hub of politics tended to make it late for the fair) had instructed its representatives, with only one dissentient, to vote against supplies until economic reform, shorter parliaments and more equal representation had been secured.[2] But now at last the country seemed to be settling down.

Unfortunately for this hope, Rockingham died after a few months of office, a victim of the influenza epidemic, and the king's choice of Shelburne as his successor annoyed his followers and drove Fox, Burke, and all the more effective of the whig leaders into opposition, leaving the ministry in a minority. To retrieve the position, the king called Chatham's son, a young lawyer completely unknown in the country but likely to inspire confidence through his father's name, to lead the commons as chancellor of the exchequer. The calculation proved, in the end, an extremely shrewd one, but it could not save the immediate situation. For Fox, to force himself back into power on terms acceptable to himself, now made common cause with North, who saw in this coalition a chance of retrieving the disastrous failures into which he had fallen through having to pursue and defend an indefensible royal policy. Now that America was out of the way, there was little to divide them that did not equally divide any other combination of ministers, and the combined strength of their followers promised a secure majority and indeed seemed to offer the only prospect of a stable ministry. The majority was used for a direct vote of censure on the government such as the king could not ignore. After many attempts to evade the issue, he found himself left with no alternative but to invite Fox and North to share the two secretaryships, with Portland (another Rockingham whig) as figurehead premier at the treasury.

It was the heaviest blow the king had yet suffered. Apart from the personal stab in the back from North, he had had to admit to power the politician he most detested, and who was associated not only with the most vehement demagogic appeals of the days of the freeholders' movement (when as a member of the city committee for Westminster he virtually stole the leadership of the movement from the more moderate Wyvill and his Yorkshiremen), but also with the most extreme views of party government and personal hostility to the crown. For the first time George had presented to him an entire ministry as a *fait accompli*, with no say at all in those junior appointments which he had formerly used with such effect as a curb on the leaders, and a 'clear intention to eliminate the king's personal will from politics altogether'. Even North now took the line that 'the appearance of power is all that a King of this country can have'.[1] It seemed as if responsible government had arrived *per saltum*, before ever the legislature to which ministers were to be responsible had been made accountable to the electorate or the electorate itself had become a fair sample of the changing community.

It was here that the weakness of the new ministry lay, and the king was not slow to seize on it. Although there is little reason to believe that the coalition in itself produced the immediate revulsion of feeling sometimes attributed to it, manœuvres and majorities at Westminster had long since ceased to impress

[1] Pares, pp. 123–4; Aspinall, loc. cit., p. 214.

the public, and the recovery of trade and prestige redounded to the credit of the monarchy rather than of the fluctuating ministries. If only an issue could be found on which the crown could appeal to the public against the ministers, the dream of a Patriot King need not even now be finally abandoned. And the coalition provided him with such an issue in its India Bill. The East India Company's patronage had long made the 'nabob vote' an important element in politics at Westminster, and now Clive's conquest of an empire there had made it doubly urgent that this patronage should not be left without restraint in the hands of an irresponsible commercial company. North's Act of 1773, the first challenge to the company's exclusive control, had not solved the problem. Fox was naturally determined that the Indian patronage should not be used as a new buttress for the Influence of the crown; but in giving control to the government of the day he laid his ministry open to the charge of a design to perpetuate itself by a fresh accession of automatic votes. The coalition majority put the measure safely through the commons, but by personal intervention the king secured its rejection in the upper house. On the very next day—just a week before the Christmas of 1783—he dismissed his ministers and called in the young Pitt, at twenty-four, as first lord of the treasury, to lead a ministry otherwise drawn exclusively from the upper house and in a hopeless minority in the commons.

For more than three months Pitt sat tight and left the initiative to the opposition, allowing its hostile majorities to pass over his head, while his unruffled courage in face of Fox's violent attacks gradually reduced their size and won him the confidence of the house and of the country at large. The issue of responsible government was now squarely joined. Pitt insisted against Fox that

> the immediate appointment or removal of ministers does not rest with this House. There is, therefore, nothing illegal in a minister's remaining in office after this House has declared against him, particularly when immediate resignation would have injured the country.

He was not, of course, denying that defeat on a major measure of policy must lead to resignation; what he would not admit was the power of the house to enforce resignation without stating one ground of distrust in the men, and without suffering ourselves to have any experience of their measures.

Lecky (while censuring the conduct of Fox) dubs this doctrine 'unconstitutional'; but Fox's counter-claim, far from having become an accepted convention of the constitution, was not yet even an official dogma of the whig party. On the other hand, Pitt came perilously near to a rejection of the doctrine of 1641 that 'there be grounds of diffidence that lie not in proof', or to Charles II's refusal in 1680 to dismiss a minister except on proven charges.[1] One remedy still lay in the hands of the opposition, as Fox was not slow to point out:

> His Majesty has undoubtedly the power of choosing his own ministers, and the House of Commons of refusing the Supplies. But were the one to take into his service any men or set of men most agreeable to the royal inclination without any regard as to how such appointments might operate on the public, might not the House with the same propriety withhold the purse of the people?

It was clear, however, that were the opposition to call into play what Burke called 'the extreme medicine of the State' it had no hope of carrying with it the country gentry, and Fox himself concluded that 'both extremes ought to be avoided, because equally injurious to the public welfare.'[2]

At last, a division in March, 1784, which reduced the opposition's majority to a single vote, decided the king on an immediate appeal to the country. The arduous task of drawing up the electoral lists which Newcastle used to call 'choosing the parliament' was one to which none of his successors at the head of the treasury was prepared to give the detailed attention so congenial to his temperament. It was now the job of the patronage secretary to the treasury, and since George III's accession this post had always been held by a king's man who did not change with changing ministries. John Robinson, North's former patronage secretary, had been originally brought in by Bute; he had 'chosen' the parliaments of 1774

[1] *Supra*, pp. 33, 62.
[2] Lecky, v. 242–55; the word 'unconstitutional' occurs in the chapter heading, not the text.

and 1780, and had been the king's unofficial agent throughout the North ministry. The king now called him in for the same purpose. As a civil servant he took it as his duty to place his knowledge and skill at the disposal of the king, whatever ministry was in power, and his lists had been handed in just before the coalition's defeat in November. It was Fox's knowledge of the 'pull' enjoyed at election time by the government in power that prompted his violent attempts to get rid of Pitt before he could use this advantage; but the king was too quick for him. For George it was equally important to strike while the iron was hot without waiting for Burke's 'economical' reforms (the operation of which was delayed by the fact that so many offices were freeholds for life) could take full effect; even now they were beginning to upset electoral calculations.[1]

Yet these official lists were by no means infallible, and even when they were correct, they could only forecast the strength of the various 'connections' in the next house—not the way members would actually vote on any issue where strong feelings were aroused in the constituencies. For as we have seen, members were still regarded as free agents, with certain obligations to patrons and an overriding obligation to help to run the country with the special interests of their own constituents in mind; attempts to bind them down to particular 'instructions' on specific issues had never cut much ice, and it had appeared again and again how majorities could fade away in the face of some vital and unforeseen issue.[2] Now it has been made abundantly clear by Mrs. George that in 1784 the feelings of the country were in fact deeply stirred and that

> the election . . . differs from all others of the century in the nature and extent of the publicity campaign which preceded and accompanied it: public meetings all over the country to vote addresses to the Crown, pamphlets and election literature of a type then rare in that it was concerned with general, not local issues.[3]

Whatever Robinson's lists might say, it is doubtful whether any parliament elected that year would have dared to do other

[1] W. T. Laprade in *E.H.R.*, xxxi. 224–37; A. S. Foord in id., lxii. 501.
[2] See, e.g., Feiling, p. 130.
[3] Trans. *R.H.S.*, IV. xxi. 133–68.

than support the king and Pitt. The election has, in fact, been described as 'the first in which the whole weight of government coincided with the whole impetus of public feeling'.[1] In some constituencies it was noted as a portent that no bribes were needed to secure the return of government candidates, and over the whole country the treasury seems to have spent far less over this election than the last. We read of patrons repudiated, of candidates coerced by county meetings. The fate of Fox's hundred and sixty 'martyrs' who lost their seats as his supporters is a commonplace; but the landslide was certainly not foreseen by Fox himself until addresses in support of the administration began to pour in a couple of months before the election—and from the very quarters where support for the 'freeholder' movement had been strongest four years back.

The recovery of the monarchy in so short a space of time from such general execration is one of the most striking phenomena of a reign of surprises. Yet what 1784 restored was no more the monarchy of 1770 than what 1660 restored had been the monarchy of 1640. The day of ministerial mouthpieces was over; the king must now share his popularity, and in the long run his authority, with a minister of outstanding talents and independent character, and that after bitter experience of the only alternatives. 'In having supported me', he told Pitt, you have 'saved the constitution.'[2] In a sense he was right, but not quite in his sense. It was emphatically a triumph on terms.

[1] Feiling, pp. 160–2.
[2] Dobrée, p. 185.

IX

The Patriot King in Adversity
1784–1810

STRONGLY as the younger Pitt might repudiate the Foxite doctrine of responsible government, his long term of office was in fact a potent factor in its final development. A prime minister virtually choosing and directing his own cabinet, a cabinet standing or falling by a common policy, an opposition ready to step into its shoes when it fell—none of these was as yet a fully recognized convention of the constitution when he died in 1806, but each was far more widely accepted and far nearer achievement than when he formed his first ministry more than twenty years earlier. His first decade of power was marked by freedom from political storms both at home and abroad such as had not been known since the reign began—scarcely indeed since the early days of Walpole. In these placid conditions the 'rules of the game' could resume their sway in politics—revised rules, it is true, but not so drastically revised as to involve any serious loss of face for either king or minister. Pitt never claimed the right to choose his colleagues. He did make a few half-hearted attempts to increase his personal following by coalescence with the Foxite whigs. Whether any permanent basis of association could ever have been found between groups which differed so widely in their principles of government—however much at one they might be on specific issues like parliamentary reform or

catholic emancipation—may be doubted; what is certain is
that for Pitt the royal veto on admitting Fox to the cabinet was
decisive, and it meant that he was thrown back increasingly
on the support of the still surviving and important group of
'king's friends'.[1]

His nearest approach to 'dictation' to the crown came after
the king's first illness, when a somewhat subdued monarch
agreed, rather than lose his minister before he had found a
trustworthy and congenial substitute, to free him from the
perpetual obstructionism of Lord Chancellor Thurlow, a man
whose 'temper' (in the words of a colleague) was 'mostly employed to perplex and to censure the measures of those he acted
with'. Even this did not put an end to the inclusion in cabinets
of ministers with legal or administrative posts (like that of lord
chancellor or chancellor of the duchy) carrying greater permanence of tenure and closer relationship with the crown, who
could be used by it to undermine ministerial policy when the
king disliked it. This state of affairs persisted till about the time
of the first Reform Bill. Yet the tussle over Thurlow has its
importance in the development of responsible government; for
from this time the crown generally used its influence on these
semi-permanent 'unpolitical' ministers to make them conform
their personal views to cabinet policy rather than to use them
as its private 'fifth column', and Pitt got it established as
another rule of the game—henceforth never violated except
under strong protest—that individual ministers must approach
the king directly only on matters concerning their own departments, not on general policy.[2]

Another rule to which Pitt firmly adhered was that, to spare
the crown from open intervention in politics by the use of its
personal influence in either house (as in Fox's India Bill)—
or in the last resort by a revival of the legislative veto—government measures must not be introduced without the royal
consent. That is why in 1801, when George categorically
refused his consent to Catholic Emancipation (to which Pitt
felt himself committed by his Irish undertakings) the minister
had no option but to resign. But by that time the king had found

---

[1] D. G. Barnes, *George III and William Pitt*, 1938, pp. 83, 192, 135–6, 470. I have in
general followed this comprehensive analysis of the relations of king and
minister.
[2] A. Aspinall in *Proc. B.A.*, xxxviii. 231–5, 250; Feiling, p. 249.

in the staunchly anti-catholic Addington a refuge from the bitter alternative of the Foxites; for so long as Pitt stuck to his principle of refraining from 'formed opposition', Addington, with support from the king's friends and the protestant country gentry, could command a clear majority, whereas fifteen years earlier to lose Pitt would have been to jump out of the frying pan into the fire. So he allowed his minister in 1785 to introduce proposals for parliamentary reform which he abhorred, in the comfortable assurance that the house would turn them down. The king was as shrewd a judge as ever of the state of parties; he did not even have to instruct his 'friends' in the house to vote against the measure (which Pitt would never have stomached), for he knew that Pitt's followers could prevail only if the whigs gave them united support (which on this issue they would not) and if the independent country gentry concurred (an even less likely contingency). Having once tested the house on reform, Pitt wisely dropped the subject, knowing that nothing was to be gained by repeating his discomfiture; but in doing so he forfeited any remaining hope of Foxite support for his government: henceforth it was war to the knife. Once more the king had shown how he could stick to the rules and still beat the politicians at their own game.[1]

Pitt for his part insisted on

> the absolute necessity, in the conduct of the affairs of this country, that there should be an avowed and real minister, possessing the chief interest in the council and the principal place in the confidence of the King.

This George had always been prepared to concede in theory, except when ministries like that of Rockingham or the Fox-North coalition forced themselves on him. Pitt, although not exactly a man after his own heart, had at least not been thrust on him, and during that first peaceful decade he played the game by him. But after 1800, when the catholic question came to the fore, Pitt had some grounds for suspecting that Dr. Addington and a 'little Court Windsor party' of unbudging protestants were poisoning the royal mind against him, and this may well have helped to precipitate his resignation; for the

---

[1]Dobrée, op. cit., pp. 192–3; Barnes, pp. 67–70, 83, 101, 133–4, 192; Feiling, p. 167; Aspinall, loc. cit., p. 239.

king had a warm personal affection for the doctor, such as he never felt for Pitt. Pitt, on the contrary, stuck to the rules and declined to advise the king on the composition of the Addington ministry which was to succeed his.[1]

A mark of confidence on which all George III's prime ministers set great store—and a recurrent cause of friction with all except his 'favourites' Bute and North—was acceptance of their advice on patronage and the creation of peers. In this respect the younger Pitt had little to complain of. During his two ministries the king consented to the creation of nearly a hundred new peers, chiefly from among industrialists and professional men, with a sprinkling of the wealthier squires. The intention—by no means a novelty, and still operative after Pitt's day—was to dilute the influence of the old, exclusive aristocracy and to secure support for the king's government from up-and-coming men of means. The old aristocracy naturally disliked it; the king, although he had withheld this mark of confidence from Fox and North, raised no objections till, about 1790, he began to murmur that the peerage was becoming 'too numerous'. But after all he had no reason to love the close cast which was always trying to keep the monarchy in fetters, and after 1793 the need for recognizing war service provided an additional motive.[2] Patronage in general, however, was a matter on which (as one of his contemporaries said) 'Pitt's virtues and infirmities peculiarly disqualify him'; he himself admitted—how Newcastle would have stared!—that it made him 'bilious' to deal with importunate beggars for place.[3]

Patronage, however, was ceasing to have the paramount place it once held in the machinery of government, and this too was a result of what Pitt achieved during his years of peace. The programme of 'economical reform' trumpeted by Burke, used as a war-cry by Wyvill and the Yorkshire freeholders, and taken in hand (with only limited success) by the Rockingham ministry, now reached a climax. Not that Pitt shared the enthusiasm of Burke or of Wyvill for curbing the

[1]Barnes, pp. 70, 301; Aspinall, loc. cit., pp. 203, 235 and n., 244; Feiling, p. 240; *History*, xxii. 252.
[2]A. S. Turberville in *History*, xxi. 350–8; Feiling, pp. 209, 279–80; Keir, *Const. Hist.*, p. 412.
[3]Aspinall, loc. cit., pp. 236–7; Feiling, pp. 165, 240.

royal authority—in this respect as in so many others he was his
father's son. What Pitt was interested in was administrative
reform for its own sake, a matter for which neither Burke nor
Fox greatly cared. Lecky puts his peace administration in
right perspective when he emphasizes its 'essentially business
character', and declares that 'no minister displayed more
industry and skill in remedying detailed abuses'. It was from
among men whose interests were administrative rather than
political that he found his chief friends and personal followers—
men like Dundas, on whom he relied in Indian affairs and (less
fortunately) in admiralty patronage and the direction of our
war effort against France; or Jenkinson, son of Bute's *protégé*,
whom as Lord Hawkesbury he placed at the head of the reconstituted board of trade, with William Eden, another 'man of
business', at his right hand to carry to a successful conclusion
negotiations for a commercial treaty with France.[1]

The bulky reports of the commission first appointed in the
closing years of North's ministry[2] were now appearing in rapid
succession, and in the business atmosphere of Pitt's government
their recommendations reached the statute book, or took shape
in orders in council, with unwonted speed. By the second year
of his ministry the main proposals on administration of the
revenue and of the navy, army and ordnance had already been
implemented, and another commission was appointed to
investigate salaries (which were now in process of being substituted for fees) in government departments.[3] This commission
ran into heavier weather; the whig doctrine of the sacredness
of freeholds, for which Locke himself had provided a philosophic basis, roused the eloquence of Fox and Burke against
measures which went far beyond their original proposals for
'economical reform', and it was a doctrine too deeply ingrained
among the independent country gentry to be ignored. There
were endless delays in fixing compensations, extinguishing
'reversions' or waiting for nature to take its course. Government had also to meet the stock arguments about the value of
patronage in bringing into politics able young men without

[1]Lecky, v. 301–2; Feiling, pp. 168–70.
[2]*Supra*, p. 141.
[3]e.g., the under-secretary in the foreign department now received a salary of
£1,500 (soon increased to £2,000) in lieu of fees and gratuities amounting, with
his fixed allowance, to £1,079 18s. 8d. (E. Jones-Parry in *E.H.R.*, xlix. 316).

family connexion, and its vital rôle (in Lord Hardwicke's words) in 'the management of the Parliament and the quiet and orderly government of the country'. Even when the reforms were purely a matter of administration, not requiring an act of parliament, they had to run the gauntlet of vested interests in the departments affected: after the commission of 1785 had made its report (which took three years), another five years passed before the principal secretaries had added their observations, and not till 1795 was the necessary order in council issued.[1]

Yet in spite of everything the citadel of Influence was tottering. By the end of the century nearly a thousand sinecures had been abolished, and others were reprieved only for the lifetime of the present owners, while hardly more than fifty placemen were left in the house of commons. Politicians were already asking themselves how government majorities were to be maintained, or how any ministry could survive on 'such a narrow system as public virtue'.[2] But public virtue was Pitt's great asset: for half a century the name of Pitt had stood in the public mind for incorruptibility, and this was perhaps his prime contribution to responsible government, although the full fruits were not reaped till after his death. All the more cock-a-hoop was the opposition when in his second ministry it was able to formulate charges of corruption against his trusted friend and agent Henry Dundas, now Lord Melville and first lord of the admiralty, in respect of his financial administration. It is true that the charges were never proved, and the impeachment, like so many of its predecessors, fizzled out; but the attack was almost literally a death-blow to Pitt.[3] What a change it all indicates in the relations of monarch, minister and parliament! Impeachment had begun as a covert attack on the untouchable king through his confidential servant; now a confidential servant too strong to yield to frontal assault is himself subjected to flank attack through his intimate agent.

The purification of politics was only one of several aspects of Pitt's policy of administrative reform which had a bearing on

[1]D. L. Keir in *Law Quarterly Review*, 1, 368–85; Halévy, *Histoire du peuple anglais au xixe siècle*, 1924, i. 7–17; *E.H.R.*, loc. cit., pp. 313–4.
[2]Feiling, pp. 165–6; A. S. Foord in *E.H.R.*, lxii. 486, 500, 504.
[3]Barnes, pp. 162–3.

responsible government. Another was the reorganization of the civil service, and its gradual banishment from politics. The commission of 1785 recommended that each department of state should be allotted one under-secretary who, to avoid 'the confusion . . . that may arise in business of such high importance, from frequent changes', was to keep his post through changing administrations; this was not to preclude the principal secretary from employing, should he so desire, a second under-secretary to assist him in 'private and confidential business' so long as he remained in office. The secretaries of state of the day still disliked any suggestion that they might be compelled to keep in office an under-secretary appointed by, and perhaps unduly devoted to, a predecessor of different political complexion, and they successfully resisted the incorporation of this proposal in the order in council giving effect to the report; but in practice there was growing up a race of able administrators whose tenure of office became permanent not because of any established rule, but because no minister could afford to dispense with their services.

At the foreign office (which set the tone) this permanent under-secretary was given, from the secretaryship of Pitt's disciple Canning, the exclusive handling of the secret service money, and he became the chief channel of diplomatic correspondence. The pressure of these duties in Napoleonic and post-Napoleonic Europe proved incompatible with attendance in the commons; from 1809 onwards he became a purely departmental official, outside parliamentary politics. This left his colleague, the 'political' secretary who came and went with the ministry, free to take up a seat in the commons; and as most foreign secretaries during the nineteenth century were peers, it gradually fell to his lot to represent his department in the lower house, though the practice was not stabilized till the second half of the century.[1] Thus Pitt's reforms had two unplanned and posthumous effects: the reduction of the influence of the crown on the one hand, the elimination of the civil service from politics on the other.

There was also a third, and in some ways a still more important effect. Administrative reorganization extended to the upper reaches of the ministries. The 'departmentalizing' of

[1] E. Jones-Parry, loc. cit., pp. 308–20.

government had been noticeable as early as the reign of Charles II, when the undifferentiated rule of the privy council began to break up;[1] it reached a climax under the younger Pitt. Apart from the important reforms in his own department of the treasury, it was he who (for example) was responsible for the division of the original two offices of principal secretary of state into the home and foreign offices; he also revived and reconstituted the board of trade, which had been abolished among the 'economies' of 1782. As the structure of the great departments of state grew firmer and more distinct, so too did that of the cabinet that embraced them. During this period we can at last draw a line, if a somewhat wobbly one, between the 'efficient' cabinet and the rest of the responsible ministry on the one hand, and on the other hand civil servants and that queer antiquarian survival the 'nominal' cabinet. It was Addington who laid down in set terms the principle that 'the number of the Cabinet should not exceed that of the persons whose responsible situations in office require their being members of it', and applied the principle to an ex-lord chancellor who tried to keep his seat in the cabinet after surrendering the seals as part of a general re-shuffle.[2]

Addington's formula is a pretty elastic one, and in application it required frequent re-interpretation. The nucleus of the cabinet was still those ancient dignitaries of the royal household who had stood first in order of court precedence since the time of Henry VIII, took pride of place in parliamentary claims when the Long Parliament was blundering its way towards control of the executive, and formed the kernel of every inner ring of counsellors (under whatever name) from the Restoration onwards. As we have seen, it was round the lord treasurer's modern representative, the first lord of the treasury, that the cabinet eventually crystallized. The other lords of the treasury were also politicians who changed with changing ministries, but remained outside the cabinet, the junior lord eventually taking the place of the patronage secretary (when he became an unpolitical civil servant) as party whip. The chancellor of the exchequer's office was also an ancient one, but it had originated in a mere clerkship, not a household dignity held by a peer,

---

[1]*Supra*, p. 53.
[2]Aspinall, loc. cit., p. 150.

and until after 1688 it remained so; George IV called it an office requiring 'ability not aristocracy'—an interesting and significant distinction. Finance was adequately represented in parliament by the first lord of the treasury, and on the occasions when he sat in the commons—for example during the whole of the Pitt-Addington period, as earlier under Walpole— he usually combined the two offices. The *régime* of aristocratic premiers that followed Pitt's death restored the chancellor's separate status but did not at first raise the office to cabinet rank. But the obvious convenience, in these conditions, of having in the commons an official spokesman of government finance, and the abolition in 1834 (as a delayed effect of Pitt's treasury reforms) of the separate office of exchequer, meant for practical purposes a gradual substitution of the chancellor for the first lord as guardian of the national finances. This left the head of the administration free for that general supervision, unhampered by departmental duties, that had been urged so long ago on the unwilling Clarendon.[1]

The lord chancellor's judicial duties, as we have seen, had always made his position in the cabinet a little anomalous, though not so anomalous as the inclusion in the coalition cabinet of 1806-7 of the chief justice of king's bench; this exceptional measure, however—taken in the interests of the balance of parties and as much disliked by the judge himself as by the commons—was never taken into precedent. Apart from the historic dignity of the lord chancellor as king's delegate when the two houses met in full parliament, his primacy in the lords made his presence in the cabinet desirable for any ministry anxious to keep its hold on parliament. Yet the conception of him as a non-party man who kept his place in successive cabinets died hard; it was justified by Wellington on the ground that a lord chancellor was a professional man, dependent on fees and salaries and generally without a landed estate to support him out of office (a view which ignores the fact that a successful lawyer can make far more in private practice than on the woolsack); it was Brougham, the lord chancellor of the Reform ministry, who broke the tradition.

[1]Powicke, Johnson and Harte, *Handbook of British Chronology*, 1939, pp. 80–2; Pares, *George III and the Politicians*, p. 148; Aspinall, loc. cit., pp. 147, 201; Keir, p. 417–8; *supra*, p. 50.

Even in our own time, the readiness of early labour governments to draw their chancellors from the liberal left shows that
the office has retained something of the character of what
William IV called 'a civil and not a political one'.[1] But if the
lord chancellor is never *ex officio* as complete a party man as
some of his colleagues, no premier ever tried to form a ministry
without him.

In the Tudor order of precedence the lord president of the
council stands next after the chancellor and treasurer, and by
the end of the eighteenth century (before the office of prime
minister had arrived at any sort of formal recognition) his
position in the cabinet counted first in point of dignity; this
was what made it natural for the American colonies when they
repudiated the monarchy, to substitute the office of president.
But of course with the decline of the privy council the president's duties had become light and mainly non-political, and
he had no departmental responsibilities. It might have been
expected, then, that when differentiation came he would move
outwards to the 'nominal' cabinet; but the great dignity of the
office (since like the lord chancellor the lord president was by
way of being a royal deputy) made it a useful one to offer to an
elder statesman, too old to be saddled with departmental
duties, whose presence was needed to give weight to the cabinet;
so he came to be regarded in the early nineteenth century as
one of its irreducible minimum. To this irreducible minimum
belonged also at that time the lord privy seal, who in dignity
came next after the lord president in cabinets of Pitt's day, as
he had in Tudor court precedence, but in respect of actual
duties had become virtually a sinecurist since so many of them
had passed over (during the two preceding centuries) to the
secretariat; by 1798 they could be discharged by a couple of
clerks working four hours a day, and even that poor remnant
disappeared within the next century—a very different story
from when James I's lord privy seal would hold up public
business for days by stealing off with the seal to his beloved
Monmouthshire![2] Active politicians disliked the post, but it too
was a convenient refuge for men of standing whom for one

[1]Aspinall, loc. cit., pp. 147, 232–5.
[2]Id., pp. 151–2, 157; Powicke, Johnson and Harte, op. cit., pp. 73–4; *Trans. Cymmrodorion Soc.*, 1948, p. 17.

reason or another it was politic to include in the government with cabinet rank but without departmental responsibility; it was at least more dignified than a mere ministry without portfolio. After all, for the government to tie up all its good debaters with departmental duties was to run the risk of letting the opposition speakers (with no such preoccupations) have it all their own way in debates. Both offices have for the same reason frequently (though no longer automatically) carried with them a seat in modern cabinets.[1]

The office of lord high admiral, though equally ancient, was traditionally equal neither in ceremonial dignity nor in political importance to these others. It was primarily a judicial post in origin, and only during the Buckingham era does its holder appear in the inner ring of Stuart counsellors; memories of that period no doubt accounted for his inclusion by the Long Parliament among public officials calling for parliamentary control. The reorganization of the navy under the two Charleses, followed by the naval wars of the eighteenth century, made the representation of the navy at the hub of government increasingly desirable. Defoe at the beginning of the century places the lord admiral on the outer rim of his central bureau, and by Pitt's time, when the office was almost permanently in commission, the first lord had become one of the 'indispensables' for any normal cabinet, the junior lords (like those of the treasury) being in the ministry but not the cabinet. But the differentiation between politics and administration—so vital to responsible government—proceeded at a more leisurely pace in the service departments than in their civil counterparts. There was one short period under Pitt and one under Addington when (contrary to Gilbertian principles) a professional sailor was made 'ruler of the king's navee'; for admirals, like generals, were still often active politicians, who found in rival political groups useful backing for professional rivalries. It was not until the Reform administration that the first lord of the admiralty got the navy under his control, and could answer to parliament for an organized department of administrators and service chiefs (or sea lords, as they came to be called) analogous to the

[1]The master of the mint was another sinecurist occasionally admitted to early nineteenth-century cabinets on personal, not official grounds (Aspinall, loc. cit., pp. 154–6).

permanent staffs at the home and foreign offices. Responsible government arrived even later in the junior service, as will appear shortly.[1]

We have seen that the secretaries of state had a shorter ancestry: the ordinance regulating their status and duties came just in time to push them in at the tail end of the Tudor order of court precedence, and the office was still not influential enough even a century later to be included in the Long Parliament's list of appointments it claimed to control. Things had so changed by Defoe's day that he would have made one of the secretaries the pivot of government, leaving the other (as was already tending to happen) to merge into the senior civil service. But the widening range of government business—especially in the field of foreign policy—and the gradual demarcation of functions between the two colleagues on a basis of equality, soon made the presence of both in the cabinet a matter of necessity, though without the primacy postulated in Defoe's scheme. The third secretary brought in in 1768 to deal with American affairs disappeared when America was lost, but he was replaced, as soon as we entered into the revolutionary struggle with France, by a secretary for war (also with cabinet rank), to whose department colonial affairs were added from 1801 till the Crimean War.

It was long before the new secretary was in a position to answer to crown or parliament for the armed forces as a whole. He had no jurisdiction over the commander-in-chief; the master of the ordnance controlled a separate department, which had acquired great power and dignity when Marlborough was master, and was loth to part with it; while military finance was under the independent control of the secretary *at* war, an official who first appeared during the interregnum as secretary to the commander-in-chief. It is symptomatic of this divided control that in the early years of the French war (though not afterwards) both commander-in-chief and secretary at war sat in the cabinet alongside the secretary of state for war, and the master of the ordnance remained an integral part of successive cabinets till 1828. It took the disasters of the Crimean war to separate the war office from the colonial office and to extend its authority by abolishing the independent

[1]Keir, *Const. Hist.*, pp. 303, 316–17, 418; Pares, p. 21; *supra*, pp. 36–7, 49, 65, 76.

office of ordnance and other competing controls; another
decade passed before the secretary *at* war disappeared; and it
was left for Gladstone (after a battle royal with the queen) to
make the secretary *for* war responsible for the whole of military
administration, including even the sphere of action of the
commander-in-chief, which had remained a royal preserve.
Only then can it be said that the principles of responsible
government were applied to the army.[1]

The secretaries for the outlying parts of the British Isles stand
on a different footing. It was Peel who first suggested in 1841
that Scotland and Ireland should be represented in the cabinet.[2]
For 140 years after the '45 rebellion Scotland had no secretary,
and even then he did not rank as a secretary of state for another
forty; but he always sat in the cabinet. The Irish secretary, on
the other hand, was technically secretary to the lord lieutenant
and therefore not an appropriate person to sit in a cabinet that
might issue orders to his own chief. The latter, although
obviously a high dignitary of state, was difficult to include in
cabinets because of his infrequent residence in London. Yet
the appointment was often of paramount political importance,
as members of the Long Parliament realized when (remembering Strafford) they included it among those to be subjected to
parliamentary control. In eighteenth and early nineteenth
century cabinets Ireland remained unrepresented except for
one brief appearance of the secretary; but in Victoria's reign,
as Irish problems grew more insistent in politics (and com-
munications less deterrent), it became increasingly common to
have the Irish secretary in the cabinet; at the height of the
home rule controversy there were two occasions when the lord
lieutenant sat there instead, as well as his chancellor. The
secretaryship for Wales is still in its infancy, and like the
secretaryship for war during its first forty years it is still
attached to an established department of state—which at least
ensures a cabinet spokesman for Welsh affairs.

The chancellor of the duchy of Lancaster was in origin a
legal official, in prestige well below the great court dignitaries,
but with a special relation to the crown arising from his
connexion with the royal duchy. In Stuart days he was an

[1]*Supra*, pp. 75–8; Keir, pp. 418, 496–7.
[2]Aspinall, loc. cit., p. 200 n.

obvious choice for one of the king's men in the commons; indeed James I's failure to save his chancellor of the duchy from expulsion at the hands of fellow-members for corrupt electioneering in the duchy was an early sign of the declining influence of 'those about the Chair'. As with the lord privy seal, his dignity increased as his duties diminished; eighteenth-century chancellors of the duchy were often peers, and often admitted to the inner cabinet as personal agents of the crown. It is in Pitt's later ministry that the transition occurs whereby they come to the chosen from among party connexions, and brought into the cabinet only when the need arises for offering a stepping stone or a consolation prize to some supporter who must be humoured.[1]

During the same transitional period dignified household officials like the lord steward, whose posts had become purely ceremonial, finally disappeared from the 'efficient' cabinet, attending only those rare and special meetings of the 'nominal' cabinet in the royal presence to which reference has already been made. Of the two remaining functions of this interesting survival, that of advising on the prerogative of mercy disappeared at the accession of Victoria, whose youthful sensibilities ministers wished to save from too intimate a contact with the harsh realities of crime; meetings for the reading of the royal speech continued, usually at the end of a privy council meeting—which led to a gradual confusion in the minds of all save experienced officials between the outer cabinet and the privy council itself—till in 1921 the accident of an early departure for Balmoral led to a discontinuance of the royal presence and the disappearance of this last relic of the older cabinet.[2]

Although the historic household offices remained the kernel of the 'efficient' cabinet, it had other elements as well. We have seen something of the propensity of the Stuart privy council to work through committees, some of which became permanent and self-contained and included added members from outside. Continued development on these lines would have made a very

[1] Aspinall, loc. cit., pp. 160–2; Willson, *Privy Councillors in the House of Commons*, p. 65. Hawkesbury (later Liverpool), Chancellor of the Duchy from 1791 to 1803, came from the circle of the 'king's friends'; his successors for the next thirty years nearly all belonged to one or other of the party 'connections' (Feiling, chs. xiii–xvii).
[2] Aspinall in *Politica*, iii. 324–44; Namier, *In the Margin of History*, pp. 105–15; E. T. Williams in *History*, xxii. 249–50.

different thing of cabinet government. Presumably the cabinet's task of co-ordinating departments would have fallen to that executive committee to which the privy council was already delegating so much of its routine business by the end of Anne's reign, and the lord president of the council would have evolved into something like a prime minister. This might well have checked the tendency to excessive 'departmentalism' which had become such a menace under Lord North and continues to give trouble today; but it is hard to see how anything like party government could have developed in this atmosphere, since the whole essence of the privy council lay in its transcendence of party. But although the actual evolution of government followed a different pattern, the Stuart boards and committees have left a permanent mark.[1]

The only one of them actually to survive the seventeenth century was the board of trade of 1696, itself a successor to the committee for trade and plantations which existed from the Restoration to 1675. Now the board of trade was concerned only with administration, and its chief activity was that collection and digestion of statistics on which Defoe laid such stress in his plan for a businesslike cabinet. Trade policy lay within the sphere of the treasury, by virtue of its control over the whole system of customs and excise; so it might have been expected that the board of trade would have remained within the ambit of the civil service rather than of politics. But the presidency of the board did not preclude a seat in the commons, and in practice most presidents were active politicians. In Pitt's day some of them were (or became) politicians of eminence: that able administrator (and future premier) Lord Liverpool occupied the post, concurrently with the chancellorship of the duchy, for a dozen years, and after Pitt's death Robinson and Huskisson, two of the competent young men he had brought into politics, maintained the tradition. So the presidency of the board of trade (still more its modern offshoot the ministry of labour) has often carried cabinet rank.[2]

Other boards, constituted later, followed the same general pattern; for example the board of control for India set up under Pitt's act of 1784, the committee of council on education

[1]*Supra*, pp. 49, 53.
[2]Aspinall in *Proc. B.A.*, xxxviii. 160 and n.

established over fifty years later, the local government board which took over the duties of the poor law commissioners in 1871, and in the next decade the board of agriculture. Each was in form a select committee of privy councillors, generally including the chancellor of the exchequer, the principal secretaries of state and the lord president, sometimes the first lord of the treasury and once (in the board of trade) the archbishop of Canterbury; but actually the boards soon ceased to meet and the president became in all but name a minister or secretary of state answering to parliament for his department. In course of time the name followed too: the president of the board of control became Indian secretary after the Mutiny and embodied the principle, established in the trial of Warren Hastings, that colonial administration is also responsible to parliament;[1] the president of the local government board (with added functions) turned into a minister of health after the first World War (when agriculture also achieved ministerial status); the president of the board of education (as the committee of council became in 1901) belatedly followed suit after the second World War. The importance of these developments lay in the principle they embodied, that every important activity of government must have its responsible spokesman in parliament if not in the cabinet.[2]

Even minor departments fell into line: the post office—first of our nationalized industries—had its spokesman from Queen Anne's time in the postmaster general, providing in our own day a precedent for mines and transport and a mouthpiece for the British Broadcasting Corporation; the commission for woods, forests and land revenues—a posthumous fruit of Pitt's reforms in the management of those crown lands brought under parliamentary supervision at the beginning of the reign— was answered for by the first commissioner; and the same applies to public works when in 1851 they were separated from 'woods and forests' and given their own board (and later ministry) with a view to tighter parliamentary control over government expenditure in building. Whether such ministers were or were not included in any cabinet depended on their personal importance and on the dominant political issues of the moment. As

[1]Keeton, *Passing of Parliament*, p. 52.
[2]Maitland, *Const. Hist.*, 1909, pp. 412–3.

ministries multiplied, so cabinets kept defying repeated efforts
to restrict them to manageable limits, just as the privy council
had done before—and with the same risk of leakages; of these
the periodic cabinet dinners which had now become a fixed
institution, with tongues loosened by wine and servants all ears,
became as fruitful a source as the 'avenues wher woemen and
others hearken' of which Clarendon had complained long ago
when the council met in private houses.[1]

Long before Pitt's administrative reforms began to reach
their fruition, the peaceful interlude in politics which had
made them possible was rudely interrupted. First came the
onset of the king's mental malady, involving the regency of the
prince who (after the fashion of Hanoverian heirs apparent)
had taken the whig opposition under his wing. That Pitt made
hasty preparations for a return to the bar is a measure of the
continuing influence of the crown in politics; no wonder he
made it his business to checkmate the jubilant Foxites when
they pressed for the automatic assumption by the regent of full
royal powers, and to insist on limitations which would cripple
any plot on the part of his *protégés* to dig themselves in for good.
But this time the attack soon passed off, and in the chastened
mood with which it left him the king declared that henceforth
his part in government would be confined to keeping 'that
superintending eye which can be effected without labour or
fatigue'. No doubt there was more than a touch in these pro-
testations of 'the devil was sick, the devil a monk would be', for
George III had no intention whatever of renouncing the
initiative, as Pitt found when the question of catholic emancipation became acute, and his successors from the very outset
of their ministry. He still expected, too, to be kept informed
of the 'tone and temper' of the cabinet discussions leading up to
the decisions conveyed to him in formal minutes.[2]

No sooner had the king recovered than the French Revolution broke out. Even this did not seriously check Pitt in his re-
forming career, nor damp his hopes of continuing peace abroad;
indeed, with France out of action for the time, those hopes rose
higher than ever. But once the revolutionary wars began in
1793, Pitt had no respite from them (except for his short period

[1]Aspinall, loc. cit., pp. 157–63, 186–7, 193; cf. *supra*, p. 49.
[2]Aspinall, loc. cit., pp. 202, 195; Pares, op. cit., p. 183; Guttmacher, pp. 260–1.

out of office) till his death thirteen years later. Reforms had to yield to the only two urgent tasks—winning the war and paying for it; and the minister had to abandon schemes he had set his heart on for his father's rôle—so much less congenial to the son —of *malleus Francorum*.[1] But of course there are significant differences between the situation in 1756–62 and that of 1793–1815. The struggle was no longer for prestige, but for existence, and for that reason the premier had the loyal support not only, like Chatham, of the country, but also—unlike him—of the crown and the commons, excepting only the small Foxite opposition. It was also on too vast and complex a scale to brook such direct interventions as had come from George III (for example) during the American war. The chief point on which king and minister differed was that to George, as to the labour element in the Churchill cabinet of 1940, the war was an ideological crusade, where no compromise was possible, while Pitt, like his great successor, looked on it more realistically as a struggle for existence and for empire. In spite of this, the king did allow Pitt to embark on peace overtures in 1795 and again in 1797, confident that no terms conceded by France could be acceptable to the old whigs, who shared the royal view of the war and without whose votes (in view of the scantiness of his personal following) he could not carry the house. George's political shrewdness had not deserted him: he was right both times. Even in strategy it has been maintained that royal criticisms of ministerial policy were often justified by events; yet when the minister made a stand the king always withdrew— a startling reversal of the seventeenth-century rôles of monarch and minister.[2]

The chief internal effect of the war so far as politics are concerned was a new alignment of parties, of great moment for the future. Burke and the old whigs, now led by Portland, with what was left of North's following, came over to the government, leaving opposition to the tiny remnant of new whigs under Fox who continued (when they did not absent themselves from the house altogether) to hold aloft the banner of parliamentary reform, party government, and peace with revolutionary

[1]Halévy, op. cit., i. 15–16n.
[2]Barnes, pp. 269–301; but Professor Aspinall points out that the negotiations of 1797 were actually begun without the king's knowledge (loc. cit., p. 212n.).

France. Because it was this coalition that eventually formed
the nucleus of the new tory party when the struggle for
parliamentary reform reached a climax, Pitt has sometimes
been called its founder. Nothing could be farther from the
truth. Pitt was as impatient of party as his father had been: he
firmly declared himself 'unconnected with any party whatever'. It was round the Portland whigs, rather than the small
but able body of Pittites, that the reconstituted party was
built, and it was never able completely to absorb Pitt's more
faithful disciples. Canning and Huskisson were to bring the
first breath of liberalism into the long and sterile tory *régime*
that followed the war; and Canning's ideas in turn were to be
transmitted, directly through Palmerston and Melbourne,
and then less directly (but far more effectively) through Gladstone—'bred under the shadow of the great name of Canning'—
to enter into the new liberalism of the nineteenth century. Pitt's
zeal for administrative reform, economy, free trade and peace
abroad found an echo in the liberal war-cry of 'peace, re-
trenchment, reform' and an enthusiastic response, as in his own
day, in the breasts of the commercial middle classes—Tenny-
son's 'niggard throats of Manchester'.[1]

It would hardly be too much to say that the legislative output
of the years following 1832—still more that of the liberalism
born of the union of Peelites, whigs and radicals—had its
remoter source in the bureaucratic tradition of the 'king's
friends' attached to Pitt, re-emerging from reaction in the 'en-
lightened' wing of the Liverpool ministry, as well as its more
proximate source in the 'philosophic radicals'; for radicalism,
at once authoritarian and levelling, has far closer affinities
with the Patriot King idea than with aristocratic whiggism,
whether that of the old whigs who formed the backbone of post-
war toryism, or even of Fox and his successors. It was tories
in 1744 and radicals in 1780 who espoused the principle of
'instructions' from electors to elected; it was Burke, the old
whig, who so strenuously repudiated the idea in his classic
speech at Bristol in the latter year; and Fox himself, despite
his flirtation with the freeholder's movement, gave the last

[1]Trevelyan, *British History of the Nineteenth Century*, 1923, p. 41; Feiling, p. 152;
    Barnes, pp. 267, 387–8, 469–70; Pares, p. 130n.; Morley, *Gladstone*, 1905,
    i. 25; Namier, *Monarchy and the Party System*, p. 25.

word to the house of commons where Pitt would have given it to the electorate.[1]

Yet as they hardened into party groups, both blocks of Pitt's disciples lost sight of his inherited belief in 'a patriot king presiding over a united people'; and here he himself (again following his father) had begun to weaken before his death. For in his second ministry, after he had at last brought himself to the point of rallying his personal followers against the feeble Addington, Mr. Feiling perceives a definite 'sharpening of party lines', such as had long been apparent on the opposition benches. For Fox and his followers had firmly established in the public mind the notion of an organized opposition, with an alternative programme and a recognized leader (outside the royal household), as a normal part of the machinery of government—an opposition not incompatible with orderly political life, however violent its language, because it had so much in common with the majority groups on such fundamental questions as property and the social order—even on the war itself once it became a struggle for national existence. It was an express repudiation of George III's principle that a politician on coming into office must disown the wild oats he had sown in opposition.[2]

Pitt has also been claimed, in rivalry with Walpole, Melbourne or Peel, as our first real prime minister. What grounds can be advanced for the claim? The obvious limitations imposed by the continued royal initiative in politics have already been dwelt on. They must not be exaggerated, of course. Pitt could never have been a tool or a mouthpiece like North, and as the tasks of government grew heavier and the king's mood (after his first illness) more subdued, George was generally glad, until some acute point of principle arose, to give the minister his head—even in patronage. Here the big exception was the dispute in 1795 over the appointment of a commander-in-chief with control over discipline and promotions, on which Pitt insisted with a view to placing all this, at so vital a time, beyond the reach of backstairs intrigue. The king yielded the point, and then spiked Pitt's guns by nominating for the post

[1]*Supra*, p. 139; Burke, *Works*, ed. Rogers 1837, i. 256–72; W. R. Brock, *Lord Liverpool and Liberal Toryism*, 1941; Feiling, p. 159; Pares, p. 134; Aspinall, loc. cit., p. 242n.
[2]Feiling, pp. 166, 240; Pares, pp. 119n., 130n.

his favourite son the duke of York. The backstairs intrigues continued with a vengeance through the duke's unspeakable mistress (but without his knowledge), till she provoked an open scandal in parliament; but although the duke's prowess in the field comes off badly in the popular nursery song, as an administrator of the army he was an outstanding success. In this respect at least the royal judgement was once more vindicated.[1]

And what of Pitt's leadership in the cabinet? 'This young man', said Dundas at the beginning of the ministry, 'does not choose to suffer it to be doubtful who is the effectual minister'; but looking back on it thirty years later, one of the young administrators Pitt brought into politics felt some reserves. He found his chief overbearing only towards opponents;

> With his friends he was far too yielding. He was led entirely by Mr. Dundas . . . I do not believe that there was ever a less united Cabinet, and nothing prospered except Mr. Pitt's never-to-be-equalled management of the House of Commons.

Part of the difficulty lay in Pitt's own temperament: to the world he presented a front of 'marble', but he was capable of inspiring in a few chosen intimates the undying devotion that the name of Pitt had evoked in the last generation—with the result that his colleagues competed for his favours in his lifetime, and after his death for recognition as sole purveyor of the authentic gospel. In addition to this, conditions of global war and universal espionage called for 'secresy and dispatch' to a degree never dreamed of even in the machinations of Charles II; there were papers that were circulated only to the heads of the foreign office and the service departments and chiefs, and times—recalling the days of the Treaty of Dover—when our ambassador to France wrote dummy dispatches for circulation to the full cabinet and genuine ones for the select inner circle.[2]

Occasionally—maybe four times during the long years of the ministry—cabinet ministers would 'contract out' of a decision

---

[1]Fortescue, *History of the British Army*, iv. 406–9, 876–80, vii. 29–31, xi. 92–3; R. Fulford, *Royal Dukes*, 1933, ch. ii.
[2]Feiling, p. 158; Aspinall, loc. cit., p. 203n., 210–12; Pares, pp. 158–61.

they disapproved by sending individual 'dissents' in writing to the king. Their very rarity suggests that joint responsibility was coming to be accepted as the normal assumption, a dissentient minority (as Professor Aspinall puts it) resigning either its place in the cabinet or its opinions. George for his part occasionally seized the opportunity to interpose his own opinion, but never to undermine the premier's authority; his overriding aim was always to promote a common front against the common peril. As had so often happened before, from William III's day to Chatham's, danger from abroad brought about a closing of the ranks and a quest for genuine leadership; yet popular as the ageing and afflicted king had now become with a sentimental public, it was round Pitt that the country rallied —country gentry as well as the increasingly important merchants and townsmen. He was the real focus of unity—'the pilot who weathered the storm', and in whose honour Pitt clubs were founded far and wide as symbols of common devotion to the national heritage. So complete was his ascendancy in his second ministry that a colleague described it as 'a government of one man alone', and when in 1806 death removed the pilot the crew felt unequal to carrying on without him.[1]

With a heavy heart, the king entrusted the government to a coalition of whigs, Pittites and Addingtonians, even withdrawing the veto he had imposed over twenty years earlier by admitting Fox as foreign secretary. But if ministers thought they could take advantage of this chastened mood to outwit him over catholic emancipation (on which his veto remained) by introducing a measure embodying much more than the mild concessions he had reluctantly authorized, they soon found their mistake. The king was adamant, and even Portland, titular leader of the old whigs, advised him to veto the measure should the ministry manage to rush it through the house. This extreme step proved unnecessary. Finding themselves outgeneralled, the so-called Ministry of All the Talents resigned after a few months of power to make way for the return of most of Pitt's last cabinet under the nominal premiership of Portland but with the Addingtonian lawyer Spencer Perceval (who had never held cabinet rank before) as leader of the commons. Although in forming his ministry Portland followed (in

[1] Aspinall, loc. cit., pp. 203, 216–17; Pares, pp. 158–9; *supra*, pp. 65, 106, 115–16.

opposition to the crown) the whig principle of *carte blanche* with junior appointments and discussion only over the cabinet itself, the house was restive under this new display of the prerogative, and Perceval could control neither it nor the cabinet— still less Portland, who was desperately ill. Yet the king still had a shot in his locker. Gauging aright the temper of the country, he dissolved parliament in April, 1807, after a session of only six months, and made his last appeal to the electorate against the commons on the catholic issue.[1] He got his majority; his 'protestant' ministry remained in power until Portland's resignation two years later, and then (after reconstitution with Perceval at the treasury) till the new premier was assassinated in 1812. But two years before this the king's mind had become finally deranged under the weight of domestic sorrows and public worries, and in 1811 his political life was brought to an end by a new Regency Act conveying regal authority to the prince of Wales under similar limitations to those imposed in Pitt's day. But Fox was now dead, and his henchmen bungled negotiations with the prince regent in such a way as to sicken him of whig 'dictation' and to ensure his continued support for what was to all intents and purposes an all-tory ministry.

Although the nominal reign of George III lasted till 1820, it is from 1811 that we must date the effective reign of George IV and the end of a classic struggle in which his father had been forced—by Act of God rather than the fortunes of war—to cede one after another of the outworks of personal monarchy, but never the inmost citadel. 'He continued', concludes Professor Pares, 'nearly till the end of his political life to do for his country what it had not yet the means of doing so well for itself'.[2] The situation his son inherited may be briefly summarized. In the first place the ascendancy of the prime minister in the cabinet had become so firmly established by the end of Pitt's career that its abeyance under his weak successors, and the virtual return to departmental government, were felt as an acute drawback by ministers; to George's son, whether as regent or as king, these conditions offered illusory openings for

---

[1] Aspinall, pp. 204–5, 231n.; Pares, pp. 111, 123; Feiling, p. 262; Michael Roberts in *E.H.R.* 1. 61–77.
[2] Pares, p. 207.

the display of a political acumen he inherited only in a limited degree, in circumstances where it could no longer have more than nuisance value in a battle of wits with his ministers. Not many years passed before exasperated ministers were ruefully citing George III as a model of constitutional propriety. It was still possible as late as the year of Pitt's death for a responsible minister to declare the very name of prime minister unconstitutional, but that was now mere pedantry; a man like Dundas, who knew from long experience what was needed for smooth and efficient administration, was perfectly well aware that 'power must rest in the person generally called the First Minister, and that Minister ought . . . to be the person at the head of the finances'. It was no longer the king, but the prime minister who normally summoned meetings of the cabinet and determined its agenda;[1] and the cabinet itself, save only in its predominantly aristocratic composition (which remained till the end of the last century), was taking on its modern shape as a directorate of working departmental ministers.

Acceptance of the idea of joint responsibility came more slowly. Fox himself repudiated it (when it suited his convenience) during the 'Talents' ministry; yet in the same debate it was warmly defended by the tory Castlereagh, and within a few years it was accepted as a commonplace by all parties. On the other hand it was still not true that defeat necessarily involved collective resignation. There were always ministers who stayed on from one ministry to the next, and the process of cabinet-making remained for some time closer to contemporary French than to contemporary British practice. Cabinet unanimity on questions which were a matter of practical politics had become an accepted convention; on questions not likely to become subjects of government legislation the widest divergence was possible, as it still is—witness protection in Balfour's cabinet, women's suffrage in Asquith's, and a host of domestic issues in war-time coalitions. The great difference lay in the fact that so many burning issues then lay outside the range of practical politics simply because of the continued vigour of the royal veto. For this reason almost every cabinet from Pitt's to the end of the reign had to leave catholic emancipation and parliamentary reform as open questions.

[1]Aspinall, loc. cit., pp. 174–6, 203–4, 214–6, 245n.; Namier, op. cit., pp. 8, 24ff.

It was on this last issue that the future of responsible government now hung. Thanks to the steady reduction of patronage the direct influence of the crown in politics had diminished to a point where (in Mr. Feiling's words) the royal name was becoming 'an incantation rather than a force', depending on peerages and honours rather than monetary rewards; and the 'king's friends' were a vanishing factor in politics, numbering less than forty of the commons in George IV's reign. Nor could the remaining ministerial patronage command, as it had once done, automatic majorities in the commons—hence the dissolution of the short-lived parliament of 1807. For by now control of elections was stronger than control of parliament. In parliament Influence in its older sense was yielding to the influence of oratory and personality, in which the government might at any moment (with a Canning in opposition) be weaker than its critics. Outside the house a good deal had been done to purify elections, and investigation into jobbery had been given a new lease of life by military failures and the duke of York scandal—so much that government could no longer keep its control of borough votes by means of its own funds, but only through the goodwill of borough-owning supporters; yet the broad truth is that ministers were becoming responsible to parliament faster than parliament to the constituencies, and much faster than the constituencies were adapting themselves to those new centres of population and forms of property which the industrial revolution was in process of creating.[1]

---

[1]Feiling, pp. 258–9, 263; *E.H.R.*, lxii. 493; Brock, *Lord Liverpool and Liberal Toryism*, ch. iv. On the decline of personal monarchy see Pares, ch. vi, Foord, loc. cit., pp. 482, 507, *passim*.

X

Reform in a Rush

1811–41

THE prince regent was by no means without political acumen, while in knowledge of and contacts with the continent he scored heavily over his unashamedly insular father. What he lacked was the patient industry, the solidity of character and the overruling patriotism that made the old king, especially in his later years, respected even where he was not loved. His son, on the other hand, drove even so sturdy a monarchist as Wellington—still more the irreverent Canning—to the point where he could speak of the king in tones of disrespect such as Fox himself would have shrunk from using of George III.[1] For the elder George always acted in what he conceived, rightly or wrongly, to be the interests of the country, whereas his son's preoccupation was at the best with the safety of the monarchy, and at the worst of his own skin. The outbreak of the French Revolution had not disturbed his friendship with Fox (who sympathized with it) as long as the Channel kept it in quarantine, but when the infection showed signs of spreading to our own shores—revealing itself, as he may well have thought, in the assassination of Perceval, the first prime minister of his permanent regency—his reaction was that of a confirmed hypochondriac.

[1]Feiling, *Second Tory Party*, p. 327; Aspinall in *Proc. Brit. Acad.*, xxxviii. 221; *E.H.R.*, xxxviii. 206; Namier, *Monarchy and Party Government*, p. 6.

The contrast appears in the way the two Georges reacted towards catholic emancipation, which both regarded as contrary to their coronation oath. To George III it was primarily a question of honour and an ingrained insular protestantism. His successor, far more of a man of the world—and far less of a man of honour—was at least no protestant bigot; how could he be after a morganatic marriage with a lady of the proscribed faith? His concern was with personal prestige and the susceptibility of Ireland—the storm-centre of the conflict—to subversive influences from France. So far as domestic politics are concerned, this question dominated the whole period of his regency and most of his reign. What the country desired was now in little doubt, for the first elections of the new era (like the last of George III's effective reign) took place in an atmosphere where opinion counted more and Influence less than perhaps at any time since the Hanoverians came in. There were still plenty of Eatanswills, of course, but feeling was running against them, and when bribery could be proved there was recent legislation to provide the remedy. Above all, the press had now become an active force in politics, which the government could influence only in a limited degree, and from which proceedings in parliament could no longer be concealed. In short, the time has arrived when the term 'public opinion' may be used without anachronism.[1] Now there is every indication that the Georges were right in their belief that public opinion was against catholic emancipation—so much so that when at last the measure became law in 1829 many indignant tories, convinced that a 'free' election would have scotched it, became converts to parliamentary reform. But public opinion was even more intent on a speedy and successful end to the long-drawn wars which were being so badly bungled by the politicians, however heroically their blunders might be redeemed on the field of battle. To non-party men—and they still formed the bulk of the population concerned in politics at all—this meant, as when danger threatened again in 1915, a coalition government which would make full use of the ablest men in politics (many of whom, like Canning, were in opposition), and postpone controversial issues like the Irish question till the war was over.

[1]Feiling, pp. 275, 294; *E.H.R.*, lxii. 487; Aspinall, *Politics and the Press*, 1949; Pares, *George III and the Politicians*, pp. 198–201.

A clear pointer was given when after Perceval's death an independent country gentleman managed to carry in the house a motion for a strong and comprehensive ministry—an unprecedented and ominous interference with the executive by an element in the house which had always stood for a monarchy free to choose its own servants. Nothing could have served better the ends of personal monarchy, and the regent made a show of compliance; but he cleverly contrived to manœuvre both whigs and Canningites into a position where the blame for the breakdown of negotiations could be thrown on them, and he could reshuffle his tory ministry under a leader of their own choice, who proved to be Lord Liverpool. In its immediate effects the strategem worked well: catholic emancipation was postponed for another seventeen years, and the regent had a 'true blue' ministry which lasted out his regency and (after reconstruction and dilution) most of his subsequent reign— almost as long a span as Pitt's first spell of power. Whether on a longer view his political *finesse* served the ends of personal monarchy may be doubted; what he had done was to consolidate the new tory party, and in so doing to make party government inevitable. In vain did he try, after Liverpool's death, to wriggle out of the toils of party so as to keep his own independence. One by one the smaller independent groups were absorbed in the two main parties, narrowing each time the sovereign's freedom of choice. And with the two-party system went all the implications of responsible government— the eccentric creed of a small minority in the last generation, but now taken for granted even by Liverpool himself. His ministry indeed owed its stability not (as George fondly imagined) to royal influence, but to the sound sense of a leader in whom lack of any brilliant gifts was amply compensated by steadiness of purpose, loyalty to colleagues and a wide experience in major and minor office which had brought home to him the essentials of good administration.[1] Under him the cabinet achieved a measure of inner cohesion and collective purpose unknown since the days of Pitt—hardly even then if Perceval was right in claiming that Pitt's was to all intents and purposes a one-man band.

[1] Aspinall in *Proc. Brit. Acad.*, loc. cit., pp. 226–7; Feiling pp. 267–9; Pares, op. cit., p. 183; M. Roberts in *E.H.R.*, li. 466–87.

The ministry was fortunate in that the war was at last taking a turn for the better, so that it was spared the backbiting and recriminations over policy and strategy that had rent its inglorious predecessors. Then with victory came the problems of social dislocation, revolt and repression, on which the regent and his tory ministers were at one. The testing time came after the regent had become king, and had reluctantly consented to broaden the cabinet by bringing in representatives of the more liberal element in the Pitt tradition. Peel, Huskisson and Robinson caused no friction, for the time seemed ripe for a resumption of mild administrative reform, and Peel at least was an unbudging 'protestant'; but Canning as foreign secretary was far too ready to brush aside the interests of foreign autocrats struggling against internal revolution when their activities jeopardized our markets abroad. This aroused the king to a fresh outburst of political activity in the threatened cause of legitimate monarchy. He had been loth to admit Canning to office at all; it was Liverpool who insisted, against several of his colleagues affronted by this 'forcing of the king's hand', that the premier must be final judge of what is needed to enable him effectively to carry on the king's government. Having yielded with an ill grace, George determined that at least he would not let this dangerous firebrand have his head at the foreign office. In Hanover he had a source of secret information on continental affairs from which his foreign minister was excluded; and he also formed the habit of entertaining foreign diplomats at week-end parties at Windsor Cottage, where he deliberately set out to checkmate his minister's schemes and to establish a counter-diplomacy of his own—with the great tactical advantage that he had access to Canning's secrets while Canning remained ignorant of his. Even Wellington, a member of the cabinet as master of the ordnance, lent himself in some degree to these intrigues; but the duke never mastered the principles of responsible government, any more than he understood Canning, whom he had initially urged the king to appoint.

It was a game that two could play at, and in the long run Canning had the better hand and a far better head for playing it. Liverpool loyally backed him up, and scotched the king's manoeuvre for breaking down the solidarity of the cabinet by individual consultations that would reveal internal fissures. More important still was Canning's mastery of the house of commons; he did not speak idly when he declared that if the king had not come to heel he would have resigned on this issue and exposed the whole business in the house—with results that could well have been fatal to monarchy. Above all, he was a master of his own job, and his diplomatic successes left the 'Cottage *coterie*' high and dry, much as Stanhope had scored over Bernstorff for the same reason more than a century earlier.[1] In 1825 George IV 'surrendered at discretion' to his minister. No one had ever scored over his father like that; but then George III learnt better than to expose himself to such a rebuff.[2]

Two years after this, Liverpool was incapacitated by illness and had to resign the premiership. Canning's standing in parliament and in the country, after his brilliant vindication of British diplomatic independence against the European auto-crats, made him the obvious successor; but the 'ultras' in the cabinet were determined (apart from the social prejudice against an actress's son) not to risk the protestant ascendancy by a premier who openly favoured the catholic claims. Welling-ton let it be known that under pressure he might take the post himself, but he knew, as did every other realist in politics, that 'the cabinet would not remain a week' if Canning left it, and Canning for his part made it clear that he must be *aut Caesar aut nullus*. For two months the administration remained without a head while frenzied negotiations went forward between the conflicting groups and personalities. The king tried to evade the issue by again asking the cabinet to choose their own leader, but this time they threw the ball back to him.

Public opinion, as revealed in the press of all colours, made itself unmistakably felt in support of Canning, and the popular hero also knew how to play on the king's fear of becoming a tool of factions. 'I have a better opinion', he wrote, 'of the real vigour of the Crown when it chooses to put forth its strength, and I am not without some reliance on the body of the people'. 'Sir,' he said to George IV, 'your father broke the domination

[1]*Supra*, p. 100.
[2]Temperley, *Foreign Policy of Canning*, 1925, ch. xi, and in *E.H.R.*, xxxviii. 207–24, xxxv. 200, 574; Aspinall, loc. cit., pp. 201, 221–2, 231, 249; Feiling, pp. 311, 317, 332; W. R. Brock, *Lord Liverpool and Liberal Toryism*, ch. vii.

of the Whigs. I hope your Majesty will not endure that of the
Tories'. That decided the king: 'No, I'll be damned if I do,'
he burst out, and he charged Canning to form a coalition
ministry in which the 'ultras'—notably Wellington, who in
pique went so far as to resign his position as commander-in-
chief—were replaced by a group of pro-catholic whigs. His
greatest *coup* was to include in it, with the revived title of lord
high admiral, the king's own sailor brother, the future William
IV, whose warm admiration for George did not extend to his
high tory sentiments. The appointment, however, was not a
success and soon had to be cancelled by the king.[1]

The crisis of 1827 reproduces many of the features of that of
1784, including the violent partisanship it provoked. Once
more the struggle resolved itself into one of an upstart minister,
backed by king and public, against an aristocratic and exclusive faction—but after an election which (unlike that of 1784)
was completely indecisive owing to the confusion of parties.[2]
And there were two other vital differences: Pitt was George
III's own choice, whereas George IV would have seized with
both hands any chance of evading a Canning ministry without
loss of face; and Canning for his part needed no exertion of
royal influence to secure his majority in the commons, whatever
the lords might say or do. But he was already a sick man when
his chance came, and his ministry was aptly dubbed by
Metternich Canning's 'hundred days'. His disciple Robinson
(now in the lords as Goderich) tried to hold it together on his
death, but although an able administrator he was no leader,
and after a few months of it the king sent in 1828 for Wellington.
With Peel as leader of the commons the duke formed a ministry
in which the 'ultras' greatly preponderated, with a few representatives of the more liberal wing of the party in minor posts—
unless (like Peel himself) they were reckoned 'safe' on the
catholic issue.

During the brief Goderich episode personal monarchy,
strengthened by reflected glory from Canning, had looked like
coming into its own again: if anyone was prime minister
during those months it was George IV. But in Wellington, no

[1]Temperley, op. cit., ch. xviii; Feiling, pp. 332, 350–7; Aspinall, loc. cit., pp. 221–
2; Pares, pp. 158–9.
[2]Feiling, pp. 330, 343.

less than in Canning, he met his match. For Wellington had learned much since his vagaries as a tyro in politics three years earlier, and he would brook no tampering with his authority as premier either from colleagues or from the crown. It was now that the long-drawn issue of catholic emancipation was brought to a head by the agitation of O'Connell, which faced the government with the alternatives of lowering its flag or landing the country in civil war. Wellington, as a good soldier, knew when to retreat, Peel was ready to follow, and the king, after trying in vain to ban the subject from cabinet discussions, had to yield; but the fact that (again unlike his father, who was not given to 'speechifying') he had trumpeted abroad so noisily his determination never to betray his coronation oath, undermined the spurious prestige he had so recently gained; it was another blow to the Patriot King.[1] Next year George IV died, and was succeeded by his more mediocre and less flamboyant brother the ex-lord high admiral.

William's accession did not by any means lead to a tame abandonment by the crown of what remained of its initiative in politics. In some ways he was a paler edition of the brother he so much admired. He had his own views on patronage, on which he was sometime tiresomely insistent. Still worse, he had his own views on foreign policy, which owing to his propensity for making indiscreet speeches could sometimes cause acute embarrassment to ministers. He also had in his private secretary (Sir Herbert Taylor) an unofficial adviser, of decided political views which were not always in accord with those of his official advisers. Luckily, however, Taylor understood and accepted the basic principles of responsible government, and his advice never landed the king in the risk of a head-on clash with ministers, while William for his part was always on his guard against 'backstairs intrigues' and 'irresponsible advisers'. In the last resort, however often the king might declare (like his niece after him) that he would 'never consent' to this or that, ministerial advice always prevailed—partly, perhaps, through Taylor's restraining influence, partly from the king's greater pliancy of character and lack of persistence, but chiefly because the issue had, in the main, been decided during the last reign, and he knew that if the gloves were off he was bound

[1]Aspinall, loc. cit., pp. 207–9, 239–41.

to lose.[1] The only real constitutional crisis of the reign was the struggle for parliamentary reform, which at last came to a head now that Canning (who had always opposed it) was dead and the bulk of his followers had drifted into the whig camp, while some even of the more rigid tories had come to believe that a mild extension of the franchise could not be worse than the 'betrayal' of the protestant ascendancy in the teeth of what they believed (with some reason) to be a hostile public opinion.

The first election of the new reign was held under the shadow of a bloodless revolution in France and acute economic distress at home, and the duke's government suffered some shrewd blows. But the results of an election were no longer so easy to interpret as they had been in the good old days when Influence was in full vigour, and the confusion of parties did not help, although, as the Canningites became merged in the whig party, the outlines of a two-party system were beginning to reappear. The duke, at any rate, thought he still had a working majority; a few half-hearted overtures were made (with little response) to renegade Canningites and moderate whigs with a view to broadening the basis of the administration. But the king's speech was framed on strict party lines and the premier plunged into so vigorous a denunciation of reform, and so uncompromising a defence of the constitution as it stood, that many of his own followers were left aghast. The weakness of his position, however, was soon revealed in debates, and defeat in a relatively minor division decided him to resign. The extent to which assumptions, held fifty years ago only by a small minority of the whig party, had now become commonplaces of politics, appears in the automatic resignation of Wellington's whole cabinet and the equally automatic invitation to Grey, who now led the whigs, to form a ministry. It stands in sharp contrast with the circumstances attending the formation of the Canning ministry only five years earlier.

It was the first time the whigs as a party had been in office since the beginning of George III's reign—a period nearly half as long again as the tory exile that preceded it. Ever since the defeat of Pitt's proposals forty-five years earlier, parliamentary reform had been a basic element in the policy

[1]Sir Charles Webster, *Foreign Policy of Palmerston*, 1951, pp. 23–8; Aspinall, loc. cit., pp. 245–51; cf. Sir S. Lee, *Edward VII*, 1927, ii. 34.

of the Foxite rump which had now become the whig party, and motions of varying scope with that end in view had been introduced and defeated in parliament with monotonous regularity. Old whigs and old tories alike set their faces against any fundamental tampering with the constitution, though they were prepared to concede such minor tinkering as measures to put down bribery and the disfranchisement of rotten boroughs which had notoriously offended in this regard. Even the new tories were at best lukewarm and at worst (as with Canning) unbudgingly hostile. So by the time the whigs got back to power, parliamentary reform had become *par excellence* the policy by which the party stood or fell, and the first major task of the new prime minister was to prepare his Reform Bill. The old conventions of the constitution were still in sufficient force and vigour to make it necessary for Grey to obtain the prior permission of the king before embodying so drastic a change in a government measure.[1] Here he experienced no difficulty, for William did not approach politics with that zeal of the convert against his own youthful errors which kept his brother at daggers drawn with the whigs, nor was he averse (remembering George IV's popularity in 1827) from the *kudos* accruing to the crown from association with a popular cause.

Grey's measure had a rough passage in the commons because, unlike Pitt's proposals of 1785, it provided for the extinction of rotten boroughs without compensation to vested interests— a betrayal of the sacred rights of property in the eyes of orthodox whig and tory alike, and acceptable in principle only to the radical 'tail', inspired by O'Connell, which had now attached itself to the whig party. Grey thereupon advised dissolution, and the king consented. By this time the country was thoroughly roused. The election, with its reform associations and its monster meetings, was another 1784 on a vaster and more violent scale, with more revolutionary issues at stake, and with hunger and unemployment, agrarian distress and industrial disputes, stalking in the background. What is most significant is that in almost every constituency candidates had to take sides on reform. The zeal of old county families that took up the cause was often of suspiciously recent origin, but in many a constituency it was the only hope of prevailing against the rival

[1]Aspinall, loc. cit., p. 238.

'interest'; and the upshot was the first election in which the country voted on a clear-cut political issue, without the intervention of royal influence, and returned a party pledged to a definite programme.

A second bill passed the commons but came to grief (as everyone expected) in the lords. Grey thereupon asked the king to create enough peers to swamp the hostile majority, as Anne had done (though Grey did not rely on the precedent)[1] in 1713; but although he had reluctantly agreed to the principle, William drew back when he found that this would mean at least fifty creations at one fell swoop, as against Queen Anne's dozen: and he was fortified by the knowledge—despite Grey's efforts to present a united front—that his reluctance was shared by some of the cabinet. The monarchy might to all intents and purposes abandon its prerogative as a source of jobs, but its character as the fountain of honour was inherent in its very nature. George III and George IV might sanction the extensive but gradual dilution of the peerage by Pitt and then by Liverpool, for if it was not to remain a closed cast it must adapt itself to the needs of changing society; but a wholesale hawking-round of honours such as Grey proposed was another matter: it threatened to cheapen the prerogative and to choke with ridicule the sentiment upholding peerage and monarchy alike. Even eighty years later the same reluctance was felt in a similar situation by George V. There was now nothing left for Grey but resignation, and the king sent for Wellington. The duke's instincts were those of a 'king's friend' rather than a party man, for his intransigence over Canning had been a personal rather than a party matter; he was ready now to eat his words and to bring in a modified reform bill—without which he knew no government could stand—if he could only get together a cabinet to support him. But Peel, as a good party man, would have none of this second betrayal of the party, and without Peel and his friends Wellington could not hope to manage the commons; so the king was thrown back on Grey.

Meanwhile the Bristol burnings, the Birmingham drillings, the threatened run on the bank and organized refusal of taxes, gave clear indication that the only alternative to 'the whole bill and nothing but the bill' was revolution. After vainly trying to

[1] *History*, xxi. 357.

induce Grey to water down his measure, the king recalled him with a virtual *carte blanche*, but he evaded the odious necessity for swamping the peerage by persuading Wellington and his followers—about a hundred in all—to absent themselves from the final divisions; it was a curious repetition in reverse of George III's manœuvres in the upper house over Fox's India Bill. Wellington's strategic withdrawal saved the lords as a balancing factor in politics for the next fifty years, no less than Walpole's successful opposition to the Peerage Bill of 1719 had averted in its day the threat of a closed aristocracy. And so the bill became law. Its effects as a whole do not concern us here, but there are certain aspects which have a close bearing on responsible government. The first is of course the disappearance of the rotten boroughs and the cleansing of the electorate—the completion, in fact, in this broader field of those 'economical reforms' which had begun with Lord North's commission of 1770. Not that either bribery or 'undue influence' disappeared by magic—we have our Dickens to remind us of that. It took a Municipal Corporations Act, a succession of Corrupt Practices Acts and a Ballot Act—to say nothing of four major extensions of the franchise—to bring into being the electoral system of today. But at least the measure of 1832 bridged the gap between commons and constituencies which had been steadily widening since the Restoration.

It did more than that: it opened the way for a new type of constituency, based on numbers rather than on corporateness. This development was of slow growth, as appeared in the chartist demand for equal electoral districts and its gradual translation into Redistribution Acts; it was only completed when the university vote was thrown to the wolves a few years ago. What the average voter still wanted for many years after 1832 was to be represented by the social leaders of his own local community—hence the very slow change in the social composition of the lower house and the equally slow appearance of the 'carpet-bagger' and the professional politician. Indeed the preponderance in politics of a leisured class was at that stage—until education, leisure and the other amenities of life ceased to be monopolies—the only means of satisfying that 'national preference for amateurs over professionals in politics'[1]

[1]Brodrick and Fotheringham, *Pol. Hist. of England*, 1906, xi. 350.

which had formed part of Clarendon's political creed and which finds its best expression in a healthy instinct for self-government and its worst in an unhealthy pride in 'muddling through'.

From this time onwards the conception of an election as a contest between rival political parties rather than rival family groups inexorably gained ground. It was helped by another indirect consequence of the Reform Bill. The adoption of a uniform franchise qualification meant the provision of local machinery for 'vetting' new claimants to the vote. As the duty of registration was placed on the shoulders of the overseers of the poor, who might well be ignorant and overburdened with other duties, voluntary 'registration societies' began to appear in the larger and more politically-conscious constituencies, with a view to contesting fraudulent claims and unjustified exclusions. It was not long before party influences were brought to bear on these organizations, each side bent on pressing the claims of its own known supporters and disputing those of opponents. In these we may see the germs of continuous party organization in the constituencies, where up to now there had never been more than sporadic *ad hoc* committees such as those which framed the 'instructions' of 1742 or arose out of the freeholders' movement of 1780. It took another fifty years to perfect these organizations, so essential to the complete structure of responsible government, but once more the first impulse was felt soon after 1832.[1]

In yet another respect the first Reform Act promoted the tendency towards political elections. It is a familiar fact that the Reform Parliament embarked on a long series of legislative reforms, and so set the fashion of making legislation the primary task of government and the test of its activity and success. This growing habit of mind brought about a subtle change in what was expected of a member of parliament: from being primarily the watchdog for his local community, whose main qualifications were local popularity, a stake in the soil and experience of public affairs, he now developed into a legislator first and foremost, whose political affiliations began to loom larger in the eyes of electors than his social standing.

[1] J. A. Thomas in *History*, xxxv. 81–98; I. Bulmer-Thomas, *The Party System in Great Britain*, 1953, p. 13.

The party system, vital to our brand of responsible government, had thus been built into the political structure—yet it was only four or five years since Palmerston had jauntily prophesied that 'Whig and Tory will soon be erased from our vocabulary' and Goderich had urged that the 'odious distinctions' should be obliterated for good.[1]

Grey was perhaps a stronger premier in his relations with the crown than in his control of his own colleagues. From the king he extorted assent to the general principle that the advice of responsible ministers, formally tendered, was binding, and that without it he would make no public statements and resort to no unofficial consultations.[2] On the other hand, within a couple of years of the passage of the Reform Act Grey's own chancellor of the exchequer, Althorp, who led in the commons, committed himself without the knowledge of premier or cabinet to concessions to O'Connell which his colleagues refused to countenance. Althorp thereupon resigned, and since Grey could no more carry on without him than Wellington without Peel, he went too. The king's choice fell on the ex-Canningite Melbourne, whom he asked to arrange a coalition with Peel. Nothing came of this, and for a few months Melbourne carried on with a reconstructed ministry, until some slighting references to the monarchy in public speeches by Lord Chancellor Brougham led to a sudden dismissal by William of the whig ministers, of whom he was now heartily sick, and who were in any case at sixes and sevens with each other. Since Peel was holidaying on the continent, the king sent for Wellington. The old soldier—except for his one lapse from duty occasioned by hatred of Canning—never refused the call of the crown, and pending his ally's return he manfully set about forming a government with himself as virtually Lord High Everything Else—which he whittled down to the foreign secretaryship as soon as Peel was there to help him fill the other posts.

At the ensuing general election the new government failed to obtain a clear majority over the whigs and their allies, but Peel carried on, issuing to the electorate in his famous Tamworth manifesto a new type of declaration of policy in which

[1]Feiling, pp. 357, 359.
[2]A. B. Keith, *Constitution of England from Victoria to George VI*, 1940, i. 105; Aspinall, loc. cit., pp. 238, 247.

he accepted the Reform Act as a final settlement and outlined a programme of moderate conservative reforms. In this way he set a seal on the new principle of legislative activity as the bait by which a government angles for electoral support, and began the process of 'educating his party' which turned tories into conservatives. Yet he still shrank from the full implications of party government, and even after defeat at an early stage in debates he appealed for support from the opposition benches for a programme of reforms based on the Tamworth manifesto, and fully in line with whig policy. But the whigs stood uncompromisingly by their principle that the party in a majority in the house must rule, irrespective of policies and programmes, and that the job of an opposition is to oppose. A succession of whig victories in the division lobby (including one on the granting of a charter to the 'godless' university of London) decided Peel that the position was hopeless. In spite of entreaties from both William IV and Wellington, he placed his resignation in the king's hands, leaving him powerless to do anything but recall Melbourne (whom he personally liked), even though it meant admitting Lord John Russell (whom he detested) as home secretary and leader of the commons. It is true that Melbourne averted a clash with the king by dropping Brougham, but never since the Fox-North coalition had the monarchy submitted so completely to dictation in the choice of ministers—'storming the closet', in the eighteenth-century phrase.

This was the ministry in power when in 1837 William IV died, and the crown passed to his niece Victoria, an eighteen-year-old girl completely inexperienced in politics. It was therefore on Melbourne, a man who accepted all the consequences of responsible government, that the task devolved of teaching the young queen her job; and it was fortunate for the smooth working of the constitution that a warm affection sprang up between them. The difficulty came when she had to part from him. Like all the Hanoverians, Victoria had been brought up in a partisan atmosphere: her father the duke of Kent had clung more firmly than his brother, William IV, to the whiggism assumed by most of George III's sons in reaction from their father. Her dealings with Melbourne convinced her of the moral superiority of the whigs, and a first brief encounter with

Peel, so sadly deficient in the courtly graces of 'Lord M.', confirmed the impression. Within two years of her accession Melbourne's majority in the house had again sunk below safety level, and he advised the queen to send for his rival. But Peel insisted that her ladies of the bedchamber, many of them wives of prominent whigs, should go out with the cabinet; for if the influence of the aristocratic 'political wives' of the eighteenth century was dead, it was by no means forgotten. William IV had set a precedent for Peel's demand by allowing his ministers to name the household officials, reserving only the right to challenge any names to which he had definite objection. But to interfere in the intimate concerns of a defenceless young queen was another matter. 'I should like to know,' was her withering comment, 'if they mean to give the *Ladies* seats in Parliament?' She flatly refused to yield, and it was Melbourne's turn to come to the rescue of the crown and to struggle on with his precarious majority for another couple of years.[1]

The tories had some ground for seeing in the turn of events the danger of another whig puppet monarchy or even of a new *régime* of 'favourites'; the country's last experience of feminine rule—over a century back and seen only through the distorting mists of time and legend—seemed to lend colour to such suspicions, and then it was the rule of a mature woman, not a susceptible girl. Victoria's letters to Melbourne, and still more what she confided about him to the intimate pages of her diary, were not without disquieting echoes of George III's 'maudlin' correspondence with Bute; but Melbourne was no Bute, and in the intervening seventy years constitutional conventions had hardened to the point where they could no longer be defied. In 1839 the government was defeated by a majority of one, and the ensuing general election confirmed the verdict in unmistakable terms. By this time too the queen had an irremovable counsellor, completely aloof from British parties, in her German husband, who so quickly mastered the conventions of responsible government and did so much to consolidate them. So this time there was no hesitation in sending for Peel and in giving his government ungrudging support.

This brings us to the time when the Durham report assumed as the immemorial basis of constitutional government those

[1]Aspinall, loc. cit., pp. 249–50; Strachey, *Queen Victoria*, 1924, pp. 72–8.

very conventions which had so recently gained general acceptance. Means had at last been found of solving the paradox that
a government which is still the queen's government can be made
removable under automatic rules, while the monarchy itself
is irremovable. The distinction is already implicit in the Long
Parliament's doctrine that the king's servants must do their
duty by the community even though the king in person should
forbid them, but it took another two centuries to evolve
machinery for putting this into practice without the constant
risk of deadlock, rebellion or civil war. Already in George IV's
reign the king, for all his 'legitimist' views of monarchy,
slipped sometimes into the way of talking of the 'government'
as an entity distinct from the monarchy.[1] The delicate line
between the monarch as man or woman and the monarch as
public functionary—which can of course be no more completely
translated from theory to practice than the Euclidian straight
line—involves also the distinctions between privy purse and
public funds, and between royal household and public administration. At each level there remain marginal cases for give-
and-take, where the monarch's personal resources in character,
judgement and experience may come to the aid of his public
prerogatives. At the top level, the choice of the prime minister
by the party had already become established usage, even before
parties acquired any fixity of organization; but this choice is
automatic only when the two-party system is in full vigour.
Discrimination between a number of competing groups or
rival leaders calls for the tact and experience of a permanent
and universally accepted arbiter from outside. Even George
IV's ham-fisted interventions in the case of Canning may well
have been at the time the only means of making effective what
was undoubtedly the country's choice.

By the beginning of Victoria's reign it was also true that the
cabinet was in general the premier's choice and not the
sovereign's.[2] If particular names were objected to, the weight
of the royal objections had to be balanced against the indis-
pensability of the minister. Melbourne could not afford to give
in over a key man like Lord John Russell, yet fifty years later
Gladstone could compromise over Labouchere or Dilke,

---

[1]*Supra*, p. 33; Pares, p. 184.
[2]Temperley, *Canning*, p. 110; Aspinall, loc. cit., p. 229; Pares, p. 110.

neither of them essential to the cabinet and both obnoxious to the queen on personal grounds. So too with minor appointments. A move on Brougham's part to whip up again in 1822 the indignation against 'the influence of the crown' which had carried Dunning's 'snap' motion more than forty years earlier fell as flat as the party's attempted resuscitation in 1830 of the old bogy of the civil list, which completely failed on investigation to yield up any more abuses.[1] The concept of a civil service which is really permanent and therefore non-political seems finally to have taken root by way of reaction to the short-lived party ministries that followed the Reform Act. Treasury patronage (contrary to popular belief) had now dwindled almost to nothing, but the various departments, though they could no longer sweep away existing staffs in favour of their own nominees, still had a good deal of freedom in filling gaps and making new appointments; and if these were now rarely made without some sort of proficiency test and period of probation, politics continued to play a part in them (especially near election time) until the relics of a system that had once dominated the whole machinery of government were swept away in the civil service reforms of 1854. In some degree the abolition of patronage weakened the links of the M.P. with his constituents as well as the control of the government of the day over the civil service, for it had long been a custom to allot a good deal of local patronage to the local member, irrespective of party. The final triumph in 1870 of open competition over private patronage was not all pure gain.[2]

On the other hand the influence of the crown acquired new meaning and worth once it had retired from the initiative in politics. Now that the head of the government was a party man with fluctuating tenure, it was all the more necessary that the head of the state should embody that stability that can come only from permanence, and the basic values in public life that transcend party and epitomize the common experience of the nation. In this new context there is still room for the Patriot King in politics.

[1] *E.H.R.*, lxii. 487; Feiling, p. 385.
[2] Edward Hughes in *History*, xxvii. 51–83; Brock, op. cit., pp. 94–102.

Epilogue

L IKE any other historical process, the development of
responsible government has no ascertainable starting
point and no foreseeable end. This study starts with the
reign of James I because it was then that a first approach was
made towards a recognition of the character of the problem; it
ends with Victoria's earliest years because by then, but hardly
before then, most of the characteristic features of our distinctive
system of responsible government had become accepted as
common ground by all parties. But although these basic
doctrines have never since been seriously challenged in
responsible quarters, their application to any particular set of
circumstances has often been in dispute. In any case the constitution cannot stand still in a changing society; from time to
time it has to meet the challenge of new factors like democracy
or the growing activity of the state. So far the structure of
responsible government has remained intact, at least in theory;
whether under the surface conditions have fundamentally
changed and whether the established conventions can in fact
meet the challenges that confront them: these are questions for
the prophet rather than the historian. In these concluding
pages it is proposed to pass in rapid review some of the principal
conflicts provoked by this process of challenge and response
since the system took shape at the beginning of Victoria's reign.

Once she had found her bearings, the new queen was by no
means disposed to accept the rôle of sleeping partner in the
constitution, nor yet of its ornamental façade. If she could no
longer hope for the last word on the choice of ministers, on

foreign policy, or even on the army and the overseas empire—the last ditches of royal prerogative—she was at least determined not to be left without a word, and a cogent one too, which ministers might ignore at their peril. In the prince consort she had a far more effective private secretary than her uncle's Sir Herbert Taylor, and behind him was at first his old tutor Baron Stockmar, with his long service to the Coburgs and his wide knowledge of central Europe. It was a tricky situation, recalling the days of George IV's 'Cottage *coterie*' and even of George I's Hanoverian advisers. For on the fall of Peel's ministry in 1846 Palmerston returned to the foreign office, which he had previously occupied for eleven years, conducting his diplomacy in the spirit of his master Canning. Now Prince Albert was no more a lover of autocracy than Palmerston was a democrat; but temperamentally the two men were poles apart, and Albert's methodical and deferential German mind was shocked by Palmerston's readiness, when it suited his conception of English interests and traditions, to hobnob with European insurgents and to cock a snook at established governments—so long, of course, as they were foreign. And what Albert said was law with the queen—he *knew*; whereas her foreign minister soon developed the habit of evading solemn remonstrances and academic lectures on Europe by conveniently forgetting to show important dispatches to the queen (which meant, of course, to Albert), or leaving no time for the royal couple to read them, or else changing them after approval.

Repeated scoldings having been met only with bland regrets and promises of amendment, the queen was roused at last in 1850 to present to Palmerston through his chief, Lord John Russell, the well-known memorandum drawn up for her by Stockmar, in which she stated what she required of her foreign secretary:

(1) That he will distinctly state what he proposes in a given case, in order that the Queen may know as distinctly to *what* she has given her Royal sanction;

(2) Having *once given* her sanction to a measure, that it be not arbitrarily altered or modified by the Minister; such an act she must consider as failing in sincerity towards the Crown, and justly to be visited by the exercise of her Constitutional right of dismissing that Minister.

The constitutional crisis that such a course might have provoked was averted by the fact that in the end Palmerston managed to exasperate his own premier. Lord John had grown weary of serving as a buffer against the royal wrath and of insinuating in the royal ear that discipline in the cabinet was his job, not hers. When in the following year Palmerston, without consulting queen or colleagues, committed them to a recognition of the *coup d'état* of Louis Napoleon, Russell's retort was to advise the queen to dismiss him. The victim soon had his 'tit for tat' by turning out the government: next year he was back in office— but not the foreign office—in a coalition government.

Meanwhile an ugly situation had developed. Palmerston was as popular with the English people as ever Canning had been, and his defiance of the European despots aroused wild enthusiasm—with a corresponding revulsion of feeling when it was found he had disappeared from the government just at a time when one of those despots, the tsar of Russia, was rapidly becoming our public enemy number one. English popular opinion a century ago did not discriminate too nicely between the various brands of European dynast, and it was not long before broadsheets hawked in London streets were spreading the rumour that

> . . . little Al, the royal pal,
> They say has turned a Russian.

When the war came, and (as usual) went ill for us in the open-ing campaigns, the clamour for Palmerston at the head of government grew too strong to be resisted. By this time the zeal of the court in the common cause had become plain to all, and it made even Palmerston acceptable there as the man most likely to bring the war to a triumphant issue. But the prince consort never relaxed his vigilance in the field of foreign policy as long as he lived. His last public act, less than three weeks before his death in 1861, was to tone down a dispatch—this time to America from Russell, now foreign secretary in Palmerston's second ministry—which in its original form might well have provoked war.[1]

[1]Strachey, *Victoria*, ch. v; Benson and Esher, *Letters of Queen Victoria*, 1908, II. chs. xvii–xx, III. pp. 469–70; B. K. Martin, *The Triumph of Lord Palmerston*, 1924, ch. iii.

After the prince's death the political initiative of the crown slackened appreciably. Victoria was by no means lacking in a will and judgement of her own (as she had shown Albert in their early married days), but without him at her elbow to sift and digest dispatches and to draft memoranda she could not keep an eye on ministers as she had done before, so she became more dependent on them; nor could the long-drawn seclusion of her widowhood fail to react on her political effectiveness. In addition to all this, the range of her initiative was narrowed by the return to the two-party system in all its rigour. From the time that Peel split his party over free trade in 1846, no group had ever commanded a clear majority, and the result was a succession of ministries that were either avowed or virtual coalitions. The active part played by the queen in cobbling together these administrations is amply attested by her letters.

Gladstone's first ministry opened a new era. His assumption of office in 1868 was the first occasion when a ministry went out and a new one came in automatically after winning a general election, without even awaiting the action of the commons. Hitherto a minority government might remain in power as long as the independent member (who still set the tone) refrained from voting it down on any issue it made a question of 'confidence'. This still left him free to enter the opposition lobby in division after division without upsetting the government—a thing he disliked doing unless he was strongly moved. Lord Liverpool remained in power for eleven years after defeat on so crucial a measure as the prolongation after the Napoleonic War of Pitt's new income tax—just as Walpole, more than eighty years earlier, had thrown his excise scheme to the wolves and gone on his way unperturbed.[1] But now followed those halcyon days immortalized by Gilbert in the familiar (and almost true) generalization that

> . . . every boy and every gal
> That's born into this world alive
> Is either a little Liberal
> Or else a little Conservative.

After the second Reform Act, and the party's subsequent defeat by the new artisan electors it had called into being,

[1] Brock, *Lord Liverpool and Liberal Toryism*, pp. 101-6.

G.R.G.—O

Disraeli became 'responsible for starting the first great party machine', with Chamberlain following close on his heels in the Gladstonian cause; and the two giants tossed the political ball back and forth for nearly twenty years, leaving the independent member to 'walk under their huge legs and peep about'. There was not much that the queen could do about it either, except to exhibit her preference for Dizzy by public snubs to his rival such as might well have shocked Albert, with his rigid standards of a monarchy above party.[1]

This period came to an end with Victoria's reappearance in public life at the Jubilee of 1887, and the almost simultaneous emergence of the Irish home rule controversy; this not only reduced Gladstone still lower in the queen's esteem (since he stood for a cause that threatened the integrity of 'her' empire), but by bringing about a new morcellization of parties it restored something of her initiative in the choice of cabinets and even of prime ministers. The years of seclusion may have restricted, but they had by no means destroyed, the queen's independent foothold in politics, and in her closing years she found a new confidential *aide* and adviser in the prince of Wales, whom she had so long held (Hanoverian-fashion) at arm's length from public affairs.[2] She still expected detailed reports on cabinet meetings, and major departures in policy still required her consent (though it was now becoming little more than a courtesy) before they could be introduced as government measures or even brought before the cabinet. The dissolution of parliament she still regarded as her special pre-rogative—her means, should occasion arise, of appealing from ministers and parliament to the people—and it was with the utmost difficulty that she was dissuaded from using it against the advice of her ministers even in the later years of her reign. And we have already seen something of the stiff struggle Gladstone had to induce her to sign the order in council placing the commander-in-chief of 'her' army under the control of a minister responsible to parliament. Resort to orders in council was itself, of course, an act of prerogative, although now exercised on the advice of responsible ministers. Gladstone

[1]I. Bulmer-Thomas, *Party System in Great Britain*, pp. 21–7; J. A. Thomas in *History*, xxxv. 91–8; Keir, p. 407n.; Aspinall, loc. cit., p. 228n.; Pares, *George III and the Politicians*, p. 192.
[2]Sir Sidney Lee, *Edward VII*, 1927, ii. 36.

incurred some damaging criticism from left-wing supporters when in pursuance of his army reforms he induced the queen to use her royal warrant for abolishing the purchase of army commissions, after legislation to that effect had been wrecked on the rock of aristocratic prejudice against turning the army from 'an occupation for gentlemen' into 'a trade for professional men'. Gladstone defended himself (ingeniously, perhaps, rather than ingenuously) by declaring that the order was in fact an amendment of an earlier order arising out of an act of parliament of George III's reign![1] What in fact he was doing was to revert to a convention in full vigour in Pitt's day, scouted by liberalism, but in our own day threatening to creep back in the train of increasing state control and congested parliamentary time: I refer to the principle that administrative reorganization, however sweeping, is a matter for the king or queen in council (in practice nowadays the minister briefed by his expert), rather than for legislative enactment.

Victoria left the crown strong both in popular affection and as an effective partner in the scheme of government. Although its actual initiative was now reduced to rare and critical junctures in politics, its counsel was still valued and respected, and its constant presence in the background of politics gave its rare interventions *proprio motu*, in time of threatened deadlock, an air of what President Harding would have called 'normalcy' rather than of the irruption of some *deus ex machinâ* from without. The republican movement which had begun to gather strength during the years of royal seclusion faded away in the jubilee paeans. Only since the publication in the present century of Victoria's letters, followed by authoritative biographies of her two successors, have we learned how much wider is the scope for monarchy in a political system like ours than is allowed in the classic account of the constitution which Bagehot wrote just as the crown was entering on its phase of temporary decline.

What remained open to criticism was the unmistakable bias of the crown, and this was to be remedied by the queen's successors. Edward VII was no party man: he seems to have got on equally well with the conservative ministers in power

---

[1] Keir, *Const. Hist.*, pp. 485–7; Pares, p. 157; *supra*, p. 167; R. C. K. Ensor, *England, 1870–1914*, 1936, pp. 8–16.

during the first half of his reign and their liberal successors—
except Lloyd George—during the second. If he had a personal
penchant, it was towards a 'set' rather than a party. He had
gained considerable experience of affairs in his mother's old
age, and on no side of his kingly duties—whether patronage or
policy, the formation of cabinets or the prerogative of mercy—
did he ever consent to become a 'rubber stamp'. On any question set before him he seldom failed to digest the facts and to
give an independent opinion. In fact the relations between
crown and minister were now to all intents and purposes those
of the first Elizabeth with Burghley or Walsingham in reverse:
it was the minister who decided, the crown who offered
advice—and if it was rejected, loyally backed the minister up
in a contrary policy. His dominant interest was in European
affairs. In this field he was singularly well informed, even if the
roots of his interest were social rather than political. He had
something of the taste for continental society of his great-uncle
George IV, but he went further by satisfying it in frequent
foreign travel, as wide in scope as was compatible with a quick
return to London in any emergency. The result was an outlook
which was neither insular, like George III's, nor narrowly
Teutonic, like that of most of the other Hanoverians. Indeed
German propaganda was at one time disposed to lay at his door
responsibility for worsening Anglo-German relations; but such
ideas were based on a gross exaggeration of his political influence. The European policy he tried to further by personal
contacts was not his own, but his government's, even if the
absence of a responsible minister at what might become crucial
conversations did at times cause disquietude. On the other hand,
it seems pretty clear that the 'hit' he made in France helped
materially to overcome ancient prejudices on both sides of the
Channel, and so to provide the basis in sentiment for the
political *rapprochement* favoured by both political parties.[1]

The king's last months were darkened by a domestic crisis
which had been blowing up ever since the liberal government
came into power, and which would have taxed to the utmost
his tact and statesmanship had he lived to see it through. As
the monarchy shed its partisanship, the house of lords moved, if

---

[1]Lee, *Edward VII*, II, chs. ii, ix, xv, xxii–xxvi, xxix; Harold Nicolson, *George V*,
1952, p. 141. George III, however, knew his Europe (Guttmacher, p. 129).

anything, in the opposite direction. Although the commons had by 1688 become the predominant partner in the legislature, the upper house remained an important factor in politics; until the present century, for example, it generally provided the majority of the cabinet, if not the premier himself. Under the early Georges it was the stronghold of the exclusive whig cast that controlled politics and the crown itself, but fortunately the attempt to perpetuate these conditions in the Peerage Bill of 1719 came to nothing. George III restored the traditional link between crown and peerage, and when his 'friends' in the commons failed him, a hint to the upper house could generally ensure the rejection of a measure he disapproved, and save him from the odium of a more direct use of the royal veto. The *locus classicus* is of course Fox's India Bill, the defeat of which in the lords brought about the downfall of the ministry; indeed for another half-century after that the lords as well as the commons might vote a government out.[1] Pitt's peerages broke down the old exclusiveness by subjecting the upper house to what became almost annual infusions of new blood; so that the house of lords which rejected the Reform Bills was by no means a partisan assembly. The late Professor Turberville showed that the older aristocracy were mostly for the bill, while those whose peerages dated back to Pitt were almost evenly divided and those of George III's earlier reign showed a small majority against; the votes that turned the scales were those of the bishops and of the Scottish and Irish elective peers.[2]

What changed the situation was the new social policy of liberalism, in which conservatives smelt danger to property and the social order. The old and even the new whigs had stood as solidly by these principles as old tories and new conservatives—if anything more so; this new development meant that the house of lords, as the repository *par excellence* of these threatened values—once common to both parties but now tending to become a party issue—gradually lost the olympian character which had made its function in the state analogous to that of the American supreme court, and became unashamedly partisan like the American senate. It was complained (with some exaggeration) that for conservative legislation the

[1]Pares, p. 40n.
[2]*History*, xxi. 354–5.

upper house was now little more than a registry, but for liberal
legislation an automatic slaughter-house. Conservative leaders
deliberately resolved in 1906 to neutralize the overwhelming
liberal victory of that year by mobilizing the lords against the
new government.[1] It was the Lloyd George budget of 1909,
embodying the social ideals of the most advanced liberal wing,
that brought matters to an issue. Edward VII frankly disliked
it and said so, but he was ready to follow the lead of his constitutional advisers; on the other hand a strong section of the
lords was spoiling for a fight, even though it meant the unprecedented step of rejecting a finance bill from the commons on
the ground that under cover of finance it embodied a social
revolution.

Asquith as premier thereupon advised dissolution, to which
the king assented; the liberals were returned, though with a
much reduced majority, and the lords, accepting this as the
verdict of the country, passed the budget. But this did not end
the matter, for the premier had given pledges that his government would not resume office without 'safeguards' that its
declared policy would be put into effect. As he no longer had
an over-all majority he was dependent on his Irish and labour
allies, the former with their heels dug in against any threat in
the upper house to balk them again of home rule, the latter
opposed to it on principle as the stronghold of wealth and
privilege. The only answer was to push through the commons
a bill drastically limiting the lords' power of veto, and this meant
either a highly improbable act of hara-kiri on the part of the
upper house, or else its coercion by the wholesale creation of
some 500 new liberal peers. Up to the time of the king's death
Asquith had neither specifically approached him on this subject
nor pledged himself *totidem verbis* to do so, but the conclusion
drawn by his followers from his deliberately ambiguous
utterances was that that was the course he would in the last
resort adopt. What King Edward's response would have been
will never be known. It seems unlikely that he would have
followed the advice of a few distinguished non-party men like
the archbishop of Canterbury and Lord Rosebery, and saved
the lords' veto by using his own. All we do know is that his
private secretary—on whose good sense he relied much when

[1] Ensor, op. cit., pp. 386–8.

either compliance or non-compliance with the demands of responsible advisers would have involved him in suspicions of partisanship—was for compliance. But in May, 1910, King Edward died, striving to the last for compromise.[1]

This was the problem inherited by George V, and he tackled it along his father's lines—by strenuous efforts towards conciliation and compromise. He had the satisfaction of persuading both sides to send delegates to a constitutional conference, which sat for nearly six months after the king's accession without achieving a settlement. This threw the ball back to the king, who was subjected to strong pressure, direct and indirect, from all sides. Even his two private secretaries gave opposite advice, Knollys taking the same line as he had with King Edward, while Bigge (afterwards Lord Stamfordham), who had been with him before his accession, strenuously opposed him.[2] Pushed by his cabinet, Asquith was now categorically asking for the large-scale creation of peers which would ensure passage for the Parliament Bill, though he agreed that the issue must first be put squarely to the electorate by another dissolution; and in order to keep the royal name out of electioneering (in which of course the king cordially concurred) he urged that the pledge should be given in advance but kept secret (which George as cordially disliked). With grave misgivings, the king gave in. He stated afterwards that he might have decided otherwise had he been aware that Balfour, as opposition leader, had let King Edward know that in such conditions he would, if invited, try to form a government;[3] but by now Balfour's hold on his party was slipping away—it was in the following year that he gave way to Bonar Law. The liberals won the election with a slight shift in the voting which resulted in a drawn battle between the main parties and left the Irish and socialists as arbiters. The hope of king and premier alike was now that once the 'pledge' was divulged (which was not till after the bill had reached its third reading in the lords, and then only to the leader of the opposition), the more responsible members of the

[1]Lee, loc. cit., ch. xxxi; Nicolson, op. cit., pp. 102–4, 125–9, 138, 234n.
[2]Further light is thrown on the relations between the king's constitutional advisers and his private secretary in another and still acuter crisis by an article in *The Times* for 29 Nov., 1955, by Lord Hardinge of Penshurst, secretary to King Edward VIII.
[3]Nicolson, pp. 129–30n.

opposition in the upper house would follow the precedent of
1832 and abstain from voting. That is precisely what happened,
but it was a near thing, and it was the most responsible decision
an English monarch had had to make since the days of George
III.[1]

The Parliament Act of 1911 virtually whittled down the
power of the upper house to that of referring back a measure
to the commons; since an affirmative vote there in three
successive sessions of the same parliament (with a total interval
of two years) could now override the lords, and an attested
financial bill by-passed them altogether, they lost the function
on which so much stress had latterly been laid—that of giving
the electorate its chance of 'second thoughts'. Further curtail-
ments followed in 1945, and none of the major parties has ever
tackled the task, foreshadowed in the preamble of 1911, of
creating a new revising chamber as effective as the lords had
once been, but commanding the confidence they had lost. It
has been argued that this new situation throws a greater
burden of responsibility on the crown, which now remains the
only channel for appealing to the public from the tyranny of a
chance majority. On this interpretation the Patriot King becomes
once more, in the last resort, the guardian of the constitution
and the *volonté générale* against the ephemeral *volonté de tous*.[2] But
since the Parliament Act also reduced the duration of parliament to five years (which in practice is rarely attained) the
contingency seemed less likely than in the days of septennial
parliaments and the reign of Influence. Yet within a few years
the Irish crisis had forced on the king the momentous decision
whether or not to accept something like this rôle as the only
apparent alternative to civil war.

By the end of 1912 the new Home Rule Bill, with other outstanding liberal measures, had passed the commons, and next
year the veto of the upper house had followed as an almost
automatic reflex. Meanwhile Ulster under the able but sinister
leadership of Carson had made clear its determination to resist
à outrance, and on the English side Bonar Law had taken steps
which threatened to commit his party to the desperate gamble.
Asquith for his part dared not draw back and disappoint his

---

[1]Nicolson, chs. ix. and x.
[2]Id., p. 400n.

Irish allies, now that the last constitutional hurdle seemed to be surmounted, of the measure of which they had been balked for a quarter of a century; but he had little stomach for the fight, and his irresolution only hastened the drift towards disaster. Then, after doubts had been thrown on the willingness of some senior army officers to sink their politics in the claims of the service should coercion become necessary, he took the bold step of assuming the duties of war minister. That such a question should have risen at all (even through gross mishandling) is a measure of the depth of this new cleavage in national life, and of the infection of English politics, with their hard-won tradition of give-and-take, with those of Ireland, where the necessary common ground did not exist. The responsibility lies jointly on Asquith's dependence on the Irish vote, and Bonar Law's reckless attempt to boost up opposition to the vote-catching liberal programme with religious prejudices from Ulster. It looked as though the long struggle to remove the services from the party arena had gone for nothing, and any day might see another Walpole dismiss another Pitt from his army commission for political opposition.

Such conditions, of course, sap the very foundations of responsible government, and present a constitutional monarch with an almost insoluble dilemma. It was a real triumph that in spite of this the man who probably came best out of the whole crisis was King George himself. He was subjected to constant pressure on this side and that, left-wing papers hinting darkly at the undue influence of 'court hangers-on', Ulster correspondents urging him not to 'hand us over to the Pope', Carson mouthing to undergraduates at the Oxford Union about the liberal party's 'trickery of the king' over the passage of the Parliament Act, the *fons et origo malorum*.[1] Through it all he kept his independence of judgement and still bent all his efforts towards an agreed solution, frequently urging speakers on both sides (through his private secretaries) to refrain from inflammatory language, and sending to Asquith in the autumn two weighty memoranda on the whole situation. 'Whatever I do,' he foresaw, 'I shall offend half the people.' He was sceptical of the extent of general enthusiasm for the measure—especially if it meant the risk of civil war, the

[1]Nicolson, pp. 221, 236. The Carson episode is from my own recollection.

imminence of which he took more seriously than did some of his
ministers. For that reason he favoured yet another general
election on this one issue, in the desperate hope that responsible
opposition leaders would accept the verdict even though
'people like Sir Edward Carson' (on whom he did not mince
his words) would certainly spurn it if it went against them. Yet
he would not dissolve parliament without the advice of his
ministers so long as they commanded a majority there, or
dismiss them while they still enjoyed his confidence—least of
all use his legislative veto, as some still urged on him. What
he feared was that 'the Government is drifting and taking me
with it'; and the drift continued, despite secret *pourparlers*
between premier and opposition leader, until the summer of
1914, when at last the king got his way and was able, with
Asquith's full support, to call to Buckingham Palace a conference of eight leaders representing all parties to the dispute.
Agreement on the principle of excluding Ulster from the
measure seemed in sight; it was on the attempt to fix the
boundaries of the excluded area that negotiations broke down.[1]

At this point crisis was swallowed up in cataclysm—no less
than the outbreak of the first World War. The Home Rule Bill
was placed on the statute book under the terms of the Parliament Act, but with it was coupled a second measure postponing
its operation till after the war, and as in 1855, all parties now
bent their energies to the common task—not least the king.
George V never had his father's bent towards diplomacy and
foreign affairs; he is said to have been 'bored with foreigners'—in
this, as in the simplicity of his life, resembling George III rather
than Edward VII. But on the home front, apart from his
general influence in maintaining and strengthening *moral*, his
experience and good sense played their unobtrusive part at
many critical junctures, whether in the reconstruction of the
cabinet or the control of the services—especially the senior
service, to which he had been bred. So too with the industrial
strife and political confusion of the inter-war years: in the
general strike of 1926 his bent for conciliation was directed
towards restraining either side from speech or action that
would drive the other to desperation; and more than once the
indecisiveness of elections and the disastrous dearth of leader-

[1]Nicolson, ch. xiv.

ship threw him back in the choice of premiers (notably with Baldwin, MacDonald and the coalition of 1931) on the individual exercise of a judgement that may have been mistaken but was never distorted by personal predilection. The acceptance as a matter of course of the first labour government probably came more easily to a man of his unpretentious habits than it would have done to a natural grandee like Edward VII; his warm sympathy with the unemployed was expressed, not in public declarations like those by which Edward VIII was to embarrass ministers during his brief reign, but less overtly in an urgent memorandum to the premier.[1]

Between them, Edward VII and George V succeeded in fitting the monarchy into the pattern of responsible government to a degree never quite attained by Victoria, with whom personal predilection, like the unphilosophic cheerfulness of Dr. Johnson's friend, was 'always breaking in'. It is from quite another quarter that responsible government has been threatened in these latter years—no less than the civil service itself. Those very qualities of permanence and detachment from politics, which had seemed to solve the problem of making the administration responsible to parliament without making administrators the prey of politicians, began to present new problems as the tasks of government grew more complex, parliamentary time in consequence more congested, the civil service more numerous and more expert, and ministers thrown into increasing dependence on it by their own absorption in party organization. A quarter of a century has passed since Lord Hewart drew attention to what he called the 'new despotism' of government departments legislating irresponsibly through administrative orders and usurping judicial functions through their administrative tribunals. Since then state monopolies have multiplied and the potentially irresponsible sway of the executive has correspondingly increased.[2]

Perhaps the most important corrective is a function of parliament which only developed after the first Reform Act, but has now become an indispensable part of its daily work: the institution of 'question time'. Although the claim of the commons to 'question and complain of all persons of what degree soever,

[1]Nicolson, pp. 140–1, 250–2, 285–93, 342, 376–9, 419–21, chs. xxi, xxvi.
[2]See Keeton, *The Passing of Parliament*, 1952, cf. *supra*, p. 189.

found grievous to the Commonwealth' goes back to the days of
Charles I, questions did not begin to appear as a recurrent item
on the notice paper till 1835, and only in 1869 did the institution take the form familiar to us today. It can be, and is, used
as a means of obstruction or of party tactics, and ministers have
evolved their own defensive mechanisms for side-stepping
awkward questions, but there can be no doubting their value
as a means of enforcing responsibility. It has been well observed
that question time

> is dreaded more than any other hour by the civil servants,
> and it keeps them up to the mark much better than any other
> way which anybody could suggest.[1]

When (as not infrequently happens) the result is to expose some
act of petty tyranny by a government department or official,
the responsible minister generally has to face a barrage from the
benches behind him as well as from those opposite. As recently
as 1954 the Crichel Down case gave grounds—not indeed for
complacency, but not for complete pessimism either—on the
future of responsible government. The high-handed action of
an official in brushing aside the claim to consideration of
former owners or tenants of land formerly requisitioned by
government, but no longer needed for its original purpose,
produced a full-dress debate in the house, the voluntary
resignation of the minister responsible (even though he was
unaware of the facts at the time and was trusted by the house),
and the proffered resignation of the junior ministers involved
(which however Sir Winston Churchill as premier refused to
receive). The statement of the minister for agriculture on this
occasion is worth quoting:

> I, as Minister, must accept full responsibility to Parliament
> for any mistake and inefficiency of officials in my Depart-
> ment . . . Any departure from this long-established rule is
> bound to bring the Civil Service right into the political
> arena.

Even more recently the house has had occasion to debate the
incidence of danger from yet another quarter: the permeation
of the civil service with party agents planted there, not by the

[1]Sir Ivor Jennings, *Parliament*, 1939, pp. 91–5; *supra*, p. 26.

ministry in power (the 'swing of the pendulum' provides a natural remedy for that), but by an agency outside of and hostile to our whole political system. Here the natural remedy is the imposition of political 'tests' such as have been used in the United States; but it is significant that in the debate on the Burgess-Maclean incident the remedy was scouted on both sides as worse than the disease.[1]

Possibly, however, the real crisis of responsible government in the present century came when the virtual abeyance of the constitution in Lloyd George's war-time coalition—which his second-in-command Bonar Law did not shrink from dubbing a 'dictatorship'—was prolonged into the years of peace. His imposing secretariat, his small war cabinet bound to him by personal, not party ties, and unfettered by departmental duties, his persistent 'by-passing' of departmental ministers even after normal cabinet government had been restored, all savour more of Defoe's blue-print of a 'prime ministry' than of modern cabinet practice. Even question-time had no terrors for him: he could leave his lieutenants to face the music, contenting himself with rare and olympian descents on a house of commons kept dependent on him by the recurrence of foreign alarums and by his personal prestige and eloquence, as well as by the slackening of party allegiances. Pitt's second war-time administration had the same inherent dangers, but he died in mid-career. It was perhaps fortunate for the future of responsible government that Lloyd George by ignoring the writing on the wall provoked a revolt of the conservative rank and file which thrust on their leader, Bonar Law, a return to the practice of party ministries.[2] Sir Winston Churchill, who had been one of Lloyd George's most strenuous backers, had the wisdom to heed the warning when his own time came. It remains true, however, that the price of responsible government, like that of liberty and every other political good, is still 'eternal vigilance'.

---

[1]Hansard, vol. 530, pp. 1182–1298 (20 July 1954), vol. 545, pp. 1488–1615 (7 Nov. 1955).

[2]R. Blake, *Unrepentant Tory*, N.Y., 1956, pp. 343–4, 357–8, 397–8, 414, 476, 501; cf. *supra*, pp. 75–7, 169. Mr. Blake's book (which appeared in England as *The Unknown Prime Minister*, 1955) also throws further light on the political initiative of George V (see, e.g., pp. 358, 390, 397n., 526).

Index

208 *Index*

Burgess-Maclean case, 205

Burghley, William Cecil, Lord, 4–5, 7, 11, 196

Burke, Edmund, 103, 139, 142, 145, 151–2, 165, 166

Bute, John Stuart, Earl of, 107, 117–21, 123, 127–9, 131, 145, 151, 152, 187

Cabal, 52–53, 55, 74

Cabinet, xiv, 30–31, 34, 40, 57–62, 65–69, 81, 100–5, 108, 115, 123–8, 141–5, 148–9, 155–64, 168–71, 175–6, 185, 188–9, 192, 194, 196, see also *Cabal, Committees of privy council, conciliabulum*

Cabinet, Inner ('Efficient'), 67, 75–76, 101, 103–4, 115, 124, 155

Cabinet, Outer ('Nominal'), 76, 102–3, 124, 157, 161

Cabinet, War, 205

Caernarvonshire, 142

Caesar, Sir Julius, 90

Cambridge, 131

Canada, ix

Canning, George; Canningites, 114, 154, 166, 172–82, 185, 188, 191, 192

Caroline, Queen (to George II), 102, 107

Carson, Sir E. (Lord), 200–2

Carteret, John, Lord, 106, 108, 112, 114

Castlereagh, Robert Stuart, Viscount (Marquis of Londonderry), 171

Catholic Emancipation, 149, 164, 169, 171, 174–5, 177

Cavaliers, 53

Cecil, Robert, Earl of Salisbury, 11–13, 53, 77

Cecil, William, Lord Burghley, see *Burghley*

Cecil, William, Earl of Exeter, see *Exeter*

Chamberlayne, Edward and John, 90–91 and n.

Chancellor, Lord, 5–7, 16, 36, 47, 57, 66, 69, 141, 149, 155–7, 185, see also *Lord Keeper*

Chancellor of duchy of Lancaster, 16, 160

Chancellor of exchequer, 57, 155, 156, 163

Chancellor of Ireland, 160

Chancery, 16, 18

Channel Islands, 90

Charles I, xiii, 17, 21–37, 39, 48, 53, 54, 61, 80, 82, 107, 117–19, 121, 129, 157

Charles II, xiii, 3, 8, 38, 46–63, 65, 67, 69, 72, 81, 86, 88, 91 and n., 104, 129, 131, 133, 145, 155, 157, 168

Chatham, see *Pitt*

Chester, 137

Churchill, Sir W., 24, 165, 204–5

Civil list, 72, 122, 142, 189

Civil service; civil servants, 5, 11, 43, 45–46, 54, 62, 63, 69, 77, 79, 81, 95, 100, 110, 125–8, 146, 152–5, 159, 189, 203–5

Civil War, see *Wars*

Clarendon, Edward Hyde, Earl of, 34–35, 47–54, 58, 59, 62, 64, 65, 67, 69, 70, 74, 79, 90–91, 104, 156, 164, 184

Clifford, Sir T., 54

Clive, Sir R., 144

Coffee houses, 84

Commander-in-chief, 159, 167, 178, 194

Commissioners (woods, forests, public works, Poor Law), 163

Committees of house of commons, 14–15, 39–41, 65, 82

Committees of privy council, 14, 35, 39, 48–49, 57, 59–60, 90, 161–2, see also *Conciliabulum*

Common law, lawyers, 10, 16, 18

Conciliabulum, 103, 119

Conduct of the Allies, 85, 132

Conservatives, see *Parties*

Constituent Assembly, 82

Corrupt Practices Acts, 183